D0044923

Just a note...
B JAMES
267-1440 GARDEN PL
DELTA BC V4M 3Z2

Behind Enemy Lines

Behind Enemy Lines

The True Story of a French Jewish Spy in Nazi Germany

MARTHE COHN

with Wendy Holden

Harmony Books New York

Published by Harmony Books, New York, New York.
Member of the Crown Publishing Group, a division of Random House, Inc.
www.randomhouse.com

HARMONY BOOKS is a registered trademark and the Harmony Books colophon is a trademark of Random House, Inc.

Printed in the United States of America

DESIGN BY BARBARA STURMAN

Library of Congress Cataloging-in-Publication Data
is available upon request.

ISBN 0-609-61054-6

10 9 8 7 6 5 4 3 2

First Edition

To my family, the living and the dead,
but especially my grandfather, mother, and
brother Fred, who were its soul

Acknowledgments

Marthe Hoffnung Cohn: Our family has recently been stricken with the loss, within three weeks, of my brother Fred and his oldest son Maurice. Fred, the oldest of eight children, was, as long as I can remember, a role model and hero to all of his siblings. During the war, though newly wed, Fred ensured the survival of his extended family while actively engaged in the Resistance in the Cantal. His son Maurice, born in February 1942, often complained about the Germans as an eighteen-month-old baby when he was repeatedly lifted from his crib and carried into hiding when the Nazis came to round up Jews. He may well have been scarred for life by these early traumas. On June 28, 2001, this highly successful professor at the Pasteur Institute in Paris committed suicide, leaving a loving wife and three beautiful children.

In 1942 my entire family was devastated by the arrest and deportation of my sister Stéphanie. In prison and in the Poitiers camp, she became the leader of her fellow prisoners. Her courage and determination were exemplary. In the letter she wrote the day she was deported from Pithiviers to Auschwitz, her chief concern was her mother. Fred carried that letter in a pocket over his heart for the rest of his life.

Briefly, I want to acknowledge the gallantry of all members of my family during those five years of terror. First, my parents, who, though torn by grief and worry during the entire war, never complained about or discouraged our participation in acts of resistance. My sister Cecile lived undeclared as a Jew in Paris and continued to work in order to help Fred feed our extended family. Like Fred, my brother Arnold was actively engaged in the Resistance in the Cantal and participated in the mad dashes to the mountains to escape arrest during the frequent roundups of Jews. The two brothers took turns carrying our grandmother on their back, as well as Jacquie and Maurice. My sister Hélène, a student at the University of Clermont-Ferrand, used her rented room as a safe house for fellow Resistance members and to print anti-German propaganda. She also transported arms and ammunition. Rosy, our baby, was a scout for the Cantal Resistance and was assigned to man a machine gun on a mountain road. Finally, my sister-in-law, Rosette, saved the village of Narnhac from being burned to the ground by the Germans after the arrest of a wounded Resistance member and the ensuing execution of the mayor and several hostages.

Of the numerous people who helped my family survive the German occupation in Poitiers, I am most grateful to my classmates, particularly Odile de Morin, and to the staff of the Red Cross Nursing School; to Monsieur Charpentier, neighbors whose names I forget, and the owners of the food stores, all of whom, at the risk of their lives, voluntarily provided shelter, forged identity documents, stored our belongings, or sold food to the "undesirables" we had become. I would be remiss not to mention my then fiancé, Jacques Delaunay, for his constant encouragement and wholehearted support of my nursing career and the planning of my family's escape. With love and sorrow, I wish to mention Jacques's parents, George and Amelie Delaunay, whose two sons—their only children—were executed by the Germans in 1943. I remember with gratitude Madame Keller in Marseille, who refused to obey Vichy's rules and ordered the Red Cross Nursing School to admit me, thus permitting me to complete my training. Most Jews who survived the war in France were helped by such non-Jews who risked their lives to save their fellow human beings. My deepest gratitude to all of these unsung heroes.

To Lieutenants Latour and Verin, thank you for training me day after day when I was assigned to your "antenna." I will always remember the gentleness and fairness of Lieutenant Tallichet and the great pleasure it was to work with him in Lindau, Bavaria. Thank you, Captain Jean Millot, the antenna chief who replaced Zimmerman; it was great to be part of your team. We worked hard, but you and your charming wife knew how to create a lively social life in the former villa of Martin Bormann, in the Officers' Club where we spent so many evenings, and in Austria's ski resorts that winter.

A special acknowledgment is due to Colonel Bouvet and his men for treating me as another commando and for believing in me. As I could not disappoint them, I found the courage to walk into Germany. For the spur to that courage, I wish to thank Captain Mollat for earlier doubting me. A note of thanks is due to Major Petit, who had enough confidence in a young woman in civilian clothes to immediately transmit the intelligence I offered to his superiors. I also thank Majors Ryussen and Rigaud, Captains Ligouzat, Metivier, and Ducournau, and Lieutenant Neu—along with Colonel Bouvet and Major Petit—for their long years of friendship, which I returned with great loyalty.

From my stint in Indochina, I vividly remember my numerous friends in the French Foreign Legion, who, among many good deeds, provided us with the equipment we needed, served as baby-sitters for Serge, and, as often as our heavy schedules permitted it, sent small tank convoys to carry us to their jungle posts for dinner. These friendly invitations eased our isolation and hardships in a country so far from home. I also want to thank Captain Suzanne Tillier, a former commando officer and chief of all of the women serving in Indochina, for her hospitality and friendship during my several visits to the South Annam capital.

Though my brother Fred had encouraged me to write this book for well over twenty-five years, it was only after my retirement in 1999 that I gave serious consideration to the project. In summer 2000 my original coauthor, Suzanne Singer, and I started writing the first chapter. It was a delightful collaboration that I thoroughly enjoyed and the beginning of a lasting friendship. When, on July 14, Bastille Day, I was conferred the Medaille Militaire by the Los Angeles French Consul General, Suzanne unleashed a blitz of publicity. Thanks to her I also met Robert A. Mirisch to whom I am immensely grateful for his competent legal advice, generosity, and integrity.

Special thanks are due to the late Ted Demers who, believing that my story merited publication, committed himself to the realization of this project. Without Ted Demers's financial, technical, and moral support, *Behind Enemy Lines* would never have been written. While both were involved in preparing the contract, my legal counsel, Robert Mirisch, marveled at the high business ethics and efficacy of Ted Demers. I deplore the untimely death of that truly traditional Maecenas.

I am also grateful to Alan Nevins of Renaissance for his efforts on my behalf. Particular thanks go to British author Wendy Holden, who took over the cowriting from Suzanne when she left to attend rabbinical school. In just eight months, our collaboration resulted in the growth and transformation of that initial chapter into a fully completed book. Thank you, Wendy, for your unusual empathy, patience, and understanding. By now you probably know more about my life than any of my close friends.

I am also grateful to Harmony Books for their encouragement at every stage of the work.

Finally, I must give thanks to my husband, Major Lloyd Cohn, for his complete support and immense patience in regard to the numerous hours I spent in front of the computer, either answering Wendy's innumerable questions or editing first drafts. Thank you, too, Stephan and Remi, who in 2000, on suddenly learning details about your mother's life during the war, commented to the media, "She was just our mom." Thanks to Stephan's wife Barbara, for being the daughter we never had. Particular thanks to my granddaughter, Anna Regina, for her unconditional love. Last May, at the age of eight, she honored me by writing my story as a project for her second-grade class.

Wendy Holden: Thanks to Val Hudson and the inimitable Alan Nevins for bringing me this project, and to Joel Gotler for facilitating it. And my special thanks to the late Ted Demers—without his perseverance, this courageous and heartfelt story would not have been told. I deplore his untimely death. Mark Lucas and all at Lucas Alexander Whitley in London, along with Karima Ridgley and all at Renaissance in Los Angeles, deserve special thanks; Shaye Areheart at Harmony for her eternal enthusiasm and professionalism; and to my husband, Chris Taylor, as always, for his unending support and invaluable constructive criticism.

Contents

Author's Note

Where possible, Marthe has remembered with extraordinary clarity exact names, dates, and locations. Where that was not possible, we have substituted details we feel are closest to the real thing. Our apologies for any minor inaccuracy this may cause.

Behind Enemy Lines

"Each of our deeds, even those as small as

the flapping of a butterfly's wings,

has great consequences."

—Rabbi Abraham J. Twerski

The Smell of Danger

There was no time to be frightened. My mission was clear. Shortly before midnight on that bitterly cold night in February 1945, I left the small French town of Thann with four officers and twenty Moroccan commandos. The men were heavily armed with machine guns, tommy guns, and grenades, and well-prepared for the weather. Posing as Martha Ulrich, a young nurse fleeing from the Allies, it was part of my subterfuge that I was neither armed nor suitably dressed. I wore simple clothes—a woollen skirt, jacket, hat, and gloves. I had knee-high socks under my ski boots, but my legs were bare above the knees.

It was very dark and intensely cold. The towering fir and pine trees dimmed what little light there was, and only the snow was distinguishable in the gloom. We set off in a long line, marching through deep drifts. The snow came halfway up the legs of the fourteen men in front of me and the ten behind me, but most of the time I sank up to my hips. My only consolation was that I was now warm. I had to use my hands to pull each leg out of the snow as I walked, but I never once faltered. I could see the men constantly watching me, ready to help if I fell, but the challenge of keeping up drove me on.

For five hours we traveled in complete silence, aware that the Germans were all around us. Sound carries surprisingly well in such a still, frosty environment. Outside Thann, with all its crooked buildings, we must have gone more than four miles up a mountain, and then down toward Amselkopf. The snowy peaks of the Vosges Mountains loomed high above us.

At the edge of a small valley my military escort stopped and stared at me, blinking in the dark. This was where they were to turn back. We were deep in the thick pine forests, trees close all around, making it almost impossible to see. Nothing was said, only hand signals were used. The guide shone his hooded flashlight on his map to remind me which narrow, icy path to take along the southern slope of the mountain. There were several, all running parallel. When I reached the second path before dawn, I was to follow the flank of the mountain for about an hour until I came to the heavily armed enemy post at the end of the pass.

"The Germans will shoot anything they can't clearly see," the guide had warned me the previous night. "You'll be no good to anyone dead."

In silence, the men waved farewell and evaporated into the trees. Lieutenant Neu, who'd become a friend, squeezed my arm.

Forcing myself to move, I stumbled on in the pitch-darkness, crossed the valley, found the second path heading east and turned onto it. As instructed, I crouched against a tree and waited until the first streaks of dawn lit the sky before moving on. I was so keyed up, I no longer felt tired, cold, or hungry.

I'd only gone a little way along the flank of the mountain when I spotted two German soldiers lying way down in the valley, covered in fir branches for camouflage. They lifted their heads but did nothing to stop me. I tilted my chin high and pretended not to have seen them. I suspected they were scouts, as intent as I was on avoiding detection.

Continuing to walk, I tried not to think of their fingers twitching on their triggers.

I knew I was very near my goal. I had to be. In my mind, I was constantly urging myself on.

Just a little farther, Marthe, I told myself silently. Stay calm, smile, cry, play the part, do whatever you have to do. Think of the colonel and how important this mission is to him and to his men.

I thought of how he'd kissed me on both cheeks the night before. Tears had welled in his eyes and he'd turned away, hoping I hadn't seen them.

Suddenly, a soldier sprang out from behind a tree just below me, his rifle pointed straight at me, its bayonet glinting. Though I'd expected this kind of welcome, I was so startled I nearly screamed. Taking a deep breath, I swallowed. Three more soldiers leaped out from behind adjacent trees, machine guns at the ready, sprigs of fir attached to their helmets.

Looking around me intensely for the first time in the half-light, I saw several soldiers dead on the ground nearby, their blood seeping into the snow after a recent skirmish.

"Don't shoot!" I cried, my hands raised in defense against their weapons.

Cross of Lorraine

The place of my birth was the cathedral city of Metz, in the northeastern region of French Lorraine, an area with a complex and tumultuous history. With the Franco-German border just thirty miles east, this frontier province had been the target of invasion for a thousand years. In 1870 the Germans annexed it for nearly fifty years.

By the time I was born, on April 13, 1920, less than two years after the end of the First World War, the map of Europe had been redrawn and Alsace-Lorraine was back in French hands. Raised as true French patriots in an area of such national significance, it was a matter of the greatest pride to us all that General de Gaulle later chose the double-barred Cross of Lorraine, above all symbols, to signify Free France.

Metz was a bustling, cosmopolitan city of pedimented and classical facades whose outlying steel factories and coal mines were manned by Poles, Italians, and Czechs. A garrison town, its streets were also full of soldiers in uniform. On the east bank of the Moselle River, it sat astride major trade routes linking Paris and Strasbourg. An independent republic in the twelfth century, it had a character all its own, with its medieval French quarter around the Gothic cathedral of St. Etienne, and the elegant "Ville Allemande" built under Prussian occupation, with its bourgeois apartment buildings. Filled with a mixture of seventeenth-century squares, Italianate streets, and grand German edifices, it was not at all the dour place one might have expected from its geography and industrial background.

My parents had effectively grown up as Germans. Living most of their lives in occupied territory, they'd only been allowed to speak German; it was taught in school, and they were under pain of arrest if they uttered even a single French *mot*. By the time I was born, French and German were spoken freely. For seven years I learned Hoch Deutsch as a second language in school. But my siblings and I spoke French to each other, our school friends, and some of our neighbors, and spoke German to my parents and most of their generation. It was like having a secret language. If we didn't want our parents to know what we were up to, we'd just chatter away merrily in French.

Our family name was Hoffnung Gutgluck, which means "Hope and Good Luck" in German, shortened to Hoffnung for ease of use. My given name was Marthe, pronounced "Mart." My grandfather on my mother's side, Moishé Bleitrach, was a marvelous man, a prominent Orthodox rabbi and a renowned Hebrew scholar. By the time I was born, he was nearly sixty, with a long beard. My earliest childhood memories are of tugging at it while he laughed a deep, sonorous laugh.

At the age of two, however, it was my mother, Regine, to whom I'd become obsessively attached. She was small, blonde, and pretty, and I adored her beyond reason. She was a warm, fun-loving woman, looking more like an older sister than a mother, and if she ever left my sight I'd become hysterical and go blue in the face with screaming. My elder brothers, Fred and Arnold, or my sister Cecile, would lift me and, with great relish, slap me on the back to restore normal breathing. By the age of four I realized that my siblings resented me carrying on and that I never gave them or my hardworking mother any peace; so—an early pacifist—I simply desisted.

Sixteen months after my birth, my younger sister Stéphanie arrived in this world, a gorgeous, chubby confection of dark brown curls, the exact opposite of me. I was tiny, skinny, pale, and very blonde, just like my mother. I was also insanely jealous.

"She may be pretty," I would tell Stéphanie's many admirers indignantly, "but I'm very bright." My jealousy soon vanished, however, when Stéphanie melted my heart and became my very own little doll to play with. Permanently cheerful, angelic to look at, she and Cecile were the most sweet-natured of us all, and I adored her. Stéphanie soon became a confidante, a friend, and a spirited childhood playmate.

In 1924 my sister Hélène arrived, a fragile pixie of a child, followed in 1925 by Rosy, our baby. Stéphanie and I were sent to school together soon afterward. But the teachers took one look at me, at the age of six, and because of my size refused to believe I was old enough to be in the first grade.

"You must go to the kindergarten with your sister," they told me, assuming I was the same age as Steph.

Despite my protests, they sat us side by side in the kindergarten to learn the alphabet. I was already reading entire books from cover to cover. Infuriated, I sulked until the teacher asked if anyone knew any songs. To my mortification, Steph raised her hand. Knowing what a dreadful voice she had (as we all did, apart from Cecile and my mother), I grabbed it and pulled it down.

"Don't put your hand up, stupid," I told her. "You know you can't sing." But the teacher had already spotted her and called Stéphanie to the front of the class. As I held my hands over my face, she launched into "Je Cherche après Titine," a popular song that made me cringe. At lunchtime I ran home to tell my mother what had happened.

"I can't possibly stay there," I told her, grimacing. "I won't. They think I'm a baby, and worst of all, Steph sang!" My mother hid her smile from me and walked me back to school in the afternoon. Taking my birth certificate with her, she proved to the staff that I was indeed old enough for the first grade. Thereafter, Stéphanie sang alone.

I hated school and wanted nothing more than to be at home, my nose buried in a book. Each time the teacher produced a new book for us to read, I'd already read it months before. I was bored and frustrated.

One day, when I'd requested new books in the town library, the librarian told me I couldn't have them. "You're far too young to read these," she told me, looking at my list and peering over her round-rimmed spectacles at me. When I complained to my oldest brother, Fred, he marched me to the library and took her on, face-to-face.

"My sister is allowed to read anything she chooses," he told her, firmly but politely. "It is for her family to decide whether or not they are suitable, when she gets them home." I loved him even more for his intervention.

Fred was the one I felt closest to as a young child. He was more like a father than a brother. Each night, after dinner, he would read aloud to us from the daily newspaper, an event I keenly anticipated. Sitting at my mother's knee, I'd listen awestruck as he recounted news of the latest political or historical events in Europe.

One story that transfixed me from an early age was the case of Shalom Schwartzbad, an immigrant Jewish watchmaker and poet who'd fled to Paris from Bessarabia (now Moldavia) in the Russian Ukraine after the 1919–20 pogroms against the Jews. Once in the French capital, Schwartzbad sought out Symon Petliura, the former general and supreme commander of the Ukrainian army who'd since become the socialist leader of the Ukrainian independence movement. His armies had been responsible for some of the most appalling brutality against Jews. One morning, Schwartzbad approached Petliura as he left his home, and shot him dead. The murder trial in Paris made international headlines. His defense lawyer, Henri Torres, turned it into a trial against Petliura and the loss of sixty thousand Jewish lives. Witness after witness gave the most harrowing evidence of what had happened under Petliura and the Cossacks. They'd burned whole villages; tortured, raped, maimed, and killed, even children. The descriptions Fred read to us were horrible. I was appalled to learn what some people could do to others, just because they were Jewish. When Fred read that the jury had acquitted the watchmaker, I wept tears of joy. From that moment on I wanted to become a lawyer and bring justice to the wronged.

Fred was kind and thoughtful, but he could also be a terrible tease. He and Arnold would often ambush us in the hallway of our apartment, jumping on us and boxing our ears. "Only sissies cry," they'd goad us. "Come on, girls, get those fists up and fight back." I realize now he was trying to teach us self-defense.

Each Thursday, Fred would chase me around the house with the huge live carp my mother had bought for our Sabbath dinner, terrifying me with its gaping mouth and goggle eyes. Terrified of fish, I was genuinely afraid. One day he cornered me in the kitchen between the stove and the wall, and I was so frightened I stopped breathing. My mother, who usually didn't interfere with our boisterous games, pulled Fred away.

"That's it," she told him firmly, reaching for me and slapping me hard on the back to restore the color to my face. "You must never torment Marthe about the fish again." And he never did.

My father, Fischel, was a brooding, difficult man whose unhappy childhood had scarred him for life and made him an awkward parent. His mother died in childbirth when he was three years old, and his father and new stepmother sent him and his baby brother, Benoit, the youngest of five children, to an orphanage. He'd had little formal education, and his only contact with his violent father was unpleasant. His stepmother had two boys of her own living at home with his older siblings, yet he and Benoit were all but disposed of. The bitterness never left him.

He met my mother when one of her seven brothers married one of his two sisters. He instantly fell in love with the pretty little blonde. He was her first boyfriend—young, good-looking, and shy—and she, too, was smitten. She'd grown up as the only girl in a large family of men, all of whom adored her, but this was different. Her father, known to us as "Grospapa," wholeheartedly disapproved. He felt my father wasn't nearly well-educated enough.

"To give my only daughter to an uneducated man is like giving her to a wild beast," he'd said. My father overheard, and hated him for the rest of his life.

Grospapa was right. They were completely mismatched. After Fred was born, my mother gave birth to a second son, Eugene, and then they had their first daughter, Cecile. Eugene died of scarlet fever when he was two, and the pain nearly tore them apart. Maman left

Papa and returned home to her parents with her two surviving children. She told him she wanted a divorce. But Papa begged her to come back, promising to be a better husband. "You have no right to take my children from me," he pleaded, and she knew he was right. More for the sake of the children than for herself, she returned, and went on to bear him five more.

At times my father could be great fun. He loved to invent stories and regale us with them. He'd play games or take us swimming in the Moselle, or for long walks in the countryside around Metz. But despite his deep affection for us, he was unreasonably jealous of our warm relationship with Maman. Part of him desperately wanted to emulate my mother's close ties to us, but he just didn't know how. When he broke down and cried as I was wheeled into the operating room as a child to have my appendix removed, I was so touched at his concern, I forgot to be frightened for myself. But rare events aside, he was more often than not moody and bad-tempered; shouting for no reason, dictating orders like a Prussian general.

When he wasn't home, the atmosphere in the house was completely different. My mother was relaxed and patient with us. We laughed a lot together, talked a great deal, and were unusually close. The seven of us still fought "like *tziganes*," as my mother would say—or Gypsies—and were often extremely noisy, but she rarely silenced us.

At the dinner table, in the presence of my father, however, we had to be well-behaved, and we felt free to talk only if he was in a good mood. We all dreaded the times when Papa would flare up for no reason, becoming unreasonably angry, screaming at my mother or at us. Once he started, he seemed unable to control himself and would go on at length, in increasingly crude language as his limited vocabulary ran out. We had to sit at the table until he'd ceased his diatribe. When he really lost his temper, he'd leave the room, telling us in a clipped voice: "If I were ever to beat you, I'd have to be much calmer than this. If I hit you now, I'd be no better than my father."

As a child, I had little understanding of his mood changes, and was angry at his unnecessary destruction of our happy family life. I'd complain about him to my mother, who'd sigh and tell me, "It could be worse. He never plays cards, he never drinks, and he never runs off with other women."

"That's a shame," I told her, and she looked at me in horror. "At least if he ran off with someone else we'd be left in peace."

Despite my anger, I also felt sorry for him. Papa seemed compelled to act the way he did, as if he had no choice in the matter. In the rare glimpses we had of how sentimental he could be, we realized that hidden beneath his gruff exterior there was a warm human being. He seemed so terribly alone, while the rest of us formed a solid block of love around my mother.

He was reasonably successful, running a small photofinishing and enlarging business—Agrandissements Photographiques Encadrements—which provided us with a comfortable five-bedroom apartment on the second floor of a building in rue du Marechal Pétain, well away from the poorer, former Jewish ghetto. When my younger sisters were old enough to go to school, my mother helped him at work and with getting through each day of his life. She had infinite patience, and was determined that our home be filled with light and laughter.

We had a live-in maid, Sophie, with whom we ate lunch in the kitchen most days. She was more like an older sister than a servant, and when she eventually left us after ten years to get married, I was so upset I became ill. Once a week Sophie would polish the wooden floors until the whole apartment smelled of wax. That scent can still take me straight back to my childhood.

We were a very religious family, observing every custom and ritual, although I'm sure my father was far less devout than my mother. On Friday nights she'd light the candles, and my father and brothers—wearing their traditional skullcaps—led the prayers. Our home was strictly kosher; we had two sets of dishes and never ate meat and dairy products at the same meal. My mother was an excellent cook and mixed Jewish specialities with French and German fare, so we'd have carp or chopped liver, soup, chicken, veal or beef roast, fresh vegetables and salad, followed by fruit. On Fridays, for the Sabbath, and on holidays, the house would be filled with the smell of baking as Maman made the special challah bread, as well as cakes and pies. Hebrew prayers would be said over wine and challah before the meal, and grace was said after. We also had to say prayers before we went to bed and immediately upon waking. My mother and Cecile had beautiful voices and would sing old Yiddish songs after dinner. We younger children knew the words but not the meaning, and sang along, grimacing as my father—who, like us, couldn't hold a tune—made up his own version.

My parents wanted us to get the best and broadest education available, and so we attended public schools, mixing freely with Catholic and Protestant children. I went to the all-girl Lycée de Jeunes Filles, as did Cecile, Stéphanie, Hélène, and Rosy. We learned to read Hebrew with a tutor at home and later at the heder. At the lycée we had religious studies with Grand Rabbi Nathan Netter. Although Church and State were strictly separated in the rest of France, since 1918 the highly devout Alsatians and Lorrains had been exempted from the Separation Law. Thus, in each school, every pupil of each religious persuasion had their respective clergy teaching them religion.

Our synagogue was in the poorest area of Metz, and we walked there in our finery every Saturday. One morning, when I was about five years old, we emerged from the synagogue to find a scruffy group of children waiting outside. They were teenagers from the wrong side of the tracks, looking for trouble.

"Dirty Jews!" one of them shouted, spitting on the ground at our feet. Others threw stones, one of which hit my shin and made me wince. The boys scattered on seeing my father's thunderous expression, but stayed close enough, gaining courage, to hurl more insults.

I looked up at my father, deeply confused, and he peered down at me. I was filled with an overwhelming sense of injustice. I couldn't believe we were being treated differently just for being Jewish. What did it matter which faith we practiced? My eyes pleaded with my father for an answer, for a fair conclusion to such an unfair situation. His eyes locked on mine, and without saying a word, he slowly removed his thick leather belt. Turning on the boys with a look of absolute rage in his eyes, he gave chase, brandishing the belt high in his right hand.

"Which one of you called us dirty Jews!" he bellowed as he lashed out at them. My mouth open, I watched him run off up the street, belt in hand, as Fred and Arnold tried to lead me home. In that moment, I think I loved my father more than I ever had.

My first experience of what it was like to be a Jew in Europe in the years before the war was followed by many more. One afternoon some years later, my mother sent me on an errand to the corner shop to buy a dozen eggs. She gave me a string bag in which to carefully place them. Just as I was nearing home, a young girl from my street whom I knew by sight, stepped forward and stood in my path.

"You're a dirty Jew," she said, her hands on her hips.

"I'm not dirty!" I replied, with great indignation.

"You are," she said, and then started catcalling: "Dirty Jew, dirty Jew, dirty Jew!"

With hardly a thought, I lifted the bag of eggs and brought it crashing down onto her head, covering her hair and clothes in broken shell and yolk. Running home, I arrived empty-handed and found my mother in the kitchen, her hands covered in flour. Certain I'd done the right thing, I told her exactly what had happened.

My mother bent down and held me to her very tightly. Brushing a strand of blonde hair from my eyes, she smiled and told me, "You were absolutely right, Marthe. You must never, ever let anyone get away with calling you such terrible names."

Few of my childhood experiences were negative, however. Despite the problems we sometimes encountered outside the home, and the atmosphere created by my father within it, I was surrounded by happy, loving siblings and an indefatigable mother who taught us to rise above our circumstances and to fill our heads with ambition and learning. "You can make a difference," she'd tell us. "Be your own person and stand up to the rest of the world."

My heroes at that time were Maurice Bellonte and Dieudonné Costes, the French airmen who flew nonstop across the Atlantic, from Paris to New York, in 1930. As I read of their exploits, I became ever more desperate to fly a plane, an ambition I'd had since I'd first seen one flying over Metz as a young girl. To my delight, the two national heroes came to our town on a nationwide tour of France. Better still, their route took them right past our home. To watch from our balcony as these living legends passed in their cavalcade was almost more excitement than I could bear. The streets were thronged with people waving little French flags. Stéphanie, Cecile, and I were crammed on the balcony with Arnold, Rosy, and Hélène, screaming at the top of our voices, along with our mother. It was the first time in my life I'd ever been allowed to raise my voice in public. I was hoarse afterward.

"One day," I told my mother in a rasping whisper as she tucked me into bed that night, "I'm going to learn how to fly a plane."

"Yes, Marthe," she told me, kissing my forehead with a smile. "You probably will."

Around that time, the entire neighborhood was abuzz with preparations for the consecration of a new Catholic chapel, St. Therese, built almost across the street from our home. When the day arrived, one of my classmates invited me to attend the ceremony. As my parents raised no objections, I went along, but stood in the back of the chapel. I could not bring myself to sit with my friend and her family in a pew; I wanted to be a spectator, not a participant. I loved the pomp, the incense, the music, the choir boys, and the beautiful vestments of the bishop and his entourage. The precise planning of the high mass, with everyone following a well-rehearsed choreography, fascinated me. Afterward, I attended mass several times in that chapel, for the communion of friends and for the consecration of the bell, another grand affair. From an early age, I was interested in learning about religions other than ours. We'd occasionally accompanied our maid Sophie, a Protestant, to her religious service. Our parents were secure enough in their belief and ours not to worry about our bonds to Judaism. While I thoroughly enjoyed these high masses at St. Therese, they had no effect on my faith.

I had a wide circle of friends, mostly from school, but the core of my life was my family, with whom I spent most of my time. Stéphanie and Cecile were my dearest and closest friends. Inseparable, we slept in the same room, went to school together, ate together, and played together. On weekends or holidays, Papa didn't let us leave the house alone, and we could only go to the cinema or the theater escorted and in daytime. Even then we always had to do a chore first, like clean out our wardrobe or drawers. Sometimes the chores would be so numerous that by the time we'd done them, it would be too late to go out, a fact my father knew only too well. I began to become bitterly resentful of his autocratic ways, and often argued with him.

"I'm going to send you to an obedience school for dogs!" he'd cry, exasperated with me.

Cecile, on the other hand, never argued, and thus often got her own way. And Stéphanie was quiet and calm and never crossed swords with anyone. She simply accepted her lot. The younger children did likewise, apart from Rosy, who was always cheeky and had her own ways of exacting revenge.

My mother would try to advise me on how to handle Papa.

"You two don't always have to be at such loggerheads," she'd tell me, sighing. "Try to be softer, like Cecile." But I never learned, and the older I got, the harder it was to accept the adverse effect Papa had on us all. It was a gamble just bringing friends home from school, because I never knew what mood he'd be in. Maman would welcome anyone, but Papa would often frighten them so badly with his gruffness that they wouldn't want to come back.

Apart from my sisters, my closest friend was Sophie Weyne, the daughter of a good friend of my mother's. She and I saw each other regularly, although, sadly, we didn't live in the same neighborhood or attend the same school. Sophie was very pretty, blonde, and great fun to be with. If I couldn't go out, then Sophie would often visit—regardless of my father—and we'd sit around the table in the dining room with Cecile and Stéphanie and Sophie's older sister, Regine, talking for hours about films, books, and occasionally boys.

There was only one boy who was interested in me as a young teenager, and he became something of a nuisance. His name was Grandidier, and he was, I believed, little more than a street kid, tall and lanky. I don't know what he saw in me, but for some reason he was besotted, and for the next two years he made my life hell. He'd stand outside our apartment, staring up at the windows for hours on end, waiting for me to emerge. When I did, he'd follow me—to school, to the shops, even to the synagogue. Stéphanie and I would hurry away from him as fast as we could. One day, he followed Cecile and me to a local fair and sat in front of us on the merry-go-round, offering to pay our fare and trying to persuade me to go out with him.

"Come now," he told me impatiently, "surely you could just come for an afternoon stroll or something? I've been waiting for over a year."

I was bothered by his intensity and told him so, calling him a delinquent.

Out of the blue he sent me a postcard, the first personal mail I'd ever received at our home. I was horrified. My father, who opened the mailbox every morning, summoned me to his study and accused me of having a boyfriend.

"You're far too young," he warned me sternly, handing me the offending postcard, in which Grandidier had expressed his undying affection. "You must never see this young man again."

"But Papa, I've hardly ever spoken a word to this boy," I cried. "I haven't been seeing him at all." Thankfully, he believed me. But young Grandidier continued to follow me for some time.

I was still much more interested in books than I was in boys. From the earliest age, in the lively, noisy household I shared, my salvation was reading. My grandfather had instilled a love of books in me, my mother was very well-educated and had been similarly inspired, and Fred felt much the same way. I was never happier than lying on my belly in the large bay window of the lounge of my parents' apartment, hiding behind the thick curtains, lost in a book. Hidden from sight, ignoring all calls for me to help with the chores, I'd revel in titles like *Ivanhoe, Robinson Crusoe, Robin Hood,* and *Swiss Family Robinson.* I loved the romances of Walter Scott, the plays of Molière, Racine, and Corneille, and the poems of Musset, Vigny, and Baudelaire.

Because of my obsession, I was a very poor student. My teachers would chastise me roundly, telling me, "Your sisters are such model students, Marthe. Stéphanie, especially, is the brightest of them all. Why can't you be the same?"

My grandfather was my strongest influence as far as education was concerned. When I was in my mid-teens, Cecile and I began to stay overnight at the apartment he shared with my grandmother. Each evening after supper we'd walk the few blocks to their home and spend the night, to keep them company. It was he, not she, we looked forward to seeing most.

My grandmother was a difficult but witty woman, with a quick mind and tongue and lively blue eyes. She'd had seven sons and always favored them over my mother, her only daughter. Later, she also favored my uncles' children over us. She'd give my cousins gifts, for instance, and never us. She'd used my mother as her servant and my grandfather as the target for her nagging. He spoiled her, and us, rotten, but often complained, when she nagged him too much: "That's what happens when you marry a pretty woman." The first time I heard him say it, I was astounded. The thought of my pious grandfather being susceptible to a woman's beauty was a revelation. I was not yet mature enough to realize that not only the young fall prey to their emotions.

My grandfather rose every morning at four o'clock to pray and study his Hebrew manuscripts, of which he had a priceless library. He'd enter into correspondence with scholars from around the world, and spent much of his time writing poetry, interpretations of Hebrew texts, and letters. Metz had a large Jewish population and Grospapa founded the Orthodox synagogue, along with all the formal Jewish institutions like the *mikvah*—the ritual bath—and the heder, or Hebrew school. He'd helped organize the Jewish cemetery in Metz, and subsequently arranged the relocation of Jewish remains previously consigned to a Catholic graveyard in a small town in Lorraine.

Each morning at around seven he'd put away his books, emerge from his library, and collect the fresh bagels delivered to their apartment. Then he'd prepare breakfast for me and Cecile, almost imperceptibly making the transition from learned scholar to doting grandparent. The two of us would sit happily at the kitchen table he'd set with bone china cups over a linen tablecloth, chatting to him and bombarding him with questions, usually either of a political nature or about Greco-Roman history, a subject of which he was particularly fond.

The example set by my grandfather, mother, and Fred led me to develop an interest in current affairs, and I devoured the morning newspaper from the age of six. Likewise, listening to my grandfather's marvelous stories of Greco-Roman history, which were interwoven with that of our Israelite forefathers, I became an avid student. I began reading books where kings, emperors, princes, and beautiful queens shared tales with gods and demigods who—unlike the God we worshiped—behaved as badly as humans. Until late in my teens I read and reread Homer and Roman history, translated in French. It was a world of historic facts mixed with imaginary events and extravagant characters. Enthralled by the unbridled imaginations of the authors, I vicariously lived the terrific adventures of divine, semimortal, and mortal Greek and Roman heroes.

Grospapa also introduced us to subjects close to his heart, such as Tzedakah (Charity) and Tolerance.

"People are intolerant because they are frightened by what they don't understand or deem different," he told me. "You must never judge a person by his religion, skin color, or beliefs. If someone needs help, you never ask his or her race or creed, you just give it. And you never boast about what you've done, or it would humiliate the person you've helped."

He then cited some story from the Bible or literature that perfectly suited the situation. I basked in his presence and the influence he had over me. He and Fred were my true role models.

Injustice, it seemed, was all around us and increasing daily. We didn't have to look far. One day my father traveled to a small village outside Metz to deliver some pictures. Entering the customer's house, he met two gendarmes who asked him for his identity papers.

"Yes, sir," my father replied respectfully to the most senior officer. "I'll show them to you right away. Just let me just put these pictures down, please."

As he attempted to lean the pictures carefully against the wall, the gendarmes for some reason took offense and arrested him. They claimed later that my father was being impudent by not complying with their request immediately. For twenty-four hours he vanished and we had no idea what had happened to him. My mother, anxious, even went to the local police station and filled out a missing persons report.

When Papa walked back into our lives the following day, he was a broken man. He was also covered in bruises. A gendarme had thrown him down a flight of stairs at the station, before beating him senseless and charging him with a lack of cooperation. His trial was set for the following month. As far as he could tell, his only crime was that he was Jewish.

Whatever else my father was, he was incredibly proud, and after the events of that night, he became physically ill with grief. He'd always had such high regard for the military and the police authorities, and was distraught at having been treated so cruelly for no reason. To have discovered the flip side of power brought his entire view of the world into question, and I think probably rekindled some unhappy memories of his time in an orphanage. Papa took to his bed soon afterward with a severe case of hepatitis and turned bright yellow. The doctor was called, but gave us little hope for a recovery. My mother was beside herself. It was weeks before the doctor declared him out of danger. But Papa's recovery was so slow that his trial had to be repeatedly delayed. When the newspapers reported, with huge headlines, that a father of seven had been unjustly beaten, the judge acquitted him.

As I reached my teens I began to ponder a number of matters that until then I had taken for granted. Strong convictions led me to become a vegetarian. My mother believed my decision to be a passing fancy but, busy as she was, she still prepared special dishes for me without ever attempting to alter my thinking.

My request to learn the Hebrew language was, however, met with great alarm. "Only boys are taught our sacred texts," she told me, shaking her head disapprovingly. "No girl has ever learned them."

"I'm tired of reciting prayers I do not understand," I told her. "I refuse to repeat the Hebrew words of our prayers like a parakeet without knowing what they mean. I don't even think of God when I murmur the prayers—all kinds of thoughts cross my mind instead. It is pure hypocrisy to pray when one's heart isn't in it."

It was hard for her to accept such a rebellion against our religious practices. No event, not even the death of her little boy, had shaken her strong and sincere religious faith. With great sorrow, she understood that I was questioning my belief in God. Afterward, she never again demanded that I pray.

Grospapa, too, chose to turn a blind eye. When he realized that Cecile and I no longer said prayers before and after every meal through choice, he diplomatically left the room at that moment so as not to make us do something we didn't want to do.

All around us the world was changing beyond recognition. Mussolini and the Fascists had risen to power in Italy. Germany had sent its troops into French Rhineland. King George V died in England. The Fascists and the Republicans were fighting in Spain. And the American black track athlete Jesse Owens was publicly snubbed by Adolf Hitler when he won a gold medal at the Berlin Olympics. In France, the fascist colonel François de la Roque became president of the Croix de Feu, which had become an extreme right-wing association espousing ultranationalistic views. De la Roque engendered the mob mentality, and there was fighting in the streets, followed by the downfall of the government. The more outspoken the politicians and warmongers became on the Jewish question, the more their blinkered outlook seemed to filter down to the masses. Spurred on by those in public life, the ordinary bigots seemed to find a voice. Finally, in 1936, Leon Blum came to power, the first Jewish (and socialist) prime minister in France, an event that caused further riots in the streets. Anti-Semitism was by then quite open, and there were demands for Jews to be removed from public life, as they had been in Germany. The news sent a chill through me, as did the growing sense of threat from Hitler and his Nazi party, but I nonetheless wholeheartedly believed in peace and rejected my brothers' constant call to arms.

"We must always find a way around war," I declared grandly. "Politicians should talk to each other. Wars maim people and destroy lives. There has to be a better way."

Fred and Arnold didn't agree. "Hitler must be stopped, and soon," they warned me ominously. "You don't understand, Marthe. You were born too late for the last war."

Despite being an excellent student, Fred had left school at seventeen and gone to Antwerp, in Holland, to learn the diamond trade. He then moved to Nancy to take over my uncle Henri's bespoke tailor shop after the Depression caused the diamond industry to slump. Arnold moved with him, to work as a cutter. Every Sunday morning Fred would travel from Nancy to Metz on the train for the sole purpose of taking us girls out for the evening. Father would never have allowed us out alone. Sophie and my other friends were insanely jealous. Fred would take off his hat to greet us and treat us like ladies as he escorted us around town. I adored him and hated it each time he left.

Bored at school, inspired by the books of Zola, Balzac, Dumas, Tolstoy, Jules Verne, and Jack London, I was eager to leave and experience something of the world before it was too late. My ambitions were unclear and swung wildly from wanting to be a lawyer to being a pilot, although I knew the chances of my feet reaching the controls were limited. Fully grown at seventeen, I was no more than four feet eleven inches tall, and considerably shorter than my brothers and sisters. Even my little mother towered over me, at five feet two inches. "I will never marry a short man," I told her, "or we'd have dwarves for children."

Maman shook her head and smiled. "Where do you get such ideas, Marthe?" she asked.

In 1937, I said a gleeful good-bye to my teachers and went to work in Cecile Modes, my sister's hat salon on the second floor of a building on the corner of the Place de la Republique and rue Serpenoise in the center of Metz. A career as a milliner had never been on my agenda, but I was glad to be free at last of the strict confines of the education system. Everybody agreed that Cecile made wonderful hats. They were concoctions of fancy for the young at heart. I have a cherished photo of my friend Sophie, her sister Regine, Cecile, and I all wearing hats that Cecile had made. At the time, we didn't have a care in the world. In retrospect, I realize how kind Cecile had been to hire me. I ruined more creations than I made, and I nearly burned the shop down when I left the electric iron on one night, searing a huge hole in the center of our worktable. But she was always very patient and never got mad at me. Perhaps she knew there were worse things in the world to get upset about.

At eighteen I went with Stéphanie, Rosy, Hélène, Sophie, and a large group of friends to La Vallée de Chevreuse summer camp near Paris. We'd been there before, with our parents, but this was the first time we were deemed responsible enough to be alone. For several blissful weeks we swam, cycled, played, and laughed together. I have dozens of black and white photographs of that holiday, in which our happiness was apparent. Little did I know it was to be the end of my childhood.

In October of that year, Germany marched into Czechoslovakia, claiming it as part of Hitler's Third Reich. A month later the whole of Germany's Jewish population—already subject to myriad rules, among them physical segregation and curfews—suffered a reign of terror without precedent, as the vast majority of the non-Jewish population looked the other way. Kristallnacht, the "Night of Broken Glass," was government-orchestrated and marked a crucial turning point in German policy regarding the "Jewish question." Hundreds of synagogues were set on fire and thousands of Jewish businesses destroyed. Gangs of Nazi youths roamed the streets and systematically smashed the windows of Jewish shops. Thousands of Jews were arrested and beaten in the streets. Ninety-one died.

We read about it with horror. We had relatives in Düsseldorf, the Farber family. The wife, Cecile, was my father's niece, and heavily pregnant with her third child when the Gestapo came to her home that night to arrest her husband. They broke everything in the house, smashed all the windows and threatened the entire family with violence. Somehow, Cecile persuaded them not to arrest her husband, and during the night they all fled. Her husband escaped to Holland. She hid in her maid's house until her baby—a little girl named Mindele—was born, and then followed him. Later, they left for Palestine, leaving Mindele with relatives in Holland. Their two sons—Josie, who was two, and Jacquie, who was three—were sent to us. Actually, Fred and Cecile traveled by train to the border to collect them from the courageous maid who'd agreed to escort them there. All risked arrest by the German police at the border station, but it was something they felt they had to do. After a few days with us, Josie was sent on to Aunt Hélène, an older sister of my father, who lived in Nancy. Jacquie remained with us. The rest of my father's family in Germany—including his elder sister Feigel, her husband, and their youngest daughter, Berthe—were arrested and deported to Poland, never to return.

Jacquie was just three years old when he arrived on our doorstep. Speaking only German, he looked around the room at us in bewilderment until his eyes fell on Hélène, then just fourteen, and he smiled. From that moment he was hooked. Hélène could do no wrong. He'd follow her around our home like a puppy, completely devoted to her. She loved having a little "brother" to play with, and thoroughly enjoyed the attention. But she had Fred's playful streak, too, and she'd often tease poor Jacquie mercilessly, telling him her hands were cold so that he'd run to her and warm them, or asking him to fetch something for her to wear. Her playfulness hid a patience I secretly admired. We were all too painfully aware that Jacquie might never see his family again, and Hélène's kindness helped to soften the loss.

After the events of Kristallnacht, we agreed as a family to help any Jew we could. It was a community decision, inspired by our young rabbi, Elie Bloch. Each Jewish family I knew was doing the same. My mother was among the most active. We'd talk endlessly about what action should be taken against the German government, since the French government seemed reluctant to do anything.

"The French and the English are equally to blame," she said. "They let Hitler walk in and take anything he wanted, and nobody seemed to have the courage to defy him."

At least ten families came to stay with us, having escaped from Germany. Their tales of life under the Nazis were terrifying, far worse than anything we'd read in the papers. They'd been denied basic human rights; had their pensions arbitrarily revoked; been stripped of their jewelry, stocks, and art works; denied the right to drive, listen to a radio, or be on the streets after dark. The walls of most shops and businesses had been plastered with posters saying, JEWS NOT WELCOME, and they'd been verbally and physically abused everywhere they went.

The more who came, the more determined we were to help them. My mother would feed and lodge them for several days, until they were ready to continue their flight; Stéphanie, Cecile, and I would try to cheer them up, and my father would help them financially. Most had fled penniless with just what they could carry, and were refused permission to withdraw money from their own bank accounts. They were en route to relatives in France, the low or Nordic countries, America or Palestine.

Despite reeling with horror at what had happened to them, I can honestly say that never for one moment did I think that the same thing would happen to us. Not in France.

"The French would never allow it," I told my worried mother confidently. I was not at all afraid. I believed that with clever politicking, Hitler could be appeased. I was delighted when we heard that the English prime minister, Neville Chamberlain, had gone to see Hitler. As I'd always claimed, it was good that they were talking. I knew Hitler was crazy, but I believed that the right people could make him see sense. I was young and ideological. I believed in human nature. I still had confidence that good would prevail.

By 1939 my ideological world was shattered. As if unprepared to carry on in the face of such international madness, my beloved grandfather's heart gave out, the day before Passover. He was seventy-six years old. With tears and heartache, on a warm spring day we buried him in the heart of the Jewish cemetery he was partially responsible for, after a three-mile walk through Metz in which we were joined by hundreds of people. Children stopped to tell us that every time Grospapa saw them, he'd give them a sweet. Poor people told how he'd regularly bring coal and food for the Sabbath, hauling heavy sacks to the third or fourth floors of their apartment buildings. So many people loved him, and we didn't even know. The world suddenly seemed a far duller place. In later years, however, we were enormously grateful that he'd never lived to see what happened in France. Wise to the end, he'd chosen dignity in death rather than the indignity of such cruel humiliations.

When Germany and Russia invaded Poland on September first of that year, and France and Britain declared war, I realized that I might have been naive in my hope for peace. My parents were more frightened than any of us. They'd lived through the First World War and knew exactly what it meant, although my father had escaped the draft because he had so many children. Back then, Maman had run to Cecile's and Fred's beds when woken by the Allied bombardments, and recited with them the Shemah. "Hear, O Israel," she'd cry, praying fervently that her babies would be spared. Her children, their fear allayed, would fall asleep, despite the noise.

Now, all around us, Frenchmen were mobilized. Fred was enlisted in Nancy and sent straight to the Maginot Line, a heavily defended line of fortification between France and Germany. Arnold was doing his national service in Tunisia, where he stayed with his regiment. My mother fretted for them both, as we all did. Then the local government in Metz issued an appeal asking all French families who could afford to move from the region to do so.

"Leave?" my father said indignantly. "And go where? All we have is in Metz. This is all we've ever known." He and Cecile both had their respective businesses, the younger children were still in school, there was my elderly grandmother to consider, and my grandfather's priceless library.

"Poitiers has been designated as the town you should move to," a harassed government official told us. "It'll only be temporary. Just until things settle down. It's a precaution. Consider it a short holiday;

go and stay with family or friends. Take only what you need. And please hurry."

My father's youngest brother, Benoit, lived in Poitiers, which was south and west of Paris, more than four hundred miles from the German border. It seemed a lifetime away. Everyone firmly believed it would never be affected by war. After a brief discussion with friends and relatives, and with the persuasive arguments of the authorities, it was agreed that we should evacuate as soon as possible.

"It's a holiday, remember," my mother assured us cheerily the next morning as we prepared to leave, "a late summer holiday. We'll be back here before we know it."

I was nineteen years old, and as I packed a few precious belongings into a small suitcase, I had mixed feelings about being forced to abandon our home. I had my friends and my job, but a new life in a city I knew nothing about seemed a great adventure, despite my apprehension of the unknown. Then there was Cecile. She'd done so well in her shop and had built up a loyal clientele. And what about Stéphanie, desperate to train as a doctor? What would happen to her? And Hélène and Rosy, both excellent students, would they be able to graduate?

Looking up, I saw Jacquie standing in the doorway to the bedroom I shared with Stéphanie and Cecile, his eyes wide with fear.

"Are the Germans coming, Marthe?" he asked me, his thumb glistening and ready to slip comfortingly back into his mouth. This innocent young child, who'd already lived through Kristallnacht, who'd watched Nazi brutes march into his home and destroy it, who'd been wrenched from his weeping mother's arms and separated from all he knew and loved, was clearly terrified.

Scolding myself for being so selfish, I ran to him and held him tightly to me. "No, Jacquie," I told him, stroking his soft brown hair. "No, they're not. I promise. The Germans will never invade France. Never."

A Foreign Country

Poitiers seemed like a foreign country to us. Sitting on a hilltop overlooking two rivers, with its surrounding villages strung out across the valley floor, it was quaint and rustic compared to industrial, cosmopolitan Metz. Prior to the influx of Jews from the east, there were only three or four Jewish families living within its predominantly Catholic community. The people didn't even know what a Jew looked like, and they were surprised, I think, to discover that we didn't have horns and tails. They were warm and friendly, though, and did all they could to welcome us. We were fellow countrymen, after all, as fearful as they were of the common enemy.

We'd arrived with only what we could carry, and began by living with Uncle Benoit and his pregnant wife Fannie in his small apartment on Place de la Liberté in the center of town. Benoit was a market trader and one of the few people my father got along with. He'd had a life tainted with tragedy, losing his first wife in a car accident, a child when it was very young, and watching his surviving son develop severe autism, refusing to speak. Despite his past, Benoit was as quiet and easygoing as my father was quick-tempered. Papa had protected Benoit from the pain of life in the orphanage, and the two brothers remained very close. In Benoit's gentle company, Papa softened visibly.

It can't have been easy for Benoit and Fannie, having nine of us, including my grandmother, suddenly descend on their home. We only stayed with them for the first few nights, before moving into empty rooms in the apartment below. Jacquie's surviving uncle, Oskar Kluger, and some other relatives from Metz joined us later. Among them was my much-loved uncle, Leon—one of my mother's younger brothers—his wife Claire and their daughter Myriam.

Leon was a businessman who'd owned a store in Metz and—like us—had been forced to leave everything behind. He was slim and good-looking, inordinately fond of my mother and respectful of my father. He was intelligent and friendly and, having grown up in a house of eight children, was very good with us all. Like all my mother's brothers, he was especially fond of me because I reminded him so much of her when she was young. We were very glad of his company in this strange new town.

For several days we slept where we could, on sofas and floors, until the government found us alternative lodgings, splitting us into twos and threes. Cecile and I shared a room in the apartment of a nice old-fashioned bourgeois family, the Laffons, who were nothing if not kind. Madame Laffon had lost a son in the First World War, and we could not do her greater service than to listen as she read out his crumpled letters from the front. Each day she read them aloud, and each day she cried as if for the first time. She carried her grief like a cross.

In the daytime we'd congregate at Benoit's apartment or go into Poitiers, and disappear off to our separate lodgings at night. We had no business to run, no income to earn, and no roof of our own over our heads. Father couldn't work; he spoke only broken French, and very few people in Poitiers spoke German. Cecile, Stéphanie, and I spent much of our time exploring the narrow winding streets of the town, with its cathedral, jewels of Romanesque churches, university, and Gallo-Romanesque remnants. We walked its warren of streets and were charmed by its fifteenth-century houses and the great hall of the dukes of Aquitaine. But none of that took very long.

After a month, and with the situation not improving across the rest of war-torn Europe, we began to realize that this was much more than a short holiday. Cecile found a furnished house with a very large walled garden in the Chauvinerie neighborhood, at the top of a steep hill north of the station and we were reunited as a family.

"Let's set up a business of our own," Maman suggested brightly one day, not long after we'd moved into our new home. "It'll bring in an income and give us something to do."

With the help of Uncle Leon, and with funds Fred gave us when he visited on leave from the Maginot Line, we rented a shop on rue de la Regratterie and set up a dry goods business, selling wholesale clothing to other stores. We called it "Etablissement Elby," after my uncle's initials, LB. Uncle Leon used his car to drive to outlying villages, visiting small general stores with our samples. Business was soon brisk, and Cecile, Leon, and I worked flat out, six days a week, to keep our customers satisfied.

While Cecile and I worked, Maman stayed home and tended to the house, Papa toured the auction houses and bought up old clocks and lamps for resale, and Hélène, Rosy, and Jacquie enrolled at local schools. Stéphanie, peaceful, quiet, unassuming, and still desperate to be a doctor, began her training as a medical student at the local university. She'd hurry home each night, her face aglow, her mind full of all she'd learned. She was bright and intelligent and extremely caring. "All I want to do is to help people," she'd say, and I'd secretly chastise myself for not being as unselfish.

The little spare time we had was spent as volunteer workers for the local refugee crisis center, an organization designed to help French refugees flooding into Poitiers from eastern France. The threat of German aggression had compelled hundreds of thousands to leave their homes. Stéphanie and I volunteered almost as soon as we arrived in Poitiers, and spent many hours at the crisis center, which was located at the train station, helping to deal with the hundreds of refugees who arrived every day. Poitiers, as a major junction on the main railroad tracks between Paris and Bordeaux, was not only designated as the place for people from Metz to evacuate to, but also as a transfer station—mainly for old men, women, and children—to stop for a day or two before being assigned to other cities farther south or west. As refugees ourselves, we had nothing but pity for these people, and Steph and I went every day to assist them with the transition and interpret for the Alsatians and Lorrains who spoke little or broken French.

We were immediately made welcome at the crisis center by several young men and women from the local youth hostel group who worked there as volunteers. Among them was Nonain, a dwarf and a communist, who was always extremely vocal about Hitler and the brutal reign of his armies.

"That bastard's a total megalomaniac," he'd rant. "He won't be satisfied until the whole of Europe is razed to the ground." He was a staunch supporter of the communist campaigns against the Fascists in Italy, Spain, and Germany, and terribly worried about the implications of the Russo-German Pact.

Through Nonain we met Heinrich, a tall, blond German who'd been forced to flee his homeland, his family, and his business because of his communist beliefs. He'd even gone to Spain and joined the Republicans fighting against Franco. Since 1936 my elder siblings and I had supported the Republican Army in Spain, both morally and financially. We liked Heinrich; we knew what it felt like to be ousted from one's home, and we had every sympathy with him. He was handsome, with strikingly blue eyes, and he had a crush on Cecile, who, in turn, completely ignored him. My parents both liked him. It gave them a rare opportunity to speak German, and he was often invited to our home for dinner, at which heated debates would ensue. I would watch him speaking movingly of his beliefs, and think how sad it was that all Germans weren't like him.

"Why aren't you nice to Heinrich?" I asked Cecile in the kitchen one night, after he'd spent another evening at our house, eating dinner with us and listening to the news on the radio.

"Because I don't trust him," she said flatly.

"But Cecile!" I cried. "You can't mistrust all Germans. Heinrich feels just the same way as we do about Hitler. He's often the first to criticize him."

"I don't care," she replied. "I still can't bring myself to trust him." And she never did.

For almost a year nothing much happened to change the daily routines of our new life deep in the French countryside. The store kept us going, the refugees kept coming and going, and our friendships with people like those in the local youth hostel group deepened. Hiking in the countryside or swimming in the Clain River, we could almost forget that our lives were under threat. We'd picnic in the park, enjoy camping with young friends, and wander home tired and happy, dreaming of further languid days.

The "phony" war was on, with the French Army, including Fred, manning the Maginot Line, and the Germans on the Siegfried Line, both sides blinking at each other. Britain had sent several hundred thousand troops to France to bolster our defenses, while in Scandinavia the brave Finns were doing their best to fight back the marauding Russians. Food rationing began for the first time since the First World War, and we were tutored in blackout routines and gas drills.

In spring 1940 the tone of war became more threatening when Hitler invaded Denmark and Norway, and Holland and Belgium fell quickly afterward to the German blitzkrieg. We thought of Jacquie's little sister Mindele somewhere in the Netherlands and feared for her safety.

Fortunately, Jacquie was too young to understand the implications of the latest German aggression, and whenever he asked after his family, we placated him with false information. But even at such a tender age, he remained bitter that his mother had "abandoned" him and his siblings. He'd reach for my mother and ask her: "*Tante,* you would never have left your children, would you?" She'd try to explain how impossible it had been for his mother, but he never seemed to understand.

We'd all huddle anxiously around the wireless every evening, waiting for the news on Radio France. We heard of Chamberlain's resignation in London, his replacement by Winston Churchill, of the advance of the German troops from Belgium into northern France and the mass evacuation of French and British forces from Dunkirk. Calais and Boulogne fell, and the entire northeast was overrun, including Metz. We thought often of our home on rue du Marechal Pétain, of the friends who'd stayed behind, and of Grospapa's priceless library. Our prime minister, Paul Reynaud, resigned, and Pétain, a First World

War hero and the man whose name adorned our home street, took over.

"We are living history," I told my mother breathlessly one night after the radio had been turned off and we sat in complete silence.

"I could do with a little less history, thank you," she replied crisply and returned to mending some socks. My father just leaned back in his armchair and closed his eyes.

Enthralled by a sense of excitement, albeit tinged with trepidation, I felt that as long as we could hold out as a nation against the Germans, our family was in a privileged and blessed position. We were well south, safely out of harm's way, living a life we'd never have imagined a year or so before, and experiencing bold new adventures. My pacifism was holding up well. But in May 1940 all that changed.

Every morning Cecile and I walked from our house, down the hill, past the railway station, then up the hill on the other side to Elby, where we'd open up and start serving our customers. Each lunchtime we'd lock up and return home to eat a meal with our parents, before returning in the afternoon. The days were long and the work hard, but we were making enough for us to live on, and I never once lost faith that the situation was only temporary, that soon we could all go home and pick up where we'd left off.

One afternoon, no different from any other, Cecile and I left the house and walked down the hill toward the railway station. "Marthe," she said, rummaging in her pocket, "you go on ahead and open up the store. I'm just popping down the tracks to see old Madame Guillaume and pay her the rent. I'll catch up with you in ten minutes."

Taking the keys to the store, I waved her good-bye and set off. The sun was shining and it was a bright, clear day. Looking up, I watched the clouds scudding across the intensely blue sky and listened to the birds singing their springtime serenades. I climbed the steps to the pedestrian bridge over the railway and peered below. The station was packed. A supply train was in and soldiers were milling about everywhere. Thousands of refugees were lining the platforms, waiting for trains to take them farther south. Their numbers had been swelled by a great many Dutch and Belgians fleeing the German invasion.

Pressing on, I checked my watch and saw that the time was 1:45.

Eager not to be late, I crossed the bridge and began to climb the steep hill on the other side. I was a few hundred yards above the railway tracks, in rue Boncennes, a residential street not far from our shop, when I heard airplanes approaching. There was nothing particularly unusual in that. But something about these planes made me stop and look up. Squinting into the bright early afternoon sun, I first noticed how low they were. There were two of them, getting lower by the second, coming straight along the railway tracks. As they neared, I realized that they were so low I could actually see the pilots sitting inside. Beneath each cockpit I could distinctly make out the Italian flag.

Enemy aircraft.

My stomach did a flip but I scolded myself for being so silly. They must be en route to somewhere else, I reasoned. This was Poitiers. It was completely undefended and, in any event, there was nothing here for them to attack. I didn't even shrink away. But when I saw the first bomb fall, when I was blown back by the explosion and saw the smoke rise in a great plume from one of the houses farther down the tracks, my heart froze. The train. The supply train. The station. The refugees. *Oh my God, Cecile!*

Then there was noise and smoke and explosions all around me. Bombs were dropping from the sky. The station disappeared under a cloud of acrid black smoke, the supply train erupting in a fireball beneath the footbridge. People were running and screaming and seeking shelter wherever they could. Looking around, I saw a middle-age couple scurry into the open doorway of a nearby house with some others, and I ran after them. Twelve of us crouched in the narrow hallway of that house, afraid to watch, flattening ourselves against the walls, our hands over our ears. My elbows pressed against my knees, I curled myself into as small a ball as possible, each new explosion shaking the ground around us, and making me almost jump out of my skin.

"It's the railway they're after!" a young man by the front door shouted back at us as we sat or stood silently, waiting. After what seemed an eternity, but was probably only a few minutes, his commentary tailed off as the explosions came less frequently and the drone of the planes subsided. With one final almighty bang signifying the demise of the last diesel locomotive on the tracks, the Italian pilots, their bomb bays empty, headed east, their mission accomplished.

Those of us hiding in the hallway emerged unsteadily, peering into the smoke and dust, afraid to believe what we'd witnessed was true. Out in the open, wide-eyed and trembling, my first and only thought was for my mother. Numb to all thoughts of the injured refugees, soldiers, or even Cecile, I knew that I had to get home as quickly as I could and tell Maman that I was safe. Walking away from my fellow survivors, I broke into a trot and headed straight for the little pedestrian bridge across which I'd come minutes earlier. Smoke and flames engulfed the train beneath it. The air was so thick I could barely see across it to the other side, but just enough to ascertain that it was still somehow intact.

People stood in shock all around me. I was the only one going anywhere. My hand to my mouth, my eyes smarting from the smoke, I started to run across the bridge. Within a few seconds of taking my first steps on its narrow walkway, however, I saw a railway worker straight ahead of me on the other side, waving his arms frantically and calling at me to stop.

"Arretez! Arretez!" he shouted. "Stay where you are!" But I simply had to get home. It was my only thought. Coughing as I ran right through the flames and the thick black smoke, I was almost blown off my feet when part of the train beneath me erupted once more. Steadying myself and hurrying on, I reached his arms as he grabbed me and pulled me quickly to one side.

"Are you completely crazy?" he shouted into my face, his eyes wide. "Didn't you see the danger? That was a munitions train. It's exploding. The whole thing could have blown up right under your feet!"

Shaking myself free, I told him: "I have to get home."

Pushing past, I plowed on, up the hill and home to my family. It took me twenty minutes to get through all the people rushing back down the hill to see what had happened and what they could do to help. When I finally reached our house, I found Maman crying and shaking with fear. She'd lived through too many bombardments not to be afraid.

"Marthe! Marthe!" she wailed, running to me in the small front garden, her arms outstretched. My face was blackened with smoke, my hair disheveled, but I was home and safe.

"I'm okay, Maman, it's all right, I'm here," I told her, patting her back reassuringly. Over her shoulder I could see Papa and little Jacquie, each clearly relieved to see me.

"*Tante, Tante,*" Jacquie called to her, "I told you they'd be all right."

Pushing me away from her, my mother looked at me with an expression of sheer horror. "But where is Cecile?" she asked.

The color drained from my cheeks, and I realized I hadn't given my sister a second thought. Seeing my mother's expression, I said: "She's fine. She wanted to go straight to the store to check that it wasn't damaged."

My mother almost collapsed with relief. "Thank God!" she cried, wringing her apron in her hands, still marked with flour from her morning's baking. Knowing that Hélène and Rosy were in school on the other side of town, she reached for my father and cried: "They're safe. Our children are safe."

As soon as I could reasonably escape, I hurried back down the hill, a huge lump in my throat. The valley was now teeming with rescuers scrambling onto the tracks to see which of the soldiers and refugees they could save. The scene was sheer carnage. Hundreds had died. Women and children were lying on the embankment, covered in blood, cradling loved ones. The train was devastated but the fires were now under control. Scanning the faces of everyone I saw, I searched for Cecile among them, praying that she'd survived. Madame Guillaume's little house was empty but undamaged. Her neighbors hadn't been so fortunate.

When I couldn't find my sister in the valley, I hurried up the hill to the store. Maybe she'd gone there, I reasoned, maybe she'd hoped to find me safe behind the counter. But there was still no sign. Unlocking the door, fumbling with the keys, I wandered in and stood there hesitantly, wondering how I could go home and face my mother and tell her that Cecile was missing.

I heard her before I saw her—a little gasp a few steps behind me. Turning, I came face-to-face with a tear-stained Cecile, her skin white. "Marthe," she whispered as I ran into her open arms. She was unscathed, having survived the bombardment by sheltering under some trees in the back garden of Madame Guillaume's house. But fearing the worst for me, she'd rushed across the tracks and searched everywhere after the planes were gone. When she couldn't find me among the injured, she'd visited every hospital and clinic that was taking in casualties. Her search fruitless, she'd decided to try the store one last time before returning home to break the news.

Locking the store for the rest of the day, we wandered home together arm in arm, weeping with relief and marveling at our escape. Although our lives had been turned upside down by the consequences of war, we'd never before experienced it firsthand or seen its arbitrary and devastating effects. Never again would I listen to the endless radio reports of bombardments across Europe without thinking of the scenes I'd witnessed in Poitiers. Just turned twenty, I came to understand that despite all my earlier optimism, our lives had been changed irrevocably. Nothing was certain anymore.

We were further shocked when Uncle Leon announced that he was leaving Poitiers for Toulouse with his wife and daughter. Grosmutter decided to leave with her son. "It's getting dangerous," Leon warned my mother. "You should all leave, too, before it's too late."

Maman shook her head. "There's far too many of us to pick up and start again," she told him. "We've already done it once. I'm not going to put the young ones through that again. We'll be fine." And so, with tears and kisses, we bid my grandmother good-bye and wished them all luck.

"See you soon," Leon said cheerily, then he kissed my mother on both cheeks.

"Perhaps," she replied softly, her eyes red-rimmed.

They left that evening in Uncle Leon's car, joining thousands of refugees pushed farther south by the ever-advancing German army. But my grandmother and her daughter-in-law Claire didn't get along, and within two weeks Cecile was summoned to collect her and bring her back to Poitiers. Cecile traveled south and spent a week in Toulouse with Uncle Leon, meeting their new friends and enjoying a change of scene. When she came back with Grosmutter, there seemed to be a new spring in her step.

A month later, in June 1940, despite all my reassurances to Jacquie, the Germans conquered France. The Maginot Line quickly fell and we were notified that Fred had been taken prisoner. There was little news of Arnold, last heard of in Tunisia, where he'd been stationed. On June 14 we heard that the Nazi troops had taken Paris and were marching up the Champs Elysées. France went into shock as a nation, and me along with it. Rage and indignation tore me apart. I was so upset and angry at the thought of the German swastika fluttering from the Eiffel Tower. My brothers had been right—there was no talking to Hitler. And now Marechal Pétain was trying to strike an armistice with him. I felt disgusted and betrayed.

"I don't know what's happening to the world," my mother complained sadly, shaking her head. For the first time in my life I thought that she looked every one of her forty-eight years.

My father's temperament hadn't improved much since our move south, and he and I still crossed swords regularly. He rarely shared his deep worries for the fate of our family under German occupation, but his mood worsened almost daily.

"You're always flying the red rag of revolution with your father," Maman would scold me. "It doesn't help that you're constantly at each other's throats."

But while Cecile and Stéphanie, Rosy and Hélène, continued to sail through their relationship with him unimpeded, I couldn't. Everything, from the way he sometimes spoke to our mother to his unreasonable gruffness to Jacquie, riled me. The raising of Jacquie became a particular issue. I couldn't bear the thought of that sad little boy being constantly harangued.

"Leave Jacquie alone!" I'd complain, time and again. "Don't you think he's been through enough?"

"I'll speak to him and anyone else in this house any way I want to," Papa would respond, frowning. "And I'll thank you not to tell me what to do. Now go to your room."

Weeks and sometimes months would pass without us saying a civil word to each other, as I froze him out with my silence. He, in turn, would address me only through Maman, saying things like: "Tell Marthe to pass the potatoes." We were each as stubborn as the other.

As our home filled with his assorted clocks and lamps, bought at knockdown prices from the auction rooms, repaired and restored but rarely sold, I became increasingly annoyed at the incessant ticking and at being woken night after night by the chimes simultaneously marking the hours. I was ashamed of his broken French, distressed by his constant moodiness, and impatient with his lack of education and crude language. It was only much later in life that I was able to look back and realize how terribly hard it must have been for him, afraid for us all and living in a strange town, with everything he'd known stripped from him. While the rest of us had grown even closer in the face of adversity, he continued to remain an outsider, looking in.

By the time the Germans arrived in Poitiers in July 1940, we were a defeated people. Our country had been split into an occupied and an unoccupied zone—known as the Zone Libre—under the suspect agreement struck by an obsequious Pétain, who'd set up a government at Vichy. Poitiers, by an accident of geography, lay in the occupied zone. The zigzag border between freedom and occupation lay less than twenty-five miles south of us, yet at the time none of us thought to try and cross it. What to? Where would we go? We'd already relocated once and the upheaval had been enormous. In the year since we'd moved, we opened a new business, found a new home, and made new friends. Who was to say that if we moved, the border—or *ligne de demarcation*—wouldn't be moved farther south, making our journey fruitless? Pétain promised his people that life wouldn't radically change under German occupation, and most people trusted and believed him.

It was around this time that our good friend Heinrich simply disappeared from our lives as if he'd never been a part of it. Nonain told us he had packed his things and fled the minute he heard the Germans were nearing Poitiers.

"He said if the Nazis caught him, he'd be arrested and shot," Nonain explained. "Poor bastard, I hope he'll be all right." I was sad that I hadn't had a chance to say good-bye to the handsome German who'd been our occasional dinner companion. I wondered if we'd ever see him again.

I saw my first Nazi that week, riding into town on his motorcycle. Cecile and I were walking from the store, going home for lunch as usual, when the khaki-colored BMW came hard around the corner, its engine revving noisily. The two of us stopped and stared at him as he approached.

My lip curling, I squeezed Cecile's arm and whispered under my breath: "I hope he breaks his neck." To our astonishment, at that moment his bike skidded from under him on the hot tarmac and he fell from it with a thump, crashing to the ground. Cecile was most impressed, but unfortunately, he was hardly hurt.

To begin with, nothing much changed in Poitiers at all, except that we saw German soldiers everywhere we went and had to be very careful what we did and said. When we did have any direct contact with them, they went out of their way to be courteous and polite, as if they were obeying strict instructions not to do anything to offend us. They wanted the French people to like and trust them, and they behaved better in France than they did anywhere else. We didn't trust them one little bit, of course, and were waiting for them to change. Sure enough, bit by bit, the mood started to alter. Pétain seemed increasingly on the Germans' side as they began a bombing campaign against London and invaded the Channel Islands. He rounded up all his old opponents, including the ex-prime minister, Leon Blum, and charged them with "causing the defeat of France." General de Gaulle, who'd rallied the Free French around the world from London and become a symbol of liberation, was sentenced to death in his absence.

The changes to our everyday lives came slowly at first, almost imperceptibly. The first, in September 1940, was that the heads of all Jewish households had to register at the town hall, giving the full name and date of birth of every family member. Failure to comply was punishable by imprisonment or death. My father, ever the law-abider, duly went on the date allotted to the first letter of our last name. H for Hoffnung fell on October 3, 1940, and—without hesitation—he registered each member of our household, as did most other Jewish fathers in France, little realizing the eventual significance of those precisely maintained lists. Our new identity papers were stamped with a red stamp and the word JUIF or JUIVE in bold type across it. All French people were issued coupons for food called *carte de rationnement.*

The tension between the Germans and the French Jews started to become tangible. My mother became more gloomy and couldn't be consoled. She saw only more doom ahead, and was right to be so pessimistic. That same month, the Vichy government decreed that all Jews had to declare their interests in businesses. Jewish shops and offices had posters declaring them as MAISON JUIVE plastered all over them. Elby was no exception. We arrived at the store one morning to find the door covered in signs advising all callers that we were Jewish. Our loyal customers couldn't have cared less.

Later that month, my brother Arnold returned to us out of the blue. All Jewish soldiers had been discharged from the French Army, and he'd been shipped home. It was good to have him back with us, and he soon took over Uncle Leon's role at Elby, adding a quiet but calming influence to the increasingly worrisome situation we were in.

Before long, Jews were banned from most professions, including teaching. Property began to be confiscated, and foreign Jews were arrested and interned. The Germans were slowly circling us, ensnaring us more and more, hoping we wouldn't take fright and bolt. New edicts were issued every day, closing Jewish businesses under new "Aryanization" rules. Everything was *Verboten* and punishable by death. French people came under some restrictions, too, but never as severe.

One day two German soldiers walked into our store. Cecile and I were serving a regular customer. The men wandered around, fingering the merchandise and mentally assessing its value. Unaware that we both spoke German, one turned to the other and said: "Let's steal this little lot off these filthy Jews. I reckon there's a tidy profit to be made here."

Furious, I abandoned my customer, ran out of the store and into the street. Looking right and left, I found what I was after—a Wehrmacht officer.

"Please, sir," I told him, "two of your men are in our store and they've no right to be here under the new Vichy rules. We could get into trouble just having them here. Please evict them for me." He did just as I asked and severely reprimanded the two villains in front of Cecile and me.

Shortly afterward we received a visit from a Frenchman who informed us that he'd been assigned by the Germans as a *gérant commissaire,* a non-Jew to take over our business. Realizing what was likely to happen, Cecile, Arnold, and I, along with Hélène, Rosy, and Stéphanie, completely emptied the store, filling suitcases with the most valuable merchandise and carrying them upstairs to the apartment of Madame Le Touchais, with whom we'd become friendly. A few days later we transferred them to the home of Madame Blondet, a former cleaning woman of my cousins', whom we knew we could trust.

"We're not to leave a thing for the Nazis," Cecile told me, her lips white. "Not a thing." I patted her shoulder with a smile.

Struggling with one of the heaviest suitcases, I walked past the imposing Notre Dame church toward Madame Blondet's home one afternoon when two German soldiers came walking toward me. Lowering my eyes, I found myself staring at their polished jackboots. Smiling hesitantly, I was at a loss for words. Before I could say anything, the largest of them picked up the case.

"Here, fräulein," he said with a smile. "Let me help you. That's far too heavy a load for such a pretty young girl."

Watching as he carried it easily several hundred yards farther on, but not too far from Madame Blondet's, I smiled my prettiest smile. "Thank you," I said, taking it from him and carrying on alone. "That's fine here."

By the time the *gérant commissaire* arrived to take over Elby a few days later, the shelves and racks were empty but for a few unsalable items. I'd have loved to have been a fly on the wall when the *commissaire* drew up an inventory of the stock.

Cecile and I were now unemployed, with a growing family to feed. We prepared to move from our home in La Chauvinerie to a house on rue de la Pierre Plastique. I started looking for work in Poitiers, but Cecile decided to take what goods she could from storage and move to Paris to set up a similar operation there. Paris seemed very far away from sleepy Poitiers. It also seemed highly dangerous. But we had relatives in the capital, including Uncle Max, my mother's youngest brother, who worked as a doctor there, and Cecile was adamant that she should go in order to send us money to live on.

"I'll be fine," she said, hugging me. "Look after everyone for me, you're the oldest girl at home now." Before any of us could object, she'd packed all that she could carry and left. I missed her terribly.

But as one door closed another opened. In December 1940, Fred arrived home. We were delighted to see him, although shocked by his appearance. We sat him down, fed him and listened, open-mouthed, as he told us his story. After the Maginot Line had fallen, he'd been captured and transferred to a prisoner-of-war camp in Strasbourg, which was the last we'd heard of him. Overhearing the German guards say that all the prisoners would be transferred to Germany the following day, he brought his escape plans forward and, wearing civilian clothes he'd secretly hidden, somehow fled and crossed the Vosges Mountains in the harshest winter on foot, walking only at night. He traveled to Nancy, contacted all his old customers, held a huge sale and sold the entire contents of his tailor's shop. Secreting the money in his clothes, he'd journeyed on to Poitiers. This money kept us going throughout the whole of the war. Thanks to Fred, thin and pale after his ordeal, we were able to survive.

At dinner on the night of Fred's return, I had a guest, Rosette Korn, a beautiful young girl and new friend of the family. I'd known her vaguely in Metz, but when the call came for families to leave for Poitiers, she'd stayed with her father Kalman, a barber, while her ailing mother was evacuated with the other patients from the Jewish hospice.

"Please, could you possibly visit my mother, Marthe?" Rosette had asked in the first of many letters to me. "She is sick and far from home. She'd be so comforted by the sight of your smiling face."

By the time Rosette and her father were forced to leave Metz and join us in June 1940, she and I had become pen pals and very good friends. She found a job working in the town hall as an interpreter.

From the moment they met that evening, we all knew that she and Fred were destined for each other, and so did they. But we also knew that Fred couldn't possibly stay in occupied France. As an escaped German POW and a Jew, he was doubly at risk. Desperate to join de Gaulle's Free French and promising to keep in touch, he and cousin Oskar Kluger left to cross the border into the Zone Libre.

Security had tightened dramatically on the demarcation line in recent weeks, and the German patrols were especially suspicious of any young men who might be in the Resistance. Women were always more easily able to slip across into unoccupied France. Later that afternoon, three hours after Fred and Oskar had left, there was a knock on the door. My father opened it to a stranger.

"My name is Monsieur Noel Degout," the middle-age man told my parents. "I'm a farmer in Dienné and I've come to tell you that your son Fred was arrested this afternoon, trying to cross the border."

Her hand to her mouth, my mother asked what happened.

"He and his cousin were crossing my land when the Germans came and caught them. They brought them to my barn to question them. I see the German soldiers very regularly, they know me, and I asked them if I could talk to the two young men. They told me their names and where they lived and asked me to get word to you. That is why I'm here. They've been taken to the Pierre Levée Prison in Poitiers. That's all I know."

My mother was beside herself. She fully believed Fred would be sent back to POW camp or worse once they discovered who he was. We visited him as soon as we could and were relieved to find them both in good health and high spirits.

"I'll be fine, Maman," Fred scolded my tearful mother. "Just you wait and see."

Fortunately, German superefficiency hadn't yet reached the occupiers of sleepy Poitiers, and Fred's captors never discovered his POW past. Nor did they realize that Oskar was a German Jew. For their attempted escape, he and Oskar were each sentenced to one month in the town prison. The prison was under French control and so we were able to visit them every day.

While Fred was incarcerated, Hélène became gravely ill. She'd fallen and hurt her knee badly and needed an operation. Her knee became infected and swelled to twice its size. Then she developed peritonitis from suspected appendicitis, and the doctors told us that all we could do was pray. The day Fred was released, he went from prison straight to her hospital bedside and remained there for twenty-four hours, holding her hand and willing her to live.

"I want to die," she told him weakly. "The pain is too much."

"You cannot die," he insisted, "you're only seventeen. You have your whole life ahead of you. You have to live." He made her survive, by simply refusing to accept her defeat.

As soon as she was out of danger, Fred tried to cross the border with Oskar again, using the farm of Monsieur Degout, who'd agreed to help them. Thankfully, they made it across and moved to St. Etienne, near Lyon, where a lovelorn Rosette soon joined Fred and they were married.

With Rosette gone, there was a vacancy at the town hall for a

German-speaking interpreter. I applied for her job and was accepted. I was lucky. I had a German name, I came from Metz, I was blonde with pale eyes and fair skin. Most of the Germans assumed I was one of them. My French boss knew I was Jewish but couldn't have cared less. The department I worked for had been newly established by order of the Germans. It was the Bureau de Requisition, designed specifically to facilitate the systematic theft of anything French by the occupying forces. Mine wasn't a pleasant job, but it was a job and—unable to earn a living in the store anymore—it was what I had to do.

Every time some greedy German decided he wanted a car, house, or furniture, it was my role to translate the "request" in French to the appropriate clerk, who'd issue the necessary requisition slip in the name of the Third Reich. It was a challenge, dealing with the enemy every day, and I was far more enthusiastic about it than I'd ever been about school or while working in Cecile's hat shop.

My French boss was Monsieur Grelet, a kindly man who liked me very much. His three interpreters were all Metz Jews, since we were the only ones in Poitiers who spoke German, but I was the only blonde with a fair complexion. (Monsieur Grelet knew how anti-Jewish the Germans were, so because I looked the least Jewish, I became his favorite.) The German commander of the Kommandantur, or military headquarters, was Captain Allemann, a Protestant minister in civilian life. He called me *mon sourire* because of my cheeky, dimpled smile. Allemann could be very tough when he wanted to be, but he seemed to like me, and I had his measure.

"Come to Berlin for a marvelous career in one of our ministries, Marthe," he said. "They could really use someone like you."

I shook my head and told him that was impossible.

"Why?" he asked, astonished that I would turn down such a golden opportunity for promotion in the new Reich.

"Because I'm French," I told him.

He laughed, his hands flat across his belly. "Don't be ridiculous," he said. "You are a true Aryan."

Exercising my dimples, I said, "No, Captain, I'm a French patriot and I intend to remain here with my fellow countrymen."

One day he ordered Monsieur Grelet and me to accompany him to the Poitiers Museum, in the vaults of the town hall, because he wanted some fine art to decorate his office. Ordering the curator to show him what was available, he chose several paintings he liked and asked me to interpret for him.

I looked askance at him and shook my head. "Aren't you ashamed of yourself?" I asked, as Monsieur Grelet—who spoke no German but understood enough to know what I was saying—gasped audibly beside me. "You come to a museum, a sanctuary for history and art, and just take what you like. What right do you have to steal what belongs to France?"

For a moment I thought Allemann would order me shot, but his face broke into a smile and he nodded slowly.

"I like you, *mon sourire*," he said. "You speak your mind. I only wish the rest of your countrymen would do likewise. If all the French were as direct and straight as you, I think I'd prefer it."

I returned his smile, relieved to still be alive. *"Danke schön,"* I replied, clicking my heels together in mock deference.

Turning on his heel, he added coldly over his shoulder, "Nevertheless, those paintings are now mine. Tell Monsieur Grelet to have them sent to my office. Immediately."

The Noose Tightens

On April 13, 1941, I celebrated my twenty-first birthday. My parents firmly believed that life should continue as normal, despite our situation, and they allowed me to invite twenty friends to the apartment we'd moved to on rue Riffault. We'd rented the lower two floors of an elegant three-story town house, an old-fashioned property with a large back garden and a wooden entrance door large enough to accommodate a horse and wagon. My birthday party was a very low-key affair, with dancing, cakes, and lemonade, and Stéphanie asked some of her fellow medical students along to make up the numbers. She was by then deeply in love with one of them, a young man by the name of André Dufour, known to everyone as Dedé.

They'd met at medical school, and Dedé, a Catholic from a devout family, had taken an instant shine to the beautiful young woman that Stéphanie had become. At twenty years old, she was one of the loveliest girls I'd ever seen. Slim and petite, with glossy dark hair and stunning brown eyes, she had the poise and bearing of someone much older. She was quiet, strong, and rarely afraid. I had every confidence that she was going to make a wonderful physician, with her compassionate outlook and kind manner. Dedé's family didn't approve of his relationship with a Jew and did all they could to discourage it. Because of their resistance, the couple were never engaged officially, but as far as Steph was concerned, Dedé was the man she was going to spend the rest of her life with.

"Just don't ask her to sing!" I joked when one of the guests sat at the piano and started to play.

One of Stéphanie's closest friends was Jacques Delaunay, the son of a senior customs official based in Saigon, Indochina. He and his younger brother Marc, a law student, had been raised in the Far East, where his mother ran an orphanage for abandoned children. The two brothers had been sent back to Poitiers in 1939 when the Japanese began to make threatening noises. They were atheists.

For some reason, Jacques took one look at me that day and decided I was to be his girl. There was no debating the issue. He'd simply made up his mind. He danced with me all afternoon, refusing to allow anyone else to cut in. He was extremely handsome, with huge dark eyes, and very tall, at least six-foot-one, and he towered over me. Even in high heels I only reached his chest.

I was very flattered by his attention, but pretended not to be interested and continued looking around the room, smiling and speaking to others as we passed. But Jacques was most insistent. A smile tugging permanently at the corner of his mouth, he never once left my side. We danced the tango, the fox-trot, and the passé double. He continued, on our first few dates, to present our ongoing relationship as a fait accompli. He was more attracted to me than I to him, but the more I saw of Jacques, the more I grew to like him.

My sisters and I had a standing invitation in the summer to swim in the Clain from the beach garden of our friends, the Giraud brothers, whom we'd met through the youth hostel group. One perfect summer afternoon when it seemed as if all thoughts of war had melted away in the shimmering heat, I was paddling in the river when some of the boys from our group decided to dive-bomb me, pushing me under and filling my mouth and nose with water. I didn't mind at all. I was a competent swimmer and a good sport and I came up laughing and spluttering.

But Jacques, who'd joined us for the first time and was on the riverbank, grew increasingly agitated. Before I could say anything to stop him, he dived in, pushing the other boys out of the way.

"Leave Marthe alone!" he cried angrily, rescuing me. "Can't you see she's had enough?"

Smoothing back my wet hair, I trod water and stared at him with a mixture of shock and delight. Nobody had ever stood up for me like that before, not even Fred. Something about his gallantry that day made me supremely happy.

After that I started to see him every day. We walked together or cycled out to the beautiful countryside around Poitiers; we went swimming or canoeing with our friends. After just a few days, and while we were picnicking alone in a forest, Jacques asked me to marry him.

"Don't be ridiculous," I told him, pulling away. "It's much too soon, we hardly know each other. And, anyway, there's a serious religious problem. You're not Jewish, and my mother would never let me marry a non-Jew."

"I'll convert, if that's what it takes," he told me, his dark eyes twinkling. "I'm not remotely religious. I was never even baptized. Neither were my parents. My grandfather was excommunicated and the priest told his customers to stay away from him. The ban ruined him. Ever since then my family doesn't recognize the Catholic Church as having any rights over us. I can never take priests seriously, with their big feet sticking out from under their robes. And, anyway, you'll soon get to know me and to realize what an eminently suitable husband I'd make."

Although I didn't say yes, from that day on I didn't protest quite as much when he told me his plans for our future together.

The war, of course, hadn't disappeared, and no matter how I tried to block it from my mind and keep it from spoiling my happiness, we were under an increasingly hostile occupation. Every day I was reminded in some way of our plight, and the atmosphere seemed to worsen dramatically after the Germans broke their pact and invaded

Russia in June 1941. I told my mother: "Don't you realize that things are only getting worse because they're losing the war with Russia? It'll all be over soon." But she wouldn't be comforted.

That summer, after Pétain had ordered the arrest of twelve thousand Jews for "plotting to hinder Franco-German cooperation," the Germans issued a series of new edicts. The noose was tightening. New rules were added almost daily, and each one had to be strictly complied with. Not content with posters plastered all over walls, homes, and on nearby trees, we were now forbidden the use of a radio, a typewriter, or a telephone, although we had all three hidden in my father's bedroom. We couldn't go to the shops until four-thirty in the afternoon, and by then everything would have been sold but for the kind shopkeepers who kept things back for us, at grave risk to themselves. We were forbidden from all public places such as squares, restaurants, gardens, cafés, libraries, and sports grounds. We couldn't take a tram, enter a cinema, or even sit in a private garden. All the restrictions made my blood boil.

One day, as Captain Allemann, the former Protestant minister, was again pestering me with another great job offer in Berlin, I knew I could no longer continue with the charade.

"I can't come because I'm Jewish," I finally blurted, flashing him one of my broadest smiles.

"But you can't be!" he protested, his mouth flapping open and shut like a giant fish. "I can smell a Jew a mile away."

"Then smell well," I told him quietly, registering the disgust in his eyes. "And that is why I can never go to Berlin."

The captain had a daughter the same age as me and always treated me in a fatherly manner. Now I'd put our working relationship to the ultimate test.

"Well, maybe somewhere deep in your past there was some great-grandparent or other who may or may not have been," he reasoned aloud, frowning hard at me, hoping that I would concur.

"No, sir," I told him defiantly. "I'm Jewish. Both my parents are Jewish. I come from a long line of Jews. My grandfather was a rabbi. I'm proud to be a Jew."

The captain's face flushed red and he waved his hand at me dismissively. "I cannot believe it!" he said, his top lip curling. "I don't want to hear it. I'm terribly disappointed in you." He walked brusquely out, slamming the door shut behind him.

I left his office upset but with my head held high. I was pleased that it had angered him so.

A few days later the tall German field gendarmes brandishing polished metal breastplates, their rifles fixed with bayonets, marched into the large open office we all shared and shouted, "All Jews out! In one hour!"

Monsieur Grelet jumped to his feet to protest. "But I cannot operate without these people," he told the senior officer. "I simply cannot function." Looking at me in desperation, he pleaded, "Let me at least keep Mademoiselle Hoffnung. I need her."

The senior officer shook his head. "I have my orders," he said stiffly. By the time Monsieur Grelet and others were finished protesting, I had less than thirty minutes to clear out my desk.

It was a terrible shock to lose my job like that. I'd always thought it was safe because of the nature of the work. There was not a single German speaker in Poitiers who wasn't Jewish.

Having packed up my belongings and grabbed my coat and hat, I decided that I wanted one last chance to confront Captain Allemann. I went to the Kommandantur and asked to see him. To my surprise, I was immediately ushered in. He stood half turned away from me, but I could see his jaw clenching and unclenching as he waited for what he no doubt expected to be my pitiful pleading to keep my job. But that wasn't what I'd come for.

"You must be terribly proud," I told him, standing ramrod straight.

His eyes flickered. "What?" he said, turning.

"You must be very proud as a German officer that German orders have just cost three people their jobs."

"I—I don't know what you mean," he faltered.

"Oh, I think you do," I replied, my eyes locking onto his. "And tell me how do you feel as a pastor when your high command instigates an order that denies people the right to work, to earn money so they can eat and have a roof over their heads? How can you accept such inhumane treatment of Jews? A few days ago you thought the world of me. How can your opinion have changed so dramatically to allow me to be made an outcast simply because of an accident of my birth?"

I'd heard from one of his assistants that he'd been reassigned and was about to leave for the Russian front. Turning as if to go, I added, for good measure, "I hope that when you're enduring the most terrible conditions in Russia, Kapitan Allemann, starving hungry and freezing cold, you'll remember what you Germans did to us, the Jews."

He stepped toward me and grabbed my arm to prevent me from leaving the room. "Fräulein," he said, his eyes sad, "as a human being all I can tell you is that I'm sorry, but as a German officer I must support my government." Slowly, gingerly, he extended his right hand. "Good-bye," he said softly.

I remembered the contempt in his eyes when he'd discovered I was Jewish. I was still smarting at being forced from my office and my job at gunpoint. Spurning his hand, I turned on my heel and left his office, slamming the door behind me. It was August 1941.

I think Jacques was secretly pleased I'd lost my job. He'd never liked me being in daily contact with the enemy, and had told me as much several times.

"But I have nothing to do now," I told him, fed up with being stuck at home all day with my parents. "No job, no money, no means of helping my family—I might as well become a student."

"That's a good idea!" he said. "What would you study?"

"Oh, I don't know," I said, absentmindedly. "Nursing, perhaps."

Jacques's face lit up. "Of course!" he cried. "That's perfect! You could become a nurse, and then when I'm a qualified doctor, we could work together. That's the most brilliant idea you've ever had, Marthe!" Leaning over, he kissed me affectionately on the nose.

From then on Jacques pestered me daily to become a nurse; as with our engagement, he simply wouldn't take no for an answer. I was worried how I would manage with my college fees without an income, but when I wrote to Fred to tell him of my plans for a new vocation, he replied, "Go ahead with your studies. I'll take care of your financial needs."

My mother could hardly believe my idea. I'd always been incapable of coping with sickness and death. When I was three years old, Maman's younger brother, Jacques, had died of complications following an appendectomy—I remembered him clearly as a young man bouncing me on his knee. At his funeral I took one look at the large box draped in black cloth in which to put calling cards and went into a screaming fit. I thought his body was somehow in the container and became hysterical. Ever since then I'd been terrified of death. I wasn't much better when it came to the sick. Hélène's knee was still bad after two more operations, and I'd run from the room every time the nun arrived to change the dressings.

Despite my mother's misgivings, on October 6, 1941, I enrolled at the local Red Cross nursing college, run by Mademoiselle Margnat, allied to the University Hospital run by the nuns, Les Soeurs de la Sagesse. On my first day my fellow students voted to name our class after Marechal Pétain. When I and a classmate, Janine Rieckert, objected, our fellow students were shocked. "What do you mean you don't approve of the name?" one asked. "Pétain is the savior of France."

"Oh no he isn't," I replied adamantly. "General de Gaulle is the name we should revere. He'll be the one to save France, you'll see."

Mademoiselle Margnat called me into her office early on and asked me to sit down. She was a kind woman who knew I was Jewish. "I don't want you to worry about anything, Mademoiselle Hoffnung," she said. "There's no prejudice here. We treat our patients regardless of their nationality or religious persuasion, and our staff are to be treated the same."

I was grateful for her kindness, and she gave me good cause to be. As the atmosphere worsened toward the end of 1941, the Gestapo began arriving unannounced at the hospital, searching for what they euphemistically called "undesirables." The senior officer would march in, brandishing a list, and ask a nun for Jews or communists by name.

"I do not recognize that name," she'd reply frostily. "We have only patients here."

But pushing past her, they'd burst into wards and private rooms, check the names on the charts on the bedstead and drag anyone on their list from their beds, still in their pajamas. The nuns would hide me in a small office near the chapel whenever the Germans came. They could have been arrested and shot for less.

One day, Mademoiselle Margnat summoned me to her office, and

I thought that perhaps the Nazis were coming back. But that wasn't the reason for her summons.

"We have a new patient, Marthe," she told me. "I need you to look after him for me. You're the only one who can."

"Certainly, Madame," I replied without hesitation. "What's wrong with him?"

She sighed and studied my face for a moment before responding. "He's a German soldier," she said.

"Yes?" I said. "And what's wrong with him?"

My new charge was Günther, a six-foot-four-inch member of the Wehrmacht who'd inadvertently poked his head out of the top of a tank being transported on a train just as the train went under a low bridge. He suffered serious head injuries and was semiconscious when he arrived. It was my job to look after him until he could be transferred to a neurosurgical ward of a German hospital. I was the only one who could, because I was the only one who spoke German.

Günther was in a bad way. He'd been seriously concussed and it had affected his mind. One minute he'd be fast asleep and the next he'd be up and about, his open-backed nightgown revealing all, wandering barefoot into the street. I'd have to find him and lead him gently back by the hand. People would laugh at us, me eighteen inches shorter and in my white uniform, leading this huge man, half dressed in his nightgown and with a bandaged head, back to his bed.

"Come now, Günther," I'd tell him gently. "We can't have you wandering the streets in the nude." He came to trust me, and he'd look down at me with a simpleton's expression and allow me to take his hand. I tried not to think of who he was or what he might have done. It was my job to take care of him, regardless. I'd never have done anything to harm him, and I took care of him to the best of my ability for several days until he was transferred back to a German hospital. I never saw him again.

That year, the remaining foreign Jews in Poitiers were rounded up and placed in a nearby camp by the Germans, who used the precisely maintained lists of names that we, as a community, had so obligingly provided. Our wonderful rabbi, Elie Bloch, who'd moved from Metz to Poitiers with his wife Georgette and young daughter Myriam, was tireless in his efforts to help those who'd been forcibly interned. He badgered the German authorities every day until they finally agreed that the children of those being held could stay in the homes of local Jews and continue their education instead of enduring a life behind barbed wire.

In the rue Riffault house we had room to spare and were allocated a fourteen-year-old Polish boy named Maurice Patawer—"Pavel," as he was known—who was understandably wary of us at first and reluctant to leave his parents. But we soon put him at ease in our extended family, and he and Jacquie became very close. Pavel's sad, silent presence among us served as a daily reminder of the German injustice.

Not that we accepted it unflinchingly. All around us people were doing what they could to undermine the enemy. Poitiers was a university town, and many of the students rejected the shame of the armistice and began their own small pockets of resistance. In the local cinema, the Castille, they showed their hostility to the occupying troops by stamping their feet, whistling, and interrupting German propaganda broadcasts. They'd open newspapers and read the sports pages rather than watch the German films, until one student was arrested for doing so. German posters were torn down and the "V for Victory" sign was written in chalk or coal on walls, doors, and pavement all over the town.

At home we embarked on our own methods of resistance. As in Metz, we helped Jewish families flee from occupied France. People we'd never met would just turn up on our doorstep, ring the bell, and ask for help.

"How did you hear about us?" we'd ask, and they'd just say they'd been told. We no longer fed them or took them in; we couldn't. The Germans were watching all the time, so we had to be extremely careful. Once we'd decided that our callers were genuine and not spies or Nazi agents, we'd give them an address, sending them to one of several local farms on the border, like the one Fred and Oskar had used successfully.

We didn't know anything about these passing strangers and we rarely discovered how they came to be in Poitiers. But the strain was etched on their faces, particularly the women, and we could tell that many of them had been traveling for some time. One thing we'd learned during the war was never to ask questions—it was safer that way. Many of our callers had come from the east and were very wary, afraid of everyone and everything. All they wanted was an address to go to, a place where they could cross the *ligne de demarcation* and get as far away from the Germans as possible.

The farmers were marvelous. Through Monsieur Degout, they let it be known they'd be glad to help anyone escape across their land, and they never asked a penny in return, despite the obvious risks to themselves. We became very friendly with some of them, but we never once thought of arranging a similar route for ourselves at that time. My parents had even traveled south, on an authorized permit I managed to acquire through the German Kommandantur, to attend Fred and Rosette's wedding. But like the good French citizens they were, they dutifully came back.

None of us ever imagined how terrible things would become. We didn't know anything, even though we listened to the radio every night. There had been rumors of labor camps and of whole villages being massacred in Poland and Czechoslovakia, but it all seemed like propaganda, since it was unconscionable to believe the Germans could be capable of such atrocities. They'd cleverly created a relaxed atmosphere in France, lulling us into a false sense of security. They made us feel that these ever more aggressive edicts they were constantly being forced to issue were in response to the behavior of a few. They tried to make us believe that we were all on the same side. For a while it worked.

The news of the Japanese attack on Pearl Harbor in December 1941 rallied our spirits. We knew that, despite the tragic loss of more than three thousand lives, it would mean an end to American isolationism and the start of a meaningful alliance as the United States entered the war. For Jacques, however, it meant something quite different. As the Japanese swept through Southeast Asia, claiming Hong Kong and threatening Singapore and Malaya, he feared for his parents in Saigon. In the next few months the Japanese seemed unstoppable, as Malaya, Singapore, and finally Saigon fell. Jacques had no means of contacting his parents and could only listen in horror to the reports of the brutal Japanese victories.

My initial elation at the Pearl Harbor attack became tempered by fears for his family, and then fears for my own as political changes in France brought about a new and threatening mood of pessimism. Only my mother suspected what might be coming, and even then she didn't realize just how bad it would be. She'd lived through a war, she remembered what it was like, and she believed the few rumors that we'd heard. It was she who'd pressed Fred to leave, she who fretted and fussed over us all. It was her mind I found myself constantly trying to put at rest.

"It's all right, Maman," I'd tell her. "We're safe here, you don't have to worry." But events continued to haunt her, not least of which was the arrest in Paris of her youngest brother, Max.

Max was a doctor, married to a Swiss woman, Fannie. They had a little girl, Ruth. Max was much younger than my mother, and Stéphanie and I had spent a summer holiday with him in Lyons when we were children, regarding him more as an older brother than an uncle. Because of the narrow age gap, we were very close. Max was an academic, a quietly spoken pacifist who was a bit of a mouse. Fannie was the difficult one, a cousin of my father's. They'd met through mutual friends and were married soon after. She was a prickly woman, emotionally fragile and hard to get along with. She'd fled south to stay with Uncle Leon in Toulouse a few months earlier, taking Ruth with her and leaving Max to run his medical practice in his apartment building on rue Vavin near the Luxembourg Garden in Paris. Fannie and the lady concierge had never gotten on well, and the woman took her revenge once Fannie left by calling the police and denouncing Max as a communist, falsely claiming he'd held secret meetings in his apartment.

Made prisoner in the bleak internment camp at Drancy, Max became gravely ill. Although only in his late thirties, he developed a tumor of the pituitary gland, manifested by acute glaucoma and acromegaly. This condition, due to a rare, excessive secretion of the growth hormone, results in violent headaches. Barely able to see, hardly able to stand, burning with a high fever, he was transferred from Drancy on the outskirts of Paris, to Hôtel Dieu, the oldest hospital in Paris, close to the cathedral of Notre Dame.

I can't remember how Maman first received word of Max's incarceration and subsequent hospitalization. Nor can I remember any family discussion about what, if anything, should be done. The first thing we knew, Maman was gone. It was late January 1942. She'd taken a train to Paris to see if she could help. I remember being terribly concerned for her. She barely spoke any French and was going alone to Paris to visit my uncle, whose associations would be very closely scrutinized by the Gestapo.

We waited for several days, with no word. Jacques, afraid I would do something stupid, forbade me to try and follow her.

"You'll help no one if you are arrested, too," he warned me. "Be patient, Marthe."

Our waiting came to an end at dinner one evening, just before the new curfew, when our little mother walked back into our lives. On her arm was Max. We crowded around them, assailing her with questions.

"We're terribly tired," she said. "It's been a long trip. Let's eat and then I'll tell you what happened."

As soon as we sat down at the table, Maman recounted her experiences in Paris. "I went straight to the hospital," she said, sipping some water. "Cecile helped me. She sends you all her love, by the way. When I arrived at the hospital I found Max in bed and clearly very sick. He told me he needed to use the bathroom, so I helped him into his dressing gown and we shuffled together along the corridor. While I was waiting for him, I noticed that there were no guards anywhere to be seen. Max was a political prisoner, and they'd obviously decided he was too weak to attempt an escape. As soon as he came out of the bathroom, I told him, 'Max, you're coming with me.' I took him by the hand and led him along a long corridor, down some stairs, and out into the street. He kept protesting that he was only in his pajamas, but I told him not to worry."

Before any of us could interrupt, she waved a hand at us and continued, "Once I was out on the street, I hailed two of those newfangled velo-taxis with a sidecar. I helped Max into it and followed in the second taxi. I took him to his apartment and found him a change of clothes. We packed a suitcase with his belongings, and as soon as we reasonably could, we boarded the next train south."

There were a hundred questions I wanted to ask. I was staggered by how foolhardy she'd been. She could so easily have been arrested for trying to help a prisoner escape. I realized she was an iron hand in a velvet glove.

"But Maman," I said, my eyes filling with tears of pride, "how on earth did you make yourself understood in Paris? You surely didn't speak German?"

"No, Marthe," she said, a twinkle in her eye. "I spoke French."

Seeing our confused reactions, she smiled. "I'm afraid, my darlings, that I've been able to speak it for years. I just didn't want you knowing or you'd stop chattering all your secrets in front of me."

Our mouths fell open.

A few days later Cecile emptied Max's apartment in Paris, clearing everything out before the concierge or the Gestapo knew what she'd done. The risk could never have been matched by the value of Max's belongings, but—as with us all—she was determined not to let the Germans have a thing.

After a few days' rest, Arnold took Max and my mother to the demarcation line. Using the same Degout family of farmers who'd helped Fred, Oskar, and Rosette escape, they managed to cross safely. Uncle Leon took in Uncle Max, and my mother and Arnold went on to visit Fred and Rosette in their new home in Arles. Waiting for them was my mother's first grandchild, Maurice Jacques, born February 3, 1942.

She and Arnold returned three weeks later, crossing once more at the Degout farm. Our brave little mother returned to us safe and sound, her task complete. She rarely spoke of what she had done and never attempted anything quite so courageous again. All she could talk about was her little grandson.

World events continued to haunt us. Hitler's panzer armies were nearing the gates of Moscow, Rommel's Afrika Korps were making sweeping advances in North Africa, and Malta was under almost constant bombardment. There seemed to be no stopping the march of Nazism, despite an Anglo-American pact and some initial successes against the Italian fleets. My mother, listening to the radio night after night with the rest of us, became more and more agitated.

"What will be left when Hitler has finished?" she'd rail. "When will it all end?"

Under increasing German pressure, Pétain's deputy, Pierre Laval, became prime minister and began openly collaborating with the enemy. He went on radio to wish victory for Germany and offered to help the Nazis round up those in the Resistance.

As Jacques continued to fret over the worrying situation for his parents on the other side of the world, I came to realize that, much closer to home, things were changing dramatically for the worse.

Badge of Pride

Every night between six-thirty and seven-thirty, the SS would come to our house to see if we were complying with the nightly curfew and the myriad other *Verboten* rules that were used as a precursor to the barbed wire with which the Germans eventually tried to surround us. The rules changed almost daily, and each one had to be strictly followed. Failure to do so led to immediate arrest and imprisonment. We'd already heard of foreign Jews being carted off in the middle of the night. Rabbi Bloch said he'd discovered some of them in the camp for foreign Jews on the outskirts of the town but that an alarming number were missing.

The same SS officers came to our house seven nights a week to tick us off their list—Adjutant Wilhelm Hipp, in charge of Jewish affairs in the city, and three or four of his gun-toting henchmen. Ours was one of the many homes they visited. Hipp was a short, ugly man who looked like a troll. He jokingly dubbed himself the "King of the Jews" among his fellow officers, and was the epitome of the worst thugs who'd joined Hitler's ranks at the height of Nazism in the 1930s. I was always surprised that he had enough intelligence to speak, let alone in broken French. I regarded him and the twin silver SS flash on his tight tunic collar with utter contempt.

Our numbers were much reduced by then. Cecile, Fred, and finally Arnold were all gone. Hipp had long suspected the farmers of helping people flee, but he had no proof and was desperate for some concrete evidence. When Arnold slipped south over the border in June 1942, at my mother's insistence, Hipp went mad, searching the house from top to bottom, his face florid, rifling our mail to see if he could find any proof of where Arnold was.

I told Hipp he'd simply vanished. "We're all very worried about him," I claimed. "We'd be grateful for any information you have." But Hipp wasn't buying it.

Not long afterward, on June 17, 1942, a gloriously hot afternoon, Noel Degout's teenage son Yves came hurrying over on his bicycle. "The Germans are at the house," he told us breathlessly, the sweat glistening on his face. "The Gestapo. They're interrogating everybody."

It seems crazy now, but we didn't even think of protecting ourselves. At the time, we didn't understand what the Nazis were capable of. No one did. We listened to the BBC secretly every night but there'd been little information about what was happening to Jews elsewhere in Europe, no inkling of what was to come. So we gave Yves a sandwich and a glass of cold milk, thanked him for his warning, and sent him on his way.

That evening, as the swallows wheeled and circled outside the window, we'd just finished dinner and were sitting at the huge polished mahogany dining table eating from an enormous bowl of cherries. One of the shopkeepers in the town had risked imprisonment just to give my mother a bagful for us children to enjoy. Father's numerous antique clocks ticked and whirred away all around our home before striking the hour of eight o'clock.

A few minutes later there was a hammering on the door and a ringing of the bell, before Hipp and his men marched in. Jacquie had been living with us for four years by then and was accustomed to the nightly visits that brought so many unhappy childhood memories flooding back. Our biggest problem was that he had a very loud mouth for a six-year-old. It was a nightly task of mine to try to make sure he didn't speak his native German in front of the SS and give away the fact that we all understood what our unwelcome visitors were saying to each other privately.

Placing my arms around his shoulders, I held him very still and whispered to him to be quiet as the jackbooted enemy soldiers marched into our dining room. Jacquie did as he was told, but chiefly because his mouth was crammed full of cherries. Before I could stop him, he'd quickly maneuvered the cherry stones with his tongue and fired them at the Germans in quick succession with surprisingly good aim. Seeing the expression on Hipp's face as one of the cherry stones fell just short of his immaculate tunic and dropped to the floor, I seized Jacquie's hand and slapped it very hard.

"*Non, Jacquie!*" I told him crossly, quashing the thought of what Hipp would have done had the cherry stone hit its target and left a small purple mark. "That isn't polite. We must always be polite, even in war."

My parents and I, Stéphanie, Jacquie, my grandmother and my two younger sisters, Hélène and Rosy, sat in silence as we waited for Hipp to tick us off his list, as usual. Pavel was understandably wary of Germans and he half hid behind the grandfather clock whenever they arrived. He shrank visibly whenever Hipp's eyes fell on him.

Hipp paraded impatiently around the elegant dining room rug, eyeing each one of us in turn. His black, knee-high boots were so shiny I could almost see my own reflection in them. But it was the look on his face, a sort of arrogant grimace, that bothered me most.

"Which one is Stéphanie?" he suddenly barked.

Without blinking, and before any of us could say anything, Stéphanie—who'd recently been ill with a chronic kidney infection—stood up shakily and took a tentative step forward.

"I am," she said, softly.

"You're under arrest," Hipp told her, taking her firmly by the arm and leading her toward the door. His sausagelike fingers gripped the bare flesh of her forearm so tightly that they left imprints. On either side of her the two armed guards closed in, their guns glinting steely gray. We all looked at Stéphanie and back at each other, but none of us dared intervene. Stéphanie nodded her acceptance of her arrest and stared at us all with an expression that told us not to worry. Her last, lingering gaze was for our little blonde mother, standing to attention in the corner of the room, her fingers clasped so firmly together that the whites of her knuckles showed through the skin.

The silence was absolute after the SS left. None of us moved from the positions we'd adopted when they first arrived. My mother broke the spell. Having remained defiant and dignified throughout, she now crumpled like a sack, folding into a chair.

"She'll never come back," she said, beating her chest with her fist. "When they take them like that, they never do."

We sat huddled together as a family, thinking only of Steph and what she meant to us all. For my part, I pictured her laughing, her head thrown back, her long hair cascading down her back as she picked apples with me from our neighbor's garden in Metz. I thought of the nights we'd lain awake giggling together in bed with Cecile, telling each other wild stories and whispering secretly of the boys we liked. I tried to reassure my mother that everything would be all right, but she was inconsolable. It was as if a light had been switched off inside her.

My father sat gray and haggard at the dining table, his lips pressed tightly shut, his head in his hands. For almost a year we'd hardly spoken a word to each other, as part of my continued defiance of his strict upbringing of Jacquie. I was stubbornly determined that our little cousin who'd been through so much already should be raised far less rigidly than we'd been, and the last time we'd spoken, I'd told my father so in no uncertain terms. Relations between us were at an all-time low. Yet in that dreadful first hour after Stéphanie was taken, I wanted nothing more than to go to him and offer him some comfort, too. Pride, however, got the better of me.

An hour and a half later we heard a car pull up in the street outside. Only the Germans had vehicles. We hoped at first that it was an SS driver, returning Stéphanie safely to us after curfew. We heard the footsteps on the pavement outside. Once again there was hammering on the door, this time with rifle butts. It was no mere soldier; it was Hipp.

"Your daughter's not cooperating with us and is very fresh," he told my father angrily, taking his arm shortly after bursting in. "I'm arresting you, too. You're coming with me."

Once again my mother, grandmother, and siblings stood rigidly at attention, silent and outwardly calm as our father grabbed his hat and was forcibly maneuvered toward the door. I could stand it no longer. I ran to him and flung my arms around his neck.

"Papa, I love you," I told him, reaching up on tiptoes to kiss his beard. To my delight, he returned my hug with equal intensity. As he was led away, he held his head high and looked lovingly across at my mother as she stood watching him go.

I could hardly bear to witness my mother's reaction when the front door had closed. Nor did I want Rosy and Hélène to see it.

"Come now, girls," I told my younger sisters brightly, "let's get washed and ready for bed with Pavel and Jacquie. You know how cross Papa will be if you're still dressed when he comes home. We'll leave Maman with Grosmutter." My grandmother, hunched with age and bewildered by events, looked at me helplessly.

Over the next few hours, there was a succession of gentle taps on our front door. Not the insensitive hammering of the Nazis this time, but the tentative knocks of friends and neighbors, all breaking curfew to see if we were all right. Word had gotten out that we'd had a visit and that someone had been arrested. Janine Rieckert, from my class in nursing school, fell into my arms when I opened the door.

"Oh, Marthe, I'm so glad to see you!" she said, her eyes bright. "I'd heard the Gestapo had been here and I was terrified you'd been taken." Relief was written on her face.

"Yes, I'm safe, Janine," I said, ushering her in. "But Stéphanie's been taken, and Papa, too. I'd have gladly gone in their place."

These kind people wished us well and urged us to be strong before scurrying home in the darkness, eager not to be caught by the roving German patrols. My mother accepted their condolences and reassurances blankly. Numb to anything but the unexpected disappearance of her beloved Steph and her husband, she sat staring at the door as if she fully expected the Nazis to march back in any minute and seize the rest of us.

When a car pulled up outside our home just before midnight, I quelled the sick feeling in my stomach. As the footsteps approached, Hélène and Rosy ran to my mother in their nightclothes. Jacquie clung to his beloved Hélène, afraid that she'd be taken, too. But the door opened and in walked my father, the color completely drained from his face. He looked as if he'd just returned from a grueling journey to a distant place.

"Where's Stéphanie?" my mother asked, crestfallen at seeing him arrive back alone.

"She's still being interrogated," my father told us, shakily finding a seat. "They took me to the same room as her and threatened me to make her talk. They wanted to know all about the Degout farm; they wanted her to implicate Monsieur Degout, but she refused point-blank. I told them she knew nothing. I did the best I could and tried to defuse the situation. I even offered myself in her place, but they had found a letter at the farm from Stéphanie. Someone left their tobacco coupon at our house before they fled and she sent it on to them at the farm, signing her name."

Tobacco coupons were a vital bartering commodity during the war, and the refugee in question would have been desperate to have it back. In sending it to him, my kind, thoughtful sister had inadvertently provided the SS with proof positive of her and the farmer's involvement in the escapes. But oh, Steph, I thought, why on earth did you sign such a letter?

"Is she strong, Papa?" I asked, fearful for her health.

"In spirit, yes," he said, his voice breaking. "She refuses to implicate Monsieur Degout. I tried to make her say the right things, to be friendly and make the Germans think she couldn't possibly be capable of anything like this, but she wouldn't. She remained stubborn and defiant throughout. She told them she'd rather die than falsely implicate anyone." He paused and lowered his head.

"But, oh Marthe," he added, his voice barely audible, "she's so terribly tired. They made her stand the whole time she was being interrogated. At one point she leaned against a desk, gripping it with both hands to steady herself, half drunk with exhaustion, and they barked at her, lashing out and telling her to straighten up."

Hot, bitter tears filled my eyes. I vowed never to forget Hipp or the men who had been so cruel to Steph. Never.

The mood in France worsened daily. Eleven days after Stéphanie's arrest, all Jews over the age of six in occupied France were ordered to wear the Star of David. Our rabbi, Elie Bloch, was among many who told us to consider it a "badge of pride." Despite his words of encouragement, it was the culmination of a growing humiliation. We were each issued one gaudy yellow six-pointed star, made of cloth, with the word JUIF or JUIVE in the middle. It had to be taken off and carefully hand-sewn onto each new item of clothing we changed into. The use of a safety pin instead of precise needlework was punishable by immediate imprisonment. Rosy, then just sixteen, was arrested in the street and threatened with incarceration for just such a flagrant infringement a few days after the edict had been issued. Her crime? To use pop studs, or snaps, instead of a needle and thread. Fortunately, she was released with a warning.

By wearing the star, we were supposed to be ostracized by others in public, but walking in the streets with our yellow badges, whole families from the local Catholic community would very often cross the street deliberately, the men to raise their hats and the women to say hello, all of them voicing their strong disapproval of the discrimination to which we were subjected.

At the hospital the chief administrator forbade me from wearing the star on my uniform, even though the remaining Jewish patients had to comply. "We'll have none of that in here," he said crisply, his eyes blazing with anger.

But the star was the least of my problems, as Stéphanie continued to occupy my mind constantly. Categorized as a political prisoner, she was sent to Poitiers prison, where Fred had been incarcerated, but this time we were not allowed to visit. July 10, 1942, was her twenty-first birthday, and instead of waltzing around our living room with Dedé, as she should have been, she was sick, in prison, and all alone. Desperate for news of her, we didn't have to wait long. Women who'd been released told us that Stéphanie—with her college education—had become their unofficial leader, keeping up morale, despite her relative youth and poor health.

"She's the most spirited of us all," one woman told me, smiling at the memory. "She shows nothing but contempt for any German who dares come near her. She organized us all into work parties and wants you to know that she's fine."

I thought of the quiet, gentle sister I thought I knew and wondered at her sudden transformation. She'd never been much of a leader at home, and the circumstances of war had clearly changed her. I wondered how I would have fared.

A month later Stéphanie was moved from the prison to the internment camp for political prisoners and foreign Jews on the outskirts of the city. Pavel's parents were among her fellow inmates. Surrounded by barbed wire and watchtowers, she was allowed just one visit a week, from one person alone, and had to sleep on a filthy mattress riddled with lice. Mostly, my mother went—my father went once and could never bear to return—and she was appalled by what she saw. Pale, thin from poor living conditions, and sick from her kidney complaint, Stéphanie was a shadow of her old self. But she was nonetheless in good spirits.

"There's so much for me to do, Maman," she told my mother breathlessly, "so many daily battles to be won. I don't mind missing medical school for a while. Not if I can be of use here." As before, she'd become a figurehead to the other women, bolstering those younger and more fearful than she and maintaining camp morale. She was using her medical experience where necessary and advising the inmates on anything from nutrition to hygiene. My pride in her swelled daily.

Run by French gendarmes, the camp's atmosphere was relatively relaxed at first, until the Gestapo began to supervise. Then things changed for the worse, and Stéphanie with it. Maman, who visited her faithfully every Friday, told me: "Marthe, I need you to go and see Hipp and tell him that Steph must have medical treatment immediately. Her kidney is making her very ill. I'm desperately worried for her. She needs to go to the hospital and get proper treatment."

I was less afraid of confronting Hipp than I was of disappointing my mother, so the very next day I went to his office at Gestapo headquarters in the center of Poitiers.

"I need to see Adjutant Hipp," I told a soldier at the door. "It is a matter of the utmost urgency." He reluctantly ushered me inside, and I repeated my request several times until I made it all the way up to Hipp's outer office and his assistant.

"Adjutant Hipp is very busy," the man in uniform barked. "What's it about?"

"I'm afraid I can't tell you," I replied. "It's a personal matter of the utmost urgency."

My ploy had little effect. Wearing my yellow star, I was unceremoniously led from the office and the headquarters and almost thrown into the street. I returned to my mother with a heavy heart and the news that I'd failed.

"Please, Marthe," she urged, taking both my hands in hers. "Try again tomorrow. I'm sure he'd listen to you if only you could get to see him."

And so it was that my new routine began. Every day after school, I'd visit his office in the hope of seeing him. After a week I was banned from the building and not even allowed to step through the main doorway. Incensed, and determined not to let my mother down, I took to waiting in the street outside, hanging around on the corner for hours, watching for Hipp to emerge.

"Okay, mister," I told him under my breath, "you've got to come out some time."

Finally he did, and I ran over to where he was about to climb into a gleaming black car. He spun round as I called his name, as did the three officers with him.

"Adjutant Hipp," I said, catching my breath and giving him the smile that had won over one of his former colleagues. "I need to talk to you. It's very important. My sister Stéphanie is in the internment camp and she desperately needs medical treatment. Please, is there anything you can do to help?"

Hipp glanced at his companions with a smirk and leaned toward me until his face was a few inches from mine.

"*Mädchen!*" he cried. "If you come one pace closer to me and bother me one more time, I'll have you arrested and thrown into the camp, too. Now get out of my sight!" He was so close I could smell the staleness of his breath.

I'd have traded places with Stéphanie in an instant, but that was never on offer. Backing away, I knew there was little to be gained from becoming a fellow prisoner. Retreating as fast as I could, I walked off and didn't stop until Hipp and his ice-cold eyes were several streets away. I vowed to myself then that after the war I would find Hipp and bring him to justice for what he had done.

There had to be another way to help Stéphanie. I thought we'd found it when Arnold wrote to tell me that one of his friends, a young man called Roland, was a French guard at the camp. Fred and Arnold had offered to pay for him to go south with Steph if he helped her escape. Fred had even found him a job. Roland had agreed to help if he could, but then the Gestapo completely took over the running of the camp and his role was no longer the same.

With the help of my classmates, I found the doctor who treated the prisoners, and, amazingly, he agreed to help us. "I'm sent a few inmates from the camp every now and again," Dr. Pacaud told me. "If you can get her on the list, I'll examine your sister and admit her to the hospital for treatment."

I told my mother that I had to visit Stéphanie that week since I had some important news for her. I went to see her, taking a basket of food Maman had prepared and some fresh underwear Stéphanie had asked for. Once through the high barbed-wire gate, the visitors were allowed to mingle freely with the inmates, and most of them sat huddled in groups in the dust, holding hands, sharing conversations, and handing over their parcels.

The camp was a former military barracks, with long rows of low wooden huts. Women were assigned to one area and men to another, but they were allowed to mix in the open arena. Cooking was done by the women in huge steel pots and consisted mainly of soups and vegetable stews. Meals were taken on long trestle tables while seated at benches. The washing and toilet facilities were primitive and often inadequate.

It had been almost two months since I'd last seen Stéphanie, and I was shocked by her appearance. Her once lustrous dark hair was lank and flat against her head. Her skin was a pasty pale yellow and her eyes sunk into their sockets. But there was a fire in her eyes I'd never seen before. She had taken up the torch of resistance and was flourishing mentally, if not physically.

"Steph, listen to me," I told her, speaking quickly and quietly in case anyone overheard us. "We haven't got long. I'm getting you out of here, it's all arranged. You must ask the camp nurse to get you on the list of people being sent to the hospital, and then Dr. Pacaud will arrange for you to be detained. Dedé and Jacques and, well, most of your classmates and mine, will all be waiting. They've been fantastic, absolutely marvelous, and between them they'll bundle you out to safety after dark and across the southern border. Then—"

Stéphanie reached out and squeezed my hand, stopping me midsentence. "Thank you, Marthe," she said, her eyes smiling. "But no."

"No, what?" I said, afraid of what she was saying.

"I can't leave here," she replied. "I have an important job to do." Waving her arm at her fellow prisoners, she added softly, "These people need me."

"But—" I began, grabbing her arm, ready to shake some sense into her.

"No buts," she said. "Besides, if I escaped, Hipp would come and arrest the whole lot of you and throw you in here, too, so what would be the point of that?"

Her words stopped me in my tracks. She was right. It hadn't occurred to me that Hipp would take his revenge on us. We'd undoubtedly be heavily penalized. No matter how I tried to reassure her, to persuade her that this was the best way to get her out and that we'd follow her as soon as we could, she wouldn't listen.

"It won't work, Marthe. It wouldn't be fair to the people here or to the rest of you. Maybe I'll be released soon anyway. Fred wasn't kept for very long, and I've hardly done anything terrible, have I? Pray for me."

The whistle sounded, signifying an end to my brief visit. The French guards hurried around under the watchful eye of the Gestapo and gathered us up to leave. Waving Steph good-bye through the wire, I wondered what to do next.

On the way home from the camp it struck me exactly what to do. Everything became clear in my mind. It was a course of action so dramatic, I wasn't sure if I was mad or not. I went to see Jacques to ask for his help. "We must all escape," I told him, saying it as if it were the simplest of undertakings. He was completely taken aback.

"But what about you and me?" he asked, frowning. "And your studies? You're only in your first year."

I looked up at him with an expression of love, and he stopped talking and looked down at me with a smile. My own throat tightened at the thought of leaving him. Holding my shoulders in his broad hands, he peered into my eyes. "Marthe, you're right. All of that can wait. You and I will still be able to see each other when we can. You'll see, in my breaks from medical school I'll get some passes to the South for sporting events or something and we'll be able to meet. I'll write every day, and when the war's over we'll be together all the time. As for your nursing studies, I'm sure you'll be able to continue them in the South. And by the time you're qualified, this stupid war will be at an end and we can work side by side as we always planned."

"But Jacques—" I began, momentarily losing confidence in my own plan.

"But nothing," he said, pulling me into his arms. "You have to leave. I can't stand by and see you treated this way. And if you go, Stéphanie will go, too. If you time it right, she can escape the same day and join you later in the unoccupied zone. You know you're right."

My next problem was how to organize such a seemingly impossible task. There were eight people to consider, from my elderly grandmother to young Jacquie. And then there was Pavel, who'd been living with us for over a year and had become part of our family. His parents had written to Rabbi Bloch to ask him to thank us for taking their son in. "He's thriving within the bosom of the Hoffnung family," his mother wrote. "We're very happy that he has been lucky enough to end up in such a place." I had to speak to Rabbi Bloch about the boy. Pavel was his responsibility, and I knew that if I just took him without asking, there could be dire repercussions for the rabbi and his family.

"No, Mademoiselle Hoffnung," he told me, shaking his head sadly after I'd explained my plan. "Absolutely not." He wore large round-rimmed glasses, and he took them off to better emphasize his point. "You cannot possibly take Pavel with you. If just one child from the camps were to disappear, then the Germans would round up all the rest and throw them back inside. It would undermine everything we've managed to achieve so far. Hard as it would be to leave him behind, you must do it, for the sake of the other children."

A heavy weight pressing on me, I walked slowly home wondering how I was going to break the news to the trusting Polish boy who'd won his way into our hearts. Worse, how would my mother react? She didn't even know I was planning our escape yet, but what would she say when I told her that not all of us could go?

By an unexpected stroke of luck, I had already solved a major problem that stood in the way of our escape. Unbeknown to my family, I had hidden in our home forged documents bearing our correct names but without the damning red stamp marked *"Juif."* Several weeks earler, Monsieur Charpentier, a clerk I'd worked with in the town hall, approached me in the rue Gambetta, the main street of Poitiers. He was a softly spoken middle-age man, a white-collar worker who'd been in charge of all the necessary paperwork for the requisitions department.

"Mademoiselle Hoffnung," he said as we crossed paths in the street, "I need to speak with you."

He fell into step and we walked on a little way until we were in a quieter area. Glancing right and left constantly, he looked thinner and older than I remembered him. His suit was threadbare in places and his shoes were old. We'd always been friendly at work. I'd taken the trouble to talk to him and thank him for his contribution when some of the others hadn't. He was charming and shy. I knew he was married, with a young family, and that he'd been appalled when we'd all been fired. He'd been one of the first to jump to his feet when the Nazis marched into our office to evict us, and had backed up Monsieur Grelet when he said he couldn't operate without me.

"I have a proposition to put to you," he said to me now, taking my arm and leading me away from the few passersby. "I've switched departments and may now be in a position to help you and your family, if you want me to."

I stopped and stared at him for a moment, trying to take in what he was telling me. "How?" I asked.

"I can provide you with the necessary forged documents should you want to go south," he said, his gray eyes blinking as he awaited my response.

"Do you know what you're saying, monsieur?" I whispered, clasping his arm. "Do you know what they'd do to you if they caught you?" I thought of the small black-and-white photograph of his wife and son that he kept on his desk.

"It's a risk I'm prepared to take," he said quietly, lowering his head, his hat in his hand.

I stood silently for a moment, examining the top of his dark hair, wondering what to say. Thoughts of Stéphanie and her weakening kidney forced my hand. "There are eight of us, Monsieur Charpentier," I said quickly, rummaging in my handbag for a pen and a piece of paper. "I'll give you the names."

He looked up and half smiled, evidently relieved that I'd decided to accept his offer. "Eight?" he said. "I had no idea there'd be so many. Very well."

I began scribbling down the names, speaking them out aloud as I did so, starting with my parents and grandmother. "Regine, Fischel, Zipporah, Stéphanie, Hélène, Rosy, Jacquie, and myself." I looked up at him and wondered for a moment if I should ask for the relevant papers for Pavel too, in case I could somehow arrange his escape later on. But with Rabbi Bloch's words still burning my ears, I decided against it.

Handing him the piece of paper, I added, "We'll gladly compensate you for this kind offer. You'll be saving our lives. We really are most grateful. You must let us know how much this will cost."

Monsieur Charpentier was staring at me through his spectacles, his mouth slightly ajar. I stopped speaking and stared back at him. Dropping his head, his hand went to his pocket for a handkerchief, with which he wiped his eyes.

"I—I'm so sorry," I said, squeezing his arm gently. "Have I said something wrong? I didn't mean to offend you. Please, monsieur, don't cry."

It took him several minutes to compose himself, but finally he raised his head and looked at me, his chin quivering. "Mademoiselle Hoffnung," he said, his voice tremulous. "I don't want your money. That's not why I offered to do this for you. I never wanted your money!"

Faltering, I stepped back and clasped my hands to my chest. "But—" I began, unable to continue.

"I'm doing this because it is what I can do," he said. "Something has to be done to save people like you. If I can help one family escape from the Germans, then I will. I can't just stand by and watch what's happening. I couldn't live with myself if I didn't at least try."

My vision of him became blurred and I bowed my head. "I—I don't know what to say," I said, almost inaudibly. "Please forgive my mistake. And thank you."

My words seemed wholly inadequate.

Crossing the Line

The night before we were due to escape, long after curfew and the nightly Gestapo visit, there was hammering on the door. My family were jumpy enough as it was. Telling them to remain calm, I opened the door gingerly. Standing on the doorstep was my classmate, Odile de Morin.

"Marthe, you have to come with me, quickly," she said, looking right and left. "We've heard through the grapevine that there's going to be a *rafle*"—a police roundup—"tonight. You must all come home with me now and sleep at my house."

"Odile!" I gasped. "Think what you're saying. That's impossible! You could be killed for even coming here to warn us. Don't be crazy. We cannot possibly ask you to risk your life."

Odile buried her head in her hands and started to cry. "Please, Marthe," she sobbed, "I can't bear it. You must come. I won't leave you here. Please listen to me. You have to accept my offer, or you may all be taken tonight."

Yet again, as with Monsieur Charpentier, I was overwhelmed. Like him, Odile refused to give up on us. With her to back me up, I eventually persuaded my reluctant parents, grandmother, and siblings to bundle together their remaining things and get ready. The house had been stripped in the previous week. Friends and neighbors, fellow students and boyfriends, had all arrived on their bicycles, and each left with a small parcel of our most precious belongings, which they promised to store until after the war. Now we stood holding what we had left, and prepared to leave Poitiers for good.

"Au revoir, Pavel," I told the plump young Pole as he stood in the empty, echoing hallway to bid each of us farewell. He was trying so hard to be brave, but his bottom lip was trembling and his blue eyes were filling with tears. Although only a teenager, he was already taller than me, and I reached up to hug him.

"I wish there was some way we could take you with us," I told him for the hundredth time, stroking his white-blond hair, "but Rabbi Bloch is right. This way you'll be able to stay with your parents and friends, and before long we'll all be reunited, you'll see."

The rabbi had agreed to come for Pavel that night, as soon as we'd left. He'd already found another family willing to take the boy in so his schooling wouldn't be interrupted. My sisters and parents all said their farewells, but Jacquie lingered longest, staring up at the quiet teenager he'd come to regard as an older brother.

"Au revoir," he said. Trying to be ever so grown up, and copying my father, he extended his hand and his friend took it in his. *"Bonne chance,"* he added, shaking his hand firmly with a smile. I turned away so neither boy could see my eyes.

It was dark as we left the house and hurried on, hiding in the shadows. Odile's elegant town house was a few blocks away. Pressed up against a wall every time we heard a car approaching, I ushered my family through the deserted streets of Poitiers, several thousand francs of the family money sewn into the lining of my clothing.

I hardly slept that night at Odile's, lying awake worrying, listening to every noise. Was it my imagination or could I hear car horns and whistles a few streets away? I hoped Pavel was safe and well with the rabbi and not in any danger. When I did eventually drift off, I dreamed we were all thrown into the same camp as Stéphanie, with Hipp on the other side of the barbed wire, laughing at our stupidity in attempting to flee when he was watching us so closely. We were hardly in the best shape as a family. Hélène, with her bad knee, couldn't cycle or walk very far. Jacquie, though terribly young, had already lived through so much upheaval and was understandably nervous. My mother was beside herself with angst for us all, and my father had been strangely subdued ever since his helplessness in the face of Stéphanie's arrest two months ago. My grandmother was my biggest concern. She was eighty, had just undergone an operation for a strangulated hernia, and could barely walk at all. A thin, tiny little woman, she was quite feeble.

"You must leave me behind, Marthe," she told me when I first informed her of my plan the day before. "I'm far too old. I'll only hinder you."

"No, Grosmutter," I told her firmly, "we'd never leave you behind. If you can't come with us, then none of us will go." I thought of my grandfather and the happy times Cecile and I had spent in their apartment in Metz, surrounded by his books. I knew he'd never rest in peace unless we took my grandmother with us. The choice was already made.

Just after first light the following morning, my father, Hélène, Rosy, Jacquie, and I left for the border, leaving my mother and grandmother to follow us later. We decided to cross separately in order to reduce the risk. We were dressed as French peasants, my father and Jacquie in their shabbiest trousers and jackets, and us girls in head scarves, long skirts, and flat shoes.

Our agreed meeting point was the village of St. Secondin, about twenty miles southeast of Poitiers, right on the border of the Zone Libre. Hélène and my father took the bus part of the way and were to walk the rest. Rosy and I were to ride our bikes all the way, taking turns to carry Jacquie on the handlebars. My mother and grandmother were due much later, on the last bus from Poitiers. My father was to lead the first of the family across the *ligne de demarcation,* while I stayed to make the most dangerous, final crossing with my mother and grandmother.

On our way south, Rosy, Jacquie, and I passed my father and Hélène limping slowly along the road. It was a fine August day, and in any other circumstance it would have felt good to be out of the city and in the sunlit countryside. "See you in the church," I said to my father as cheerily as I could, before we cycled on, looking around all the while for roving German patrols or anyone who might turn us over to the Gestapo for the handsome bounties.

We arrived in St. Secondin a few minutes later and, having hidden our bicycles, made our way to the church. Papa and Hélène arrived soon afterward, and I left them all in the vestibule before going in search of the priest, Father Christian de Chaunac, who was from an old family of local nobles. He was young, handsome, and imposing, with brown eyes and hair.

"I need your help, Father," I said simply. He was the cousin of one of my classmates, Elisabeth Sechet, and I'd been told that if I mentioned her name, all would be well.

The priest was very tall and looked straight down his nose at me. "Elisabeth already contacted me," he said. "I've been expecting you. I'll help you because it is the right thing to do. But you should know this from the outset—I'd never trust a Jew."

"How can you say that?" I asked, appalled. "We'd rather be killed than betray you to the Germans if we were caught!"

"Don't you know the story of Judas?" The priest sneered. "I don't trust Jews because they always squeal. If any of you are arrested, I feel sure you'll tell the Germans it was I who helped you."

Years of hurt and anger at this long-held Catholic view of Jews bubbled to the surface in me. I remembered reading the catechisms of my friends at school in Metz and being horrified by the condemnation of all Jews as responsible for the crucifixion of Jesus on the basis of Judas Iscariot's behavior. Now I was desperately trying to contain my fury in front of this man who was my family's one hope now after we'd fled Poitiers and thrown away our yellow stars.

"We're not Judas!" I cried, my face reddening. "That happened thousands of years ago. We have nothing to do with Judas. And anyway, how can you reconcile feeling such terrible contempt for all Jews while your faith is based on the teachings of Jesus and the belief that Jesus is the son of God? Don't you know that Jesus was a Jew?"

The priest shrugged his shoulders as if he didn't believe me. "I've told you I'll help you," he said coldly. "It's the Christian thing to do."

There was nothing I would have liked more than to tell him that my family no longer needed his help and that we'd somehow manage without him. But I couldn't. I knew nothing of St. Secondin. I had no idea where the German patrols were, and I dared not approach anyone else for fear of being denounced.

The atmosphere between us decidedly frosty, the priest eventually agreed to scout the area to see if there were any patrols in the vicinity. He was gone about ten minutes before he returned, his shoes dusty, a sheen of sweat on his face.

"There's hardly anyone about," he said to my father. "I saw no patrols. Go now, quickly."

There was hardly time to say good-bye. I hugged Papa, Hélène, Rosy, and Jacquie and pushed them out of the huge arched doorway of the church. The priest had told them the best route to take by foot across the fields. "See you on the other side," I whispered to my bedraggled family, my voice cracking. Rosy, then seventeen and several inches taller than me but looking much younger, with her elfin face, turned and looked back, her big brown eyes wide.

The church was the safest place to wait, and I sat on a pew to one side. Staring up at the stained-glass window, I saw how the August sunlight poured through it and painted the stone floor pretty colors. It was about ten in the morning and I had a long day ahead of me. Shivering with cold in my light summer clothes, I prayed to God with all my childhood convictions to deliver my family safely. "I know I haven't always been as good as I should, Lord," I said, "but I'm begging you now, please help them and keep them safe."

I thought of my last meeting with Jacques, of how he'd held me and kissed me and told me how much he loved me. "I don't want you to go but I know that you must," he'd said, his face buried in my hair. "But please, my darling, be careful. I can't lose you. I couldn't survive it. We have a whole lifetime ahead of us, remember?"

"Yes, Jacques, yes," I'd replied, fighting back the tears.

I also relived my last visit to Stéphanie a few days earlier, when she'd finally agreed to come away with us.

"Thank you, Marthe," she'd said at first, her eyes smiling down at me. "But I've told you, I can't leave these people, they need me."

"Yes, you can," I said, afraid of what she was saying. "I've arranged it for the whole family. It's not just you this time, we'll all be leaving together."

"I can't just abandon all my friends here," she told me, her gaze distant.

"Stéphanie," I'd said, grabbing her arm, ready to shake some sense into her. "We need you, too. Maman is just not the same without you. It'll break her heart if you don't come with us. Please, you must listen to reason."

My words seemed to hit home. Wincing in pain from her kidney, leaning slightly to one side because of it, she knew I was right. It hadn't occurred to her that our mother's needs might actually be greater than those in the camp.

"Dedé will be waiting for you," I told her, smiling warmly. "He's been worried about you, too. We all have. Steph, you must grab this chance while you can. It may be the last time we can arrange this."

The whistle had sounded all too soon. Holding Stéphanie to me, feeling her bones through her clothes, I wished her good luck.

My last sight of her was standing a few feet away, her thin frame hunched over the basket of food, clothes, and books I'd taken her.

"See you in a few days," I'd whispered into her ear. I could still feel the warmth of her breath on my neck.

My memory of her was interrupted by the sound of the heavy church door creaking open. A woman I recognized as a former customer of ours from Elby, and who lived in St. Secondin, hurried in, her head covered by a scarf.

"Mademoiselle Hoffnung," she cried, grabbing both my hands. "Father de Chaunac told me you were here. Mademoiselle, I'm afraid I have some terrible news. We've only just heard. The Germans have just arrested a whole family as they tried to cross the border. There were children."

Words cannot describe my feelings at that moment. I thought I would die. So that was it. I'd unwittingly dispatched my family to certain death. I'd kissed them and waved them good-bye and sat in the sanctuary of a church while they faced bayonets and Gestapo interrogators. My father, Hélène, little Rosy, Jacquie. I'd never see them again.

No one could comfort me; no one could even talk to me. My eyes were pressed shut. I never prayed as fervently in my life as I did in that church. For hours on end I made deals with God, offering my own life in exchange, if only he'd save my family.

"Dear God, please help me. Take me. Do what you will with me, but help them," I begged, tears splashing my clasped hands. "Lord, don't let it be them."

The woman did her best to console me. She said she hadn't seen the family; she tried to reassure me, to tell me that it might not be mine after all. But I couldn't see beyond her news. What other family was in the area at that precise moment, trying to cross? It had to be them. Worse still, my mother and grandmother were on their way, oblivious to the fate of the rest of their family, expecting to cross with me at dusk. Stéphanie, too, was due to join us later that night or early the following morning, having agreed to escape only once we were all safe. I knew that none of them would cross if they thought the others were in German hands. My mother and Stéphanie especially would rather be imprisoned with them in occupied France than live free in unoccupied France without them.

I was dying inside and I didn't know what to do. When the priest saw my face, he softened. He promised to go to the Germans, to try to see the arrested family so he could confirm their identities once and for all. "I'll leave immediately," he promised. "Try and keep hold of yourself." But he returned after half an hour without success. The detainees were being kept in a locked barn until the Gestapo chiefs could arrive and interrogate them. The gruff German soldiers guarding them had refused to let him see them.

"Keep faith," he urged. "God will provide."

Taking pity on me shivering uncontrollably in the cool church, Father de Chaunac insisted I move to his presbytery. His old housekeeper was entrusted with my care and told to give me something to eat. But I sat at her kitchen table, numb, pushing away the plate of food she offered me. "I can't," I told her. "I'm fasting." Not a morsel of food or a drop of water had passed my lips since the previous night, as was our custom when faced with ordeals.

Unable to stand any more anxiety, I begged her to give me some work. "Please," I told her, "I need to be busy." She gave me some of the priest's sacred garments to embroider. And that's how I spent the rest of that interminable day, sewing, waiting, thinking, debating it all over and over in my mind as the clock ticked slowly on.

The priest came to see me regularly, causing me to prick my finger each time, but he had no more news and could offer me little comfort. "What should I do?" I asked him, sucking the blood from my fingertip.

"Save those members of your family that you still can," he said. "There's still a chance for you, and for them."

By six o'clock I'd come to a decision. I'd let them all come. I'd clean myself up and meet Maman and Grosmutter at the six-thirty bus, as planned, and wouldn't tell them a thing.

"Please don't mention anything about the family who was arrested this morning," I told the priest. "My mother is not to know."

"I understand, mademoiselle," he said, giving my arm a gentle squeeze. His kind gesture after his initial harshness almost finished me off.

At six-fifteen I made my way to the church, my footsteps leaden. Watching from the doorway, I saw the bus arrive and my frail grandmother emerge, tiny and barely able to walk. She was on the arm of my mother, who looked smaller and more vulnerable than I'd ever remembered her. Swallowing hard, I met them with a false smile and ushered them quickly toward the church, where the priest was waiting.

Once we were safely inside, the priest once again disappeared to scout the area for patrols. Sitting with the two women, I closed my eyes and prayed for one last time. "Please, Lord," I whispered. "Don't fail me now."

The door creaking open heralded the priest's return. "I saw no patrols," he said firmly, watching my eyes. "Go now. And God bless."

Our escape route was via a small street leading to unoccupied France, about three hundred yards beyond the village sign. I retrieved my bicycle from its hiding place and sat my grandmother awkwardly on the seat before setting slowly off, pushing the handlebars. My mother walked alongside and held onto my grandmother, keeping her steady with an arm around her waist. We had nothing but the clothes we were wearing and a stubborn determination to succeed.

The light was fading as we made our way toward the border. Crossing via the open fields, well away from view, would have been a far safer option, but was impossible because of my grandmother and the bike. We had to stay in the village, walking slowly down a street, fully exposed, our intention to head for the border patently clear. I knew it was extremely risky, but I had little choice. The street was a little more than five hundred yards long, and I fervently hoped that no one would spot us and summon the authorities before we made it across.

As we turned left into that street, the border straight ahead of us, my inner turmoil was almost more than I could bear. The thought of my father, sisters, and Jacquie enduring God knew what in a nearby barn made me feel physically sick. My knees and hands trembled and my mind raced with the dreadful consequences of what I'd done and was now doing. Fear seeped from every pore.

Wheeling our way slowly along the first open stretch, I saw that the street was lined down the left hand side with the humble houses of the local farmers, poor French peasants who scratched what meager existence they could from the land. Many of their younger male relatives were prisoners of war in Germany or had fled south. Deprived of their sons, they'd carried on working the wheat fields as best they could, only to see their best produce snatched by the Germans for themselves. Like the rest of us, whose living had been denied us, they existed on what little they could hide from the occupying forces.

The Germans quickly realized their strategic importance in living on the border and offered the farmers huge sums of money to denounce those trying to flee from occupied France. Most, like Monsieur Degout, were disgusted by the offer. But the posters were everywhere in Poitiers, offering thousands of francs. The Gestapo had been most generous with its rewards, almost a year's income for an average impecunious farmer. It could afford to be—after all, it had stolen from France.

As we neared the houses, a shutter banged open in the warm summer evening breeze. A dog barked close by and made me jump. Every window seemed to hide unknown eyes. Every shadow on every wall looked sinister. The front wheel of the bicycle squeaked far too loudly.

In front of every house, the farmers sat huddled together in small groups, smoking clay pipes and talking softly, their faces as careworn as their clothes. Their wives stood in the gardens a few steps down, shelling peas, relaxing or sharing the day's news with the younger womenfolk. Behind their homes their hardworking livestock—horses and oxen—chewed the long summer grass and shook the flies from their ears. In other circumstances, in another time, it would have been an idyllic rural scene.

"Dear God," I prayed under my breath, "protect us now."

I forced my gaze forward, trying not to make eye contact with these people as we approached their homes. But I pictured us in their eyes—three women, three strangers, one clearly extremely frail, making a solitary crossing so close to nightfall in such an isolated spot. Only those fleeing from the German authorities would risk such a journey.

Taking a deep breath, I turned to look at the farmers again. Maybe direct eye contact would help after all, I reasoned. Maybe my silent pleas would be etched across my face. I might already have lost four members of my family today, my eyes told them, please help me save these two old women who've never done anybody any harm.

One by one as we approached, the men stopped smoking and the women stopped talking, and they all turned to stare back at us. There was near silence as we squeaked along with our bicycle, watching them watching us.

An old man in a dark shirt and working trousers stood up from his rickety old wooden chair as we passed his house and stared at us intently. I returned his gaze, my hands clammy on the handlebars. Without saying a word, he suddenly dropped onto one knee and, hand on his chest, lowered his head in prayer. Next to him, his wife knelt on both knees in the dirt and made the sign of the cross. At the next house, two men fell similarly to their knees and began praying for us, their soft murmurings carried to us on the summer evening breeze.

A teenage girl, not much younger than I, stopped scratching the neck of her much-loved horse and clasped her hands together in prayer. And so on, along the row, men and women, desperately poor, urgently in need of the money they could so easily have earned from us as a reward, each one saying a prayer to guide us on our way.

I could hardly believe my eyes. It was so beautiful, the humanity of it. Tears rolled down my cheeks as I nodded my head in silent thanks to each and every one we passed. How could I, even for the shortest minute, have doubted them, these kind, simple people who were as much oppressed by the Nazis as we were? Lowering my head, I pressed on, taking my mother and grandmother to unoccupied France and, I hoped, to safety.

We crossed the line without incident and made our way in the dusk toward the rendezvous point of Usson-du-Poitou. All the way, my mother asked me when we'd be meeting the others and what time Stéphanie was due. "I won't be at peace until we're all together again," she told me. "How much farther is it now?"

After a while I ran out of answers. My relief at having escaped occupied France was waning and I began to feel the burden of our losses. My neck and shoulders ached, my limbs grew heavy, I developed a temperature and began to feel unwell. "I don't know, Maman," I told her wearily, my head swimming in the dim evening light. "Let's just see what happens when we get there."

I thought my eyes were deceiving me when I spotted four people standing by the old stone well in the town square. Blinking, wiping the sweat from my forehead with the back of my hand, I stopped and stared as I heard my mother, as through a fog, call out their names.

"Hélène, Rosy, Jacquie!" she cried. They all embraced in the center of that dimly lit village. Unable to speak, I went from one to the other, kissing their faces a dozen times over, barely able to believe they'd made it safely across.

Another family had been arrested trying to cross the border that morning. The Germans must have been happy with their day's quota and been so tied up with paperwork that they hadn't bothered to look for any more Jews. I was never able to find out who they were or what happened to them, but they were undoubtedly my family's sacrificial lambs. May they rest in peace.

My fever worsened that evening and I began to shiver and ache all over. We found lodgings in a small hotel in the village and I went straight to bed, but couldn't sleep. All the next day we waited, my father and Rosy scouting the town to see if they could see Stéphanie anywhere, but each time they came back to report that there was no sign of her. Our bus for Lussac-les-Chateaux and the train station was due to leave that evening at seven, but by six o'clock she still hadn't arrived.

"We must go," my father told me, suddenly purposeful. "It isn't safe to stay here. We're too close to the border. We must be on that train."

Lying in bed, weak and exhausted, I tried to argue. "But she could arrive any minute," I protested hoarsely. "I told her we'd try and meet her here."

My mother sat on the edge of my bed, her face pale. "Marthe," she said, taking my hand. "You've done all you can. You've succeeded in getting us out. You were always so sure that it would work, and it has. Stéphanie can join us later. She knows we're going to stay with Fred. She's probably in hiding somewhere with Dedé for a few days until it's safer. Don't worry, she'll find us."

Reluctantly, I was finally persuaded to board the bus and then the night train south, in the hope that Stéphanie would join us in a day or two. Just before we left, I sent Fred and Arnold a short telegram to let them know we were on our way: ALL ACROSS EXCEPT STÉPHANIE. EXPECT US SOON.

We traveled east to Montluçon, a mining town, where my father's older sister, Hélène Bleitrach, welcomed us with open arms. For the first time in four years, Jacquie was reunited with his younger brother, Josie, whom Aunt Hélène had been caring for since 1938. Both their parents were still in Palestine, waiting for the war to end so their children could be sent to them. Being reunited with Josie was a difficult time for Jacquie, and he became very upset with his parents again for leaving their children behind. Maman had become his surrogate mother in the four years he'd been with us, and though we'd all done our best to keep him from judging his parents harshly, he continued to do so.

"*Tante, Tante,*" he cried, not for the first time, clinging to my mother's skirt. "You'd never have left us as my mother did, would you?"

My mother crouched down and took both his hands. "You have to understand, Jacquie, she and your father were unable to take you with them. It was a difficult and frightening time. She was heavily pregnant and couldn't travel. She did the best she could for you, she sent you to us."

"Please can we take Josie with us when we leave?" Jacquie asked. "Don't leave him behind like Pavel." My mother tried to explain that Josie was settled with his aunt and it wouldn't be fair to move him again. Walking out of that house without him, though, was I think one of the hardest things she ever had to do.

When we arrived in Arles on the train three days later, our brothers and sister-in-law were all waiting to greet us. Fred lifted me down and into his arms, a huge beam across his face. "Marthe!" he cried. "I could hardly believe it when I received your telegram. I said to Rosette and Arnold, 'There's only one person who could have pulled this off and that's Marthe.' Well done."

As he lowered me onto the platform, I blushed. I'd never have thought it was possible a few years earlier, but war and obligation had unexpectedly turned me into someone Fred could be proud of.

We settled into the tiny house that Arnold, Fred, Rosette, and their baby son Maurice all shared, and we managed the best we could, although it wasn't easy. Arles is a large city north of the Camargue marshland delta and was chosen by Fred because Rosette had a sister there. Her mother was still in the hospice in Poitiers, and her father was determined to remain with his wife.

It was two long weeks before we finally heard news of Stéphanie. The first of many letters arrived for me from Jacques. He'd sent it from the medical school and addressed it to "Jacqueline Lenôtre," the name we'd agreed upon before I left. Jacqueline because it was the female equivalent of Jacques, and Lenôtre because it was the name of the seventeenth-century gardener André Lenôtre, a man I admired very much, who'd designed the gardens at Versailles. The letter said:

> DEAR MADEMOISELLE LENÔTRE,
> *Thank you for your interest in the patient with the kidney complaint. I am sorry to inform you that she was unable to transfer*

to this hospital due to some last minute irregularities and has now been transferred to an establishment in Paris for further treatment. I shall forward you more details as soon as I have them.

Yours sincerely,
DR. JACQUES DELAUNAY

Through follow-up letters from Jacques we discovered that, on the morning of our escape, and possibly because he'd found our house empty in the *rafle* of the previous night, Hipp went to the camp and saw Stéphanie waiting to be sent to the hospital with some other sick inmates.

"No one goes to the hospital today," he decreed. She was so close to being sent, but instead was confined to the barracks. Furthermore, when Hipp realized that we had all escaped, he had her transferred far away, to the notorious Drancy camp on the outskirts of Paris, the very same internment camp for political prisoners that Uncle Max had told us so many horrible stories about.

The news shattered our temporary happiness. My mother, torn between her joy at being reunited with her sons and her grief for Steph, was inconsolable. "How can I eat, how can I sleep, when my little girl is somewhere like that?" she wailed. "I'll never feel joy again until she's back with us."

I especially carried the burden of guilt on my shoulders. It had been my plan, my idea. I was the one who'd orchestrated it all and who'd thought I'd been so clever in thinking of everything. But I hadn't. I'd failed Stéphanie. Not only was she not free, she was now in an even worse situation because of me. Clutching the forged document that Monsieur Charpentier had so generously made for her, the one that bore her photograph but no Jewish stamp, I wondered how I'd ever get through another day until she was back in the bosom of our family.

Broken Promises

On November 11, 1942, in response to the American army landing in North Africa, the Germans and the Italians occupied Vichy France. Just three months after our escape, we were behind enemy lines once more. The false documents Monsieur Charpentier supplied were never more valuable. Untainted by the JUIF stamp, we were able to pass ourselves off as non-Jews whenever anyone stopped to ask for our papers, and to lead less dangerous lives in the more relaxed atmosphere of southern France. But we couldn't be complacent. Whichever way we looked at it, we were suddenly in the presence of the enemy again, although mostly Italians supervised by Germans. We didn't trust the Italians and we certainly didn't like them for allying themselves to Hitler, but they were a far better option and not nearly so barbaric.

None of us could work; our papers were only good enough for

random checks in the street, not for close scrutiny. Once you took a job, you had to prove you weren't Jewish, which was much more difficult. Fortunately, Jews never had to wear the yellow star in the South; it would never have been tolerated. I don't know what I'd have done had I ever been directly confronted about my religion. As a child, I'd read of people being martyred for keeping their faith, and it had always impressed me. I would never have denounced my faith or said I was a Catholic if someone asked me directly. I couldn't have. I just hoped no one would ever ask.

Our only hope was for an end to the war. We still listened to the BBC nightly, reveling in the Allied victories at El Alamein and Stalingrad. We hoped the tide was turning, with the Germans pushed back in North Africa and in the East. When the brave sailors scuttled the French fleet in Toulon, many of them dying in fending off the encircling Germans, we wept tears of pride. De Gaulle broadcast to us across the airwaves. "France heard the guns of Toulon," he said, "the explosions, the desperate shots fired in a last stand. A tremor of pain, of pity, of rage shook the whole country. On to victory. There is no other road."

Our priority was Stéphanie. My parents, in particular, lived in a state of permanent distress about her, as we all did. Maman was pale and tired from lack of sleep, and Papa's eyes were sunken into their sockets. It had been over eight weeks since we'd seen her, and there'd been so few words. Finally, two brief letters from her filtered through from the camp she'd been transferred to at Drancy. One was written to Cecile in Paris, and the other to her fiancé Dedé in Poitiers. She couldn't have risked writing to us in Arles. Cecile told us that the camp was a series of five-story buildings quite close to a main road. Banned from sending mail, prisoners threw letters through the bars of their windows to the street below in the hope that a kind passerby would buy stamps and send them. It was a haphazard and dangerous arrangement, but many letters did get through this way, and we can only imagine that Steph's came via the same route.

In them, she wrote of her eagerness to be free. "The life here is atrocious," she said. "I long to be with you all, please do everything you can to get me out. Tell Maman I'm well and think of her often." As children, we'd developed a childish code in which to write secrets to each other, with little dots written over key letters to identify them in order. It wasn't very sophisticated, and the Germans could easily have cracked it if they'd been at all interested. Using it now allowed Stéphanie to write more freely than she might otherwise have done, secretly informing us that if she were to be sent to a labor camp, as she'd been told she soon would be, she'd do all she could to sabotage the German war effort and undermine its systems. "I cannot just stand by and allow this inhumane treatment of people to happen," she wrote secretly.

We agonized constantly over what we could do and how we could help her. Visitors were not allowed, and we knew nobody who could get her out of Drancy. Dedé was helpless, trapped in Poitiers, and we were living a life of subterfuge in the South. Fred, especially, did all he could to secure her release, making inquiries through friends in the Resistance all over France, but there was nothing anyone could do.

In the autumn of 1942 there was more bad news. Uncle Max, the sickly doctor whom Maman had single-handedly saved from his hospital bed in Paris, was rearrested at his new home in Marseille in a *rafle* of four thousand Jews. He was sent to Les Milles camp for foreign Jews and political prisoners near Aubagne, Provence. His wife, Fannie, ever difficult, became sick with worry and wrote to my mother asking for help.

It fell upon me, as the eldest daughter at home, to go to Marseille and look after Fannie. "She's begged for some company and help with little Ruth," my mother told me, her eyes sad. "I know you're restless here, Marthe, and I know you'd like to finish your nurse's training, so I thought that maybe in Marseille you could help poor Fannie and make some inquiries about another course?"

My plans to resume my nursing course had already partly foundered. With some money from Fred, I'd traveled to Montpellier, not far from Arles, and tried to enroll in a reputable Red Cross school. I was interviewed by Mademoiselle Le Bon, the principal, on whose door was a large sign that read: PLEASE SHUT THIS DOOR BEHIND YOU.

Examining my papers closely, she asked me why I'd left Poitiers halfway through my course. Seeing me hesitate, she frowned and asked directly: "Are you Jewish?"

"Yes," I said, unable to lie.

"Then I'm sorry, but I can't take you," she replied, standing up and returning my papers as if to dismiss me. "I don't take Jews."

My face burning, I jumped to my feet in anger. "Are you French or German?" I asked, tired of the endless bigotry.

Mademoiselle Le Bon flushed. "French," she replied, "very French. But I still cannot take a Jew. I am not allowed to accept any."

"There are no such rules in this part of France," I countered, my temper rising.

"I don't care about rules," she responded tartly, "I just don't want any Jews in my school."

Stepping closer to her, I wagged a finger at her. "When de Gaulle has won the war," I told her, "I shall come back and ask you to repeat what you have just said."

Knowing that I could get no further, I turned and left her office, leaving the door wide open.

After such a demoralizing experience, the thought of moving to Marseille and trying another school while living with the difficult Fannie did nothing to raise my spirits, but I knew that it was my duty to go. I packed my few belongings and took a train to Marseille.

There was little to eat in the port city, apart from root vegetables and sweet potatoes, and people were starving in the streets. Fred gave me money for food but there was little to buy. The Germans and Italians took the best of everything to feed themselves and their own. The streets were full of destitutes, who had no money or coupons, no papers and no means of existence. They lay, literally dying, their eyes closed against the tide of humanity passing them by.

When I arrived, I found Fannie in a state of physical and mental collapse. Swiss born, she was unable to cope with Max's second arrest in as many years, and was happy to leave me completely in charge. As well as caring for her and Ruth, who was ten, I had to take a three-hour bus ride every day to visit Uncle Max at Les Milles, taking him food, medicine, and clean clothes.

Fannie and her daughter shared a large apartment with another family, the Neufelds, and their son Jacques. He was a businessman we'd known in Metz who'd once been in love with Cecile and had very much wanted to marry her, but she'd turned him down.

Hearing that Stéphanie was being held in Drancy, he told me he knew a lawyer, a Spaniard, who worked closely with corrupt Germans and who might be able to help. With Monsieur Neufeld at my side, I went to see the Spaniard in a grubby hotel in the center of Marseille.

"My sister is being held in Drancy," I told him. "We need to get her out."

"It will cost a great deal of money," the Spaniard replied with a huge grin, rising from a disheveled pile of papers in front of him to kiss my hand. "Do you have money, mademoiselle?"

"Yes," I said firmly, removing my hand from his grasp.

The Spaniard smiled, revealing beautiful teeth. "Then of course I can help you," he said.

For the extortionate sum of twenty thousand francs, he promised that he would have Stéphanie out of Drancy within a few days. I contacted Fred, who managed to raise the cash and came to Marseille to deliver it. With Jacques Neufeld as my bodyguard, I handed it over.

"How will you arrange it?" I asked, nervous at parting with such a large sum.

"That's for me to know and you to find out," the Spaniard said, counting the cash carefully. "I'll be in touch when it's done."

Days passed without news, then a week. I feared terribly for Steph. A hundred times I nearly went back to the Spaniard's office to demand our money back, but each time Fred urged caution. "Give the man a chance," he wrote. "These things take time."

But when two weeks had passed without result, I could stand it no longer. With Jacques Neufeld to back me up, we returned to the Spaniard and found him in exactly the same position as when we'd last left him. I wondered if he ever moved from that airless room.

Jacques was wonderful. Before I could even speak, he hammered his fist on the Spaniard's desk. "You're running a scam," he said. "You're preying on the weak and the helpless. I'll have no compunction about denouncing you to the proper authorities as a con man. We want every penny of the money this young lady gave to you, and we want it now."

To my astonishment, the Spaniard rose from his chair, opened a safe beside him, and handed every penny back to me. The money looked as if it had never been touched. I wondered at his nerve. Leaving his hotel, I blinked back the tears.

Despite winning a moral victory, I knew we were now even further away from freeing Stéphanie. Soon afterward, we heard from Jacques that she'd been moved from Drancy to a camp at Pithiviers, near Orléans. Pithiviers seemed especially poignant. It was the place she'd spent her last vacation before she was arrested, staying with a girlfriend for a few days of much-needed rest. A treasured family photograph showed her cradling baby chickens on her friend's farm, smiling happily into the camera and looking as if she didn't have a care in the world.

From Pithiviers, Stéphanie was able to smuggle out one letter, thanks to the kindness of a nurse who, on learning that she was a medical student and that I was a nurse, agreed to risk her life by doing so. Pithiviers was terribly overcrowded, Steph said. "There's never enough food to go around, and we have to share what we have," she wrote.

A few weeks later, via a letter from Jacques, we learned that Stéphanie had been deported to an unknown destination on September 21, the day of Yom Kippur.

Continuing to visit Uncle Max at the camp, I was one of the few visitors from the outside. Most of the inmates were foreigners a long way from their homes and families. And those who were French had warned their loved ones to keep away because of the risk of being arrested for just knowing them.

"We need to think of a way to get you out," I told Max repeatedly at the camp. "What can you do to help me, Uncle?"

But Max was a timid man, not inclined to action. "There's nothing you can do," he'd say, shaking his head sadly. "This time there's no rescuing me."

After considerable pressure from me, he finally came up with the idea of ingesting ipecac, a medicine made from a Brazilian plant that makes anyone who takes it vomit violently. "If they see the blood, they might hospitalize me again," he suggested nervously. "Then, maybe, it would be easier to get me out."

"Brilliant!" I told him. "Now, how do I get hold of this ipecac?"

He wrote me a series of prescriptions from a pad I'd smuggled in to him, and I went to several pharmacists in Marseille to get as much of it as I could. Each time I asked for it, I was closely questioned. "What do you want this for, mademoiselle?" they'd ask suspiciously.

I told them I needed it for my sick grandmother and that it was very urgent. Reluctantly, they gave it to me, and I managed to smuggle it in to Max in tiny packets. But losing courage daily, he never swallowed the drugs I'd risked so much to acquire.

By now Fannie was suffering from violent mood swings. Her mind was unable to cope with war and she was almost completely incapable of doing anything for herself. Her deep religious faith was all that kept her going. Knowing that I had to contact her family in Switzerland and ask for their help, I went to a post office and booked the call. Such an action was extremely hazardous. The Gestapo monitored all international calls and I'd have to be very careful what I said. Although I carried false papers, I would be under close scrutiny for making such a call in such a public place. Rabbi Bloch's wife, Georgette, was arrested and deported with her six-year-old daughter Myriam for doing something similar in Poitiers, I learned much later. But I had no choice.

I went to a booth and waited for the call to be connected. There was an unusual amount of clicking on the line before the operator put me through to one of Fannie's brothers in Switzerland.

"Hello," I said. "This is Fannie's niece. I'm calling to tell you that her husband is dangerously ill and that it's very contagious. It would be far better if she and her daughter could come home immediately. I wondered if you could possibly arrange it?"

Her brother understood the message immediately, and within a few days a man arrived on our doorstep, ready to take them home. He was a stranger, a guide the family had paid to do the job, and he wanted to leave with his charges straight away. But it was a Friday.

"I can't go on a Friday," Fannie told me, aghast. "It's the start of the Sabbath."

Seeing the exasperation on the guide's face, knowing that he wouldn't linger a day longer, I took her firmly by the shoulders.

"Fannie," I said, as if speaking to a child. "I respect and understand your devotion to the faith, but the Jewish laws say that it is all right to break the Sabbath if your life is in danger. That's the case now. If you and Ruth don't leave with the guide tonight, you'll be arrested and thrown into the same camp as Max." I wouldn't let her argue, and within a few hours they'd packed a few things and were being led out of the door.

"Au revoir, Ruth," I told the long-suffering little girl I'd grown very fond of, kissing her on both cheeks. *"Bonne chance."*

A few days later, on one of my routine visits to Max, I arrived at the camp to find a train had pulled in. I could hear the wailing as I neared the barbed wire—the unmistakable sound of women screaming and crying for their children. I quickened my pace and hurried to the gate, my throat suddenly dry.

"No visitors today," a guard snapped. "You'll have to come back tomorrow."

"But I must see my uncle," I protested, holding up a bag. "He needs his medication; he's a very sick man. I insist."

"Then wait in there," the guard said gruffly, pointing to a shabby office building on the periphery of the main exercise area.

Trying to ignore the piteous cries from the other side of the wire, I walked to the shack and stepped inside. Up against a window stood five French guards, men I'd come to know from my regular visits to the camp. They were generally kind to the inmates and not at all happy with the strict Gestapo methods. Turning to look at me as I walked in, their eyes were full of tears and they bowed their heads in shame.

Running to the window where they stood, I peered out into the big open arena. The Gestapo, along with the first deputy of the prefect of Marseille, a man I recognized, was supervising the imminent deportation. As I'd done with Hipp and Stéphanie, I'd approached him when I'd first arrived in Marseille to beg for the release of my uncle on medical grounds, a request—like Hipp—he'd refused out of hand. Beyond him and the Gestapo were hundreds of men, women, and children, all being herded onto the waiting train. The women were lined up on one side and the men on the other, scores of them about to be loaded into cattle cars designed to house just a dozen animals each. Every prisoner wore their outdoor clothes and carried one small suitcase of belongings.

I'd been going to the camp almost every day for three weeks and I knew some of them by sight. There was old Madame Friedman, who'd lost her husband; young Isaak Rozenzweig, with his prominent ears; Monsieur Feuerman, who acted as a go-between; and the entire Schwartz family, their young children no more than toddlers, standing in the middle of the melee, screaming their confusion and distress. Most of those being deported appeared to be the foreign Jews, people who'd fled German persecution across Europe, only to find themselves being snared after all. The German soldiers were rough and unfeeling, laughing in the faces of the women who were crying and holding out their hands for their men, who were being dragged to the other side.

The tough French policemen from Marseille wept openly as they watched. "We never wanted to be a part of this, mademoiselle," one told me, his eyes moist. "We refused to help and that's why they put us in here."

My eyes were drawn back to the compelling scene unfolding before me. I simply couldn't tear myself away. "We must all watch and remember," I told the policemen softly. "We shall be the ones to bear witness."

It took over an hour to load the several hundred people onto the cattle cars, during which time I stood watching helplessly. I couldn't leave. I couldn't do anything. I knew I couldn't protest or they'd have put me on the train too. They wouldn't let me near, and so I stood transfixed at the window. I saw the deputy from the prefecture laughing as the Germans wrenched crying babies from the arms of their screaming mothers. I watched it all, tears streaming down my face.

I thought of Stéphanie incarcerated in Drancy, and hoped it would never be like this for her. I heard the cattle car doors slide shut and the heavy bolts drawn. I could almost smell the reeking urine, feces, and sweat those inside would have to endure for those long days it would take to get to wherever they were being sent.

Most of all, I watched to see if my uncle had been loaded onto the train. "Have you seen my uncle?" I asked one of the policemen suddenly, rousing myself. "Is he on this train?"

"I think so," another replied. "I saw him being put into one of the first cars." My spirits plummeted as I watched the train pull slowly away, its dirty old steam locomotives straining under the weight of all that crammed-in humanity.

I continued to stare unblinkingly as the Germans marched out of the camp, leaving the few surviving camp inmates scattered in the center of the area. The dirt floor was strewn with hats and scarves, small items of treasured personal belongings and photographs that had become separated from their owners in the confusion. I focused on the people left behind; I watched their shattered expressions as they wandered aimlessly about, staring at the empty space where the train had been as if they could will it to return. I thought I was hallucinating when I recognized my uncle's distinctively slim figure amidst the crowd, his hands held in fists at his sides. He was forty years old but looked at least twenty years older. Determined to speak to him, I had to use all my powers of persuasion to get the guards to bring him into that little office.

"Marthe, Marthe, did you see? Did you see what they did?" he cried, shaking his head and clinging to the low wooden table at which we both sat. "I can't believe how they treated us." His face was etched with strain.

"I saw, Uncle." I nodded, my skin still tight with the salt of my tears.

"I was on the train," he added, "I was actually put on the train, squashed in with all the others. It was only because Monsieur Feuerman told them I didn't belong there that I was taken off again." He looked gaunt. He couldn't even be happy to be saved. As a physician, a scholar, and a beautiful human being, he was unable to comprehend that his fellow men could act in such a way.

The scenes I'd witnessed that afternoon shook me equally. They were images that were to haunt me for the rest of my life. I realized, for the first time, that although I'd foolishly thought we were much safer in the South of France, the long arm of Adolf Hitler stretched all the way to the Mediterranean Sea and beyond.

Less than a week later, when I arrived as usual at the camp gates, I found the place almost deserted. Earlier that morning another train had come, this time for the remaining inmates, including Uncle Max.

"But where has he been taken?" I asked, desperately scanning the empty camp in the hope that the guards were somehow mistaken.

"To Gurs, a camp in the Pyrenees," one of the guards told me glumly. "But where he'll be sent from there is anybody's guess."

Two days later Uncle Leon arrived on my doorstep. He'd moved to St. Etienne from Toulouse when the whole of France was occupied and had come to visit Max. It was my sad task to tell him that his brother had been deported to another camp.

"No matter," my uncle said, with the same cheerfulness that had kept Cecile and me in good spirits the entire time we ran Elby with him. "I'll go and see him there instead."

True to his word, he went to visit him, and discovered that friends from Metz were in charge of the care of the camp and were allowed unlimited access to the inmates. Leon, like his sister—my mother—before him, seized his chance and persuaded these friends to help him free Max. And so it was, for the second time, that Uncle Max was sprung from imprisonment and certain death, this time lying in the foot well of a service vehicle waved through the gates by the guards. Leon then managed to get him into Switzerland.

Poor Uncle Leon. A year after helping his brother escape, he was walking in the main street of St. Etienne when the Gestapo arrived in force for a surprise *rafle* of Jews. Checking his papers, they arrested him and detained him in a camp. He was held there for several weeks and, like Stéphanie, was offered the chance of escape but turned it down. Soon afterward he was deported to a camp somewhere in Poland. We had no idea where.

Fred, fearing for the rest of the family—being so close to Marseille, with all its *rafles* and troop movements—decided it was time to move away. He chose an area known as the Cantal, southwest of Clermont-Ferrand, in Auvergne, where there was a far smaller chance of seeing Germans than in a city on the Rhone. He found a big house in the beautiful high mountain resort of Vic-sur-Cère, at the head of one of the deep wooded valleys radiating out from the volcanic Monts du Cantal. There were only two roads into the resort, all but deserted because of the war, and he had patrols watching them twenty-four hours a day. As soon as any Germans came through, he had a mobilization plan and places for every Jewish family in the area to hide.

He and Rosette, their young son Maurice, Arnold, my parents, grandmother, Rosy, and Jacquie all moved to there from Arles, while I remained in Marseille. Hélène went with them initially, but after a few months she left the mountains for Clermont-Ferrand, where she enrolled in the university as a philosophy student. Fred, still supporting us all, told her that nothing should stand in the way of her education.

Trying to keep myself busy, I went to the closest Red Cross office and asked to see the person in charge, a Frenchwoman by the name of Madame Keller. I'd heard good things about her. She was an Alsatian and had a daughter who became a nurse but who later died suddenly. In fact, it was in her daughter's memory that Madame Keller took up nursing, and eventually became regional director of the Red Cross. Having made an appointment, I walked into her office, introduced myself, and blurted: "I have a problem. I'm a trainee nurse who wants to finish my studies and graduate, but I'm Jewish."

Madame Keller smiled and invited me to sit down. "Why should that be a problem?" she said kindly. I told her what had happened in Montpellier, and she was horrified. Patting my hand reassuringly, she said: "You shall graduate, Mademoiselle Hoffnung, and one day we shall be Free French again."

She picked up the telephone and called the principal of the local Red Cross school. "I have in front of me a young woman from Poitiers who completed one year of nursing training before escaping into unoccupied France because she is Jewish," she said. "I want her to be taken on by your school. I don't want to hear any objections; I want her accepted, period. I am sending her to you now."

The principal, Mademoiselle Chabannes, and her assistant, Mademoiselle Martin-Laval, were waiting for me, stony-faced. Leading me into a small office and closing the door, they rounded on me.

"We will never accept a Jew in this school," the principal spat, staring down at me, "so don't even think about applying. And if you should dare to go back to Madame Keller and complain, it'll be all the worse for you."

Saying nothing, I rose from my seat and quietly left the room. It took me half an hour to make my way back to Madame Keller. In my presence once more, she picked up the telephone. "If this girl is not both accepted and treated decently," she warned them, when I'd told her of my reception, "you'll both be fired."

And so, in November 1942, I enrolled at the school to finish my nurse's training, the only Jew among forty girls. I learned later that Mademoiselle Martin-Laval's brother, a physician, was the chief of the local Milice, the much despised volunteer police force which implemented Vichy and Nazi dictates. Despite Madame Keller's warning, the staff were horrible and did everything they could to make me leave. They wouldn't speak to me or tell me what I was supposed to do, and whenever they could be, they were rude and cruel. The other students didn't understand. None of them knew I was Jewish, and they didn't appreciate my situation. I rented a room, first from a woman who later volunteered for the service for foreign workers in Germany, and then from a widow.

Food became even scarcer, and along with my fellow students, I existed on the patients' leftovers and dishes made from root vegetables normally served to cattle. I was always very grateful for the cheese and food parcels regularly sent by Fred. He and Arnold did the gardening in their mountain retreat, growing fruits and vegetables. Neither had ever worked with the land before, but they became proficient market gardeners, providing enough food for themselves and the rest of the family, and bartering spare produce with the dairy farmers for cheese, butter, and milk.

I resolved from the start to ignore the unpleasantness of the hospital staff and to be as cheerful and helpful as I could be. Our patients were railroad workers, and whenever they were asked what they thought of the students nursing them, they always said kind things about me. "Mademoiselle Hoffnung is the most cheerful of them all," they would say. "We love to see her smile." Gradually, the hostility toward me softened a little and life became a bit more bearable.

A surprise visit by Jacques couldn't have been better timed. It was February 1943, and he wrote and told me he'd be coming to Marseille for a day and a night, having told his parents he was playing in a basketball game with his team. I asked my landlady if my fiancé could sleep in a spare bedroom, and she agreed. I was excited about his visit. Despite the frustratingly long delays in the mail service, now censored by the Germans, I'd written to him every day since we'd escaped, and he'd written back hundreds of letters under my pseudonym of Jacqueline Lenôtre, always signing off with "a thousand tender kisses." Our love for each other had never waned, but it had been six months since he'd held me in his arms, and I ached for him. I was twenty-two years old.

His parents were safely home from Saigon, having managed to find passage on the last ship out, and he'd told them all about me.

We'd never met, but his mother sent me her best wishes and her hopes that one day we'd meet. She asked him about me constantly, and was eager to know what I was like. He'd told her I was Jewish, "as small as a little bird," and blonde, but he still hadn't found the courage to tell her it was me he was visiting in Marseille, not a basketball court.

When the train from Poitiers finally pulled into the station at Marseille, I thought I would burst. Our last meeting had been so highly charged, saying good-bye the night before I'd led my family into unoccupied France. Now here he was, walking toward me, a huge grin on his face, his arms open wide.

"*Chérie,*" he said, engulfing me in his embrace. I must have kissed his face a hundred times. We spent that idyllic afternoon walking and talking, as lovers do. Like every young French couple, we strolled arm in arm, stopping only to kiss. My landlady prepared us a meal that night with some delicious ingredients sent by Fred. It was a feast, by Marseille standards, but I think Jacques—ever the hungry young student—thought it a little meager.

When my landlady had diplomatically retired to bed, the two of us stayed up talking most of the night. There was so much to catch up on, so much to tell him, things I couldn't have explained in our coded letters—how we'd escaped, what had happened to Uncle Max, our attempts to free Stéphanie, our anguish at not hearing from her since her deportation, and my trials getting into nursing.

"It's so good to see you, Jacques," I whispered, kissing him tenderly once more. "I wish we could stay like this forever."

He, in turn, told me the news from Poitiers, of his parents' dramatic escape from Indochina, and how his younger brother Marc had become very active politically. He brought greetings from Dedé, too, who sent word via Jacques that he hadn't heard from Stéphanie since her deportation, either.

Before we knew it, the first streaks of light were heralding the dawn, and Jacques was due back at the station to catch his homeward train. It felt so cruel, to have had such a short time with him, but I was grateful for it nonetheless.

"I'll see you at Easter, Marthe," he promised. "I'll meet you in Vic-sur-Cère when you go to visit your parents." I could hardly wait.

The time dragged interminably until Easter, but eventually the day came when I was to leave for the mountains and meet Jacques again. I was accompanied by Juliette Fontaine, the young daughter of a family Fred and Rosette had known in Arles, whom they'd invited to spend the Easter break with them. The trains crawled along. A journey that would have taken a few hours in peacetime now took days. We were to spend all day traveling north and then stay a night at a hotel in a little town north of Montélimar, before catching the morning train to Vic-sur-Cère. Jacques was meeting us at the overnight stop, before traveling on with us.

Finding a seat, Juliette and I settled into what seemed an interminable journey, getting up only to use the bathroom or stretch our legs. Standing in the corridor of the train a few hours into the trip, I noticed a man in the next compartment trying to attract our attention by waving his hand. Two other civilians, a priest, two German soldiers, and an officer accompanied him. Thinking they were all German, I ignored him and told Juliette to look away. "Don't take any notice," I said. "They're just being fresh."

But glancing back in their direction a few minutes later, I saw that the man who was desperately trying to attract my attention was signaling a gesture of imaginary handcuffs on his wrists. Suddenly taking it all in, I realized that he, the priest, and the two civilians were prisoners of the German soldiers.

Soon afterward one of the soldiers wandered out into the corridor and I immediately engaged him in conversation. Speaking German, I asked him where he was going and who he was traveling with. "Political prisoners," he told me, yawning. "They're being transferred to Paris."

Shortly afterward his superior, a noncommissioned officer who'd been conversing with a French girl for much of the journey, disappeared with her into an empty compartment. His soldiers relaxed visibly when he left, and allowed one of their prisoners to stand in the corridor for a few minutes. "What can I do to help?" I asked him, speaking quickly in French.

The soldiers lit cigarettes and ignored us. After all, I was only a girl.

Continuing to speak quickly, I added, "Why don't you take advantage of the situation and try to escape? The train's going slowly enough. I could distract the soldiers while you jump out of the bathroom window."

The prisoners discussed my plan among themselves and seemed prepared to do it, but the priest vetoed the idea. "No," he told the others in a whisper. "We shouldn't even try. God will help us."

The escape plan ditched, I offered to at least contact their families for them and tell them where they were being taken. Writing down the names and addresses of wives, parents, and loved ones, I spent as much time as the soldiers would allow with these men whose only crime had been to join the Resistance struggle against the occupying forces.

By the time we reached our station, all thoughts of Jacques had been forgotten; such was my concern for these prisoners. "God be with you," I told each of them sadly as I waved farewell.

Jacques was waiting for me on the platform. Rushing to the train, he lifted me up into his arms and spun me around before lowering me to the ground. But all I could think of were the prisoners. Instead of returning his gleeful embrace, I could only talk of them.

"It's so terrible, Jacques," I complained. "I so wanted to do something to help them, but there was nothing I could do." As the train pulled out of the station, I watched it go with a dark sense of foreboding.

Vic-sur-Cère helped lift my spirits. It was beautiful spring weather and everything looked so green. The birds were singing, the cows were in the pastures, and sheep were grazing in the high meadows. Jacques stayed with us for a whole week. My parents, who already liked him very much, welcomed him warmly. My mother, still in such torment over the fate of Stéphanie, was heartened at least by Jacques's promises to convert to Judaism when we married. It was something that the devout Dedé would never have agreed to if he and Steph were ever reunited.

It was the first time Fred had met Jacques, and he took to him instantly. In just a few days Jacques became one of the family. Little Jacquie was particularly fond of the new grown-up in our midst, and held his hand tightly wherever we went. We went hiking in the mountains, took happy family snapshots, and tried to pretend that there wasn't a war on. But no matter how we tried, the absence of Stéphanie and the constant threat of German patrols kept it at the forefront of our minds.

Much of the week was spent discussing the unfortunate prisoners I'd met and what more could be done in the way of active resistance against the Germans. Fred and Arnold were already heavily involved, organizing Allied air drops of arms and munitions, and knew many of the senior Resistance men. I wanted to do my part, too. Hélène, back from Clermont-Ferrand for the Easter break, was also surprisingly active. A pretty young thing, she lived two floors above a Gestapo office, and yet she had a printing press in her room, on which she printed propaganda posters. She also traveled around the region with a rucksack on her back, full of arms for the Resistance.

"I was stopped by a French policeman once," she told us. "He barred my way and asked, 'What's in your rucksack?' I nearly died of fright, but all I could think of was to beam a huge smile at him. Softening visibly, the policeman told me, 'Nobody with such a smile could do anything wrong. Go on your way.' And off I went to safely deliver my important packages."

One day, in the university library, she told us, the SS walked in to look for Jews. Hélène's professor stood up and objected to them marching into somewhere so sacred. They shot him dead right in front of the students. The SS rounded up all the students and threw them in jail overnight. The Jewish students were detained, but Hélène was released because her papers didn't have the Jewish stamp. As she told us the story, I silently thanked Monsieur Charpentier once more.

"So what can I do in Marseille?" I asked Hélène, still reeling from the idea of my little sister being such an active member of the Resistance.

"Nothing, I hope," Jacques intervened swiftly. "You're far too precious, Marthe. I absolutely forbid you from doing anything foolish."

Fred listened to Jacques's vehement response and looked thoughtful. "And what about you, Jacques?" he asked quietly.

Jacques looked across at me and then at Fred. "I haven't made up my mind, yet," he said, swallowing. "I, er, haven't fully committed myself to any active group."

Smiling my support, I squeezed his hand.

The end of our Easter sojourn came all too soon, and before I knew it I was back in Marseille, back at nursing school living on left-overs, miles from all the people I knew and loved.

A month later, in my lonely bedroom, I opened a newspaper and read that four members of the Resistance, including a priest, recently transferred from the South of France, had been executed by a firing squad in Paris.

"Oh, how terrible," I cried aloud, alone in my room. "Now, do you see Jacques?" I railed to no one. "We have to do something. We can't just sit back and watch anymore."

Shattered Dreams

I only had to wait a few months before seeing Jacques again. In July 1943 he would be spending a week in Paris, completing part of his final medical exams in the university hospital program to become a nonresident doctor at the hospital. He and Dedé would be traveling to the capital to compete for a coveted place, and Jacques suggested that I either take some time off school and visit Cecile or try to get a student placement there for the same period.

Because I'd become a model nurse by then and had finally warmed the cold hearts of the staff, they agreed. Cecile's new boyfriend arranged a position in the pediatric department of the Enfants Malades de Paris under Dr. Debré. I managed to get the relevant passes and traveled by train to Paris. The Germans carefully checked my forged identity card on the train and gave it back to me with a smile.

It was wonderful to be reunited with Cecile after nearly two years. She looked great. Ever since her arrival in Paris, she'd been living falsely as a non-Jew, having gone to city hall and claimed that she'd lost her original papers. After questioning her closely, they made her up a new one without the stamp JUIVE. She was very pleased to see me, and took me back to the apartment she'd found on rue Chauvert, near the École Militaire.

"It's small, but it's safe," she told me. I noticed how she constantly looked right and left as we made our way through the busy streets from the station. I was overwhelmed by how many German soldiers and vehicles there were everywhere.

The studio apartment was tiny but comfortable, and Cecile made me very welcome. We were to share the only bed. It was just like being a little girl again. She was earning enough to support herself from selling clothing to a Turkish Jew named Joe Gerson, who sold them on the black market. What little extra she made, she sent to Fred. She introduced me to her boyfriend, Jacques Lefevre, who lived on Boulevard St. Germain and who'd arranged my pediatric placement. He was a medical student, the non-Jewish son of a lawyer, and had been raised in Saigon, like my Jacques. Cecile had first met him in Toulouse in August 1940, when she went to collect my grandmother from Uncle Leon's. He was in the army there, having been drafted after his first year in medical school. He'd asked for her address and started writing to her immediately. When she moved to Paris, he'd already returned there to complete his studies, and he and Cecile soon became an item. Jacques Lefevre was utterly devoted to Cecile and wanted to marry her desperately.

"We could at least get engaged," he'd suggest, but Cecile always refused.

"I can't possibly make any such plans while our beloved country is under occupation," she stated. Jacques would nod dejectedly and hope for peace soon.

The impending visit of my Jacques was, however, all I could think of. I was as jumpy as a schoolgirl on a first date. Cecile helped me get everything ready before he arrived, and I chose a favorite dress. Jacques seemed taller and more gaunt when I saw him in the doorway of her apartment, but he held me tightly and kissed me tenderly and I was so happy to be back in his arms. Within a few minutes of our long-awaited reunion, however, I could tell there were more pressing matters on his mind.

Saying little, he took me to a café on Boulevard St. Germain, guiding me to a seat on an empty corner of the terrace. "Something's happened, Marthe," he told me, taking my hand, his face pale.

I wondered for one horrible moment if he'd met someone else. I thought back to the day we'd first met, my twenty-first birthday party, when he'd danced with me all afternoon. He was such a handsome young man; I wouldn't have been surprised if he'd fallen in love with someone closer to home.

"What is it, Jacques?" I now asked, bracing myself for the speech I half expected. Inwardly, I chastised myself, knowing I should have expected this. Apart from our brief time together in Marseille and Vic-sur-Cère, we'd been separated for almost a year. He was only flesh and blood, I told myself, biting my top lip.

"I'm in some trouble," Jacques said, struggling with his words.

"What kind of trouble?" I asked, smiling with relief that it wasn't what I'd thought. He was calm, intelligent, and kind. How bad could it be?

"Murder," he said, focusing intently on my face.

I laughed involuntarily. "Murder, Jacques? Don't be silly!" I punched him playfully in the ribs.

"I mean it, Marthe," he said, his face burning. "Since I saw you last in the mountains, I joined the Resistance group run by Marc, and between us we killed a man."

"This isn't funny, Jacques," I said, feeling a tightening in my chest. "This isn't funny at all."

"No, Marthe, I know it isn't," he replied, lowering his eyes. "But I'm afraid I'm not joking. I'm sorry, but it's true."

He proceeded to tell me, in as even a voice as he could, how he'd been encouraged by his brother Marc, the idealistic law student, to help set up their own little Resistance unit. With three friends, including one I knew—Eloi Rieckert, the brother of my classmate Janine—they'd organized several attacks of sabotage and disruption. Under Marc's leadership, the group became ever more ambitious, and in May of that year, less than a month after I'd last seen him, they hatched a plan to kidnap Dr. Michel Guerin, a leading Nazi collaborator and anti-Semite, who embodied all that they hated.

Their plan was to ambush and kidnap the doctor, take his keys, search his house, and burn all his compromising documents so he could denounce no one else. They lured him to an address on the pretext of treating an elderly woman patient, but the plan went wrong.

"There was a terrible struggle," Jacques told me, the memory of that night evidently still raw. "Dr. Guerin produced a gun and fired it three times. I was just the lookout; I heard the shots and ran to where the rest of them were. Marc and the others panicked. They hit him over the head with a cosh, thinking to quiet him before anyone came, but the wooden handle of the cosh broke." He paused and took a deep breath. "Then there was a knife—someone produced a knife and they stabbed him. Marc, too. We ran away. We left him lying in a pool of blood and we ran away. He died on the operating table later that night, but not before he'd told the authorities exactly what had happened."

I was stunned by what Jacques was telling me as he sat stroking my hand. It was a beautiful, hot, sunny day, but listening to him, I drew my cardigan around me. I watched couples locked in embraces, I saw the breeze shimmer the leaves in the trees and heard the murmur of passersby. For a moment I was unable to distinguish reality from the nightmare of what Jacques was saying. I found it almost impossible to believe that my gentle fiancé could have participated in such a barbaric attack. He was such a levelheaded young man, this could never have happened in peacetime. I hated what war had done to him, how much the German atrocities had exacted on all of us. I suspected that his impulsive, ideological brother had led him on, but I knew that didn't make his situation any less grave.

"They had no choice but to kill him, Marthe," Jacques said, his eyes pleading with me to understand. "They had to silence him and his wretched gun."

"But to commit murder!" I told him, watching the birds hopping around on the ground near to where we sat. "How horrible!"

"It wasn't supposed to happen like that," he countered, "I didn't allow it. I just couldn't stop it. There was nothing I could do!"

"You're a medical student, Jacques," I reminded him. "The man who died was a doctor, and a Frenchman."

"But he was even more dangerous to other Frenchman than the Germans!" he answered hotly. Expecting my unconditional approval, Jacques was appalled by my reaction. Every one of my arguments seemed to burn him.

I was overcome by sadness; his story felt like a huge burden on my shoulders. "You can't go back to Poitiers now," I told him, trying hard to focus. "You'll be arrested." I thought of what I'd seen the Germans do to the deportees at the camp in Aubagne, and tried not to think how much worse it would be for someone in the Resistance. My memory of the four prisoners on the train was still fresh.

"You must go south, Jacques, make your way to Spain. I'll meet you there. Fred will arrange everything." My mind was taking logical little steps, pushing all thoughts of the murder away.

"I have to go back, Marthe," Jacques told me abruptly, standing and taking me firmly by the shoulders. At over six feet tall, he'd always towered over me physically, and now he seemed taller and stronger than ever.

"My whole family is still there," he said, his brown eyes sad, "and Marc is equally at risk. He and I later joined forces with the communists and attacked a German supply train. The Gestapo are hunting us for that alone. I can't just abandon him. I promised him we'd stick together on this. I'll go back and say good-bye to my parents, and then Marc and I and the others will arrange our escape as soon as we can."

Somehow, Jacques managed to complete his examination—doing well, he thought—and prepared to leave Paris. He promised to write to me every day. After a last few bittersweet days, both of us achingly tense and trying hard not to think about what lay ahead, he came to the hospital where I worked to say good-bye.

"I love you, Marthe Hoffnung," he told me, bending to kiss my forehead. "Be brave." I attempted a smile and kissed him back, once on each cheek.

"Adieu, chérie," he said, picking up his bag and turning to go. I shivered involuntarily as I watched his receding figure became smaller and smaller in the distance, a tiny dot merging into the summer crowd.

Now that Jacques was gone, I returned to Cecile's apartment alone and pulled out a crumpled letter Dedé had given me just before he, too, had left for Poitiers. Pressing it into my hand, Dedé had said: "I know this may not be a good time, Marthe, but I thought you'd like to have this. It's the last letter Steph sent me from Pithiviers, ten months ago. She says she's about to be sent to a labor camp in Metz, which is why I suppose we haven't heard from her since. She told me in a previous letter that she'd broken her ankle somehow, but apart from that she seemed in good spirits."

Taking the letter and slipping it into my pocket, I'd thanked Dedé warmly. But not even good news from Stéphanie and the thought of her being in our hometown of Metz could lift me. Now I forced myself to read it.

The handwriting was small and spidery. The paper was cheap and thin. The letter was dated September 21, 1942, the Jewish festival of Yom Kippur.

> *We leave today for an unknown destination, there are rumors that we are going to Compiegne near Paris. I'm still not able to walk, and ignore how I will walk, or how I will be transported because there is no question that I can walk. Please write to my parents and tell them that I left brave and confident, which is true. You know that for the great ordeals I'm always very strong. Please tell them not to send me any packages unless they've already done so. I've received your package, for which I thank you kindly. Unfortunately, the envelopes, paper, and lamp will be taken from me. Already, my fountain pen has been taken. I thank you for the cigarettes. I spent the night smoking because they will also be taken. It is six* A.M. *and I still have three to smoke. I will try to send you news as soon as I'm able. Please continue to take what steps you can to get me freed.*
>
> *My dear Dedé, I hope that this is not good-bye, because I have the will to keep going. If I have the chance, one day I'll describe for you the scenes we lived through yesterday and that we will go through again today. Don't worry about me; there is only one thing that bothers me terribly, which is to be disabled. Too bad . . . The most beautiful thing they can do is to make us leave on Yom Kippur. The fasting will only be easier and the prayers said with even more conviction. Tell my little mother that*

Regine Hoffnung, my mother, as a young woman, and Fishel Hoffnung, my father, as a young man.

A family picture at the swimming pool in Metz in the summer of 1936: Counterclockwise from the bottom left: Arnold (1916); Stéphanie (1921); Fred (1911); Rosy (1925); Hélène (1924); and me (1920). Missing is my sister Cecile (1915).

Spring 1936 in Metz, wearing a straw hat made by Cecile.

In Metz in 1937 at the very modern, at that time, Olympic-size pool where I spent a great deal of time practicing.
I was a good swimmer and participated in competitions.

Jacquie Farber in 1938 (three years old) shortly after his arrival in Metz from Düsseldorf, where he had witnessed the trashing of his home by the Gestapo on *Kristallnacht*.

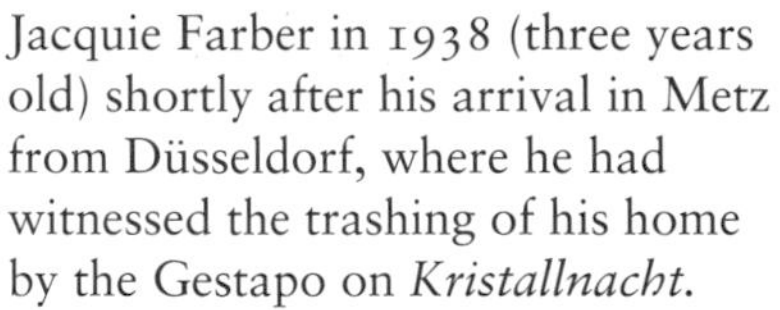

Stéphanie (seventeen years old) at the Metz swimming pool in summer 1938.

In Metz, 1938, resting in a field during a hike.

Serge Lenay in Brittany, at the age of seven, with family friends, prior to his trip to Indochina.

CARTE D'IDENTITÉ

Nom :

Prénoms :

Profession : Étudiante

Née le : 12 juillet 1921

à Metz

Département : Moselle

Nationalité : Française

Domicile :

13 FRANCS

Stéphanie: 8 Rue de la Pierre Plastique, Poitiers. Her identity card as a student when we were living at that address from late 1940 to early 1941. She was twenty years old.

Marc *(left)* and Jacques Delaunay in Poitiers, circa 1941.

Fred Hoffnung, my oldest brother, and his wife, Rosette, on their wedding day in St. Etienne in 1941 after having successfully crossed the Ligne of Demarcation.

Summer 1941: I am sitting on the left, next to Jacques Delaunay. We had enjoyed an outing with a group of friends in the countryside that day and were having lunch in a small village café.

Above: My official nursing school picture taken in the fall of 1941 in Poitiers. From the right: Mademoiselle Falaise, our instructor; Mademoiselle Margnat, the headmistress; and me. *Right:* Fall 1941 as a student nurse in Poitiers (the picture was apposed to my school records).

Jacques Delaunay, my then fiancé, and me in Poitiers in the winter of 1941, leaving a basketball game in which Jacques had participated. I am again wearing a hat made by Cecile.

ÉTAT FRANÇAIS
CARTE D'IDENTITÉ
Nom Hofnung
Prénoms Marthe
Domicile 21 rue de Provence Marseille
Profession Infirmière
Née le 13 Avril 1920
à Metz Dpt Moselle
fille de Michel
et de Blatrath Régine
Nationalité Française
Signature du titulaire.

SIGNALEMENT
Taille 1m 50
Visage ovale
Teint clair
Cheveux Blonds
Moustaches
Front ord
Yeux verts
Nez rect moyen
Bouche moyenne
Menton rond
Signes particuliers

My November 20, 1943, identity card established in Marseille in exchange for the one Monsieur Charpentier had provided without the red stamp and the inscription JUIVE (Jew) in Poitiers, 1942. This new card allowed me to safely travel to Paris and to live there until the Liberation.

Jacques and me in Vic-sur-Cère during Easter break in 1943. We were celebrating Passover with my family. During that holiday, we hiked in the gorgeous mountains of Cantal situated in the heart of Auvergne. That day we sat on the top of the world.

Left: In civilian clothes in 1945 at our "antenna," an intelligence section of the headquarters of the General Delattre de Tassigny First French Army. *Right:* In uniform in 1945, wearing on the left side of my chest the ribbon of the Croix de Guerre with two silver stars, and on my left pocket, the pin of the Commandos d'Afrique. Colonel Bouvet had awarded me both the title of honorary commando and the pin the day he decorated me with the first of my two Croix de Guerre silver stars in front of his troops somewhere in Alsace.

Captain Paul Ligouzat, the intelligence officer of the Commandos d'Afrique, and me on a ferry crossing the Lake of Konstanz in 1945, after my return from a mission in Germany.

Captain Louis Lenay (left), Serge's father, in the jungle somewhere in Indochina, circa 1946–1947. (The picture was given to me by Serge when I met him and his family in Paris, in November 2001.)

A passport established in Indochina prior to my return to France in 1948. I am wearing a colonial uniform.

SIGNALEMENT

Taille: 1m50
Cheveux: blonds
Sourcils:
Front:
Yeux:
Nez:
Bouche: Moustache:
Barbe:
Menton:
Visage:
Teint:
Signes particuliers:
Accompagné de .... enfants.

Nom	Prénoms	Date de naissance

— 2 —

Spring 1949 in Poitiers, shortly after my arrival there.

1950 in Vichy on vacation.

Left: In Poitiers in 1950. *Right:* I am (at left) with a friend ready for the Annual Ball of the Poitiers Section of the Rhin et Danube Veterans Society which, as their social worker, I organized in 1951.

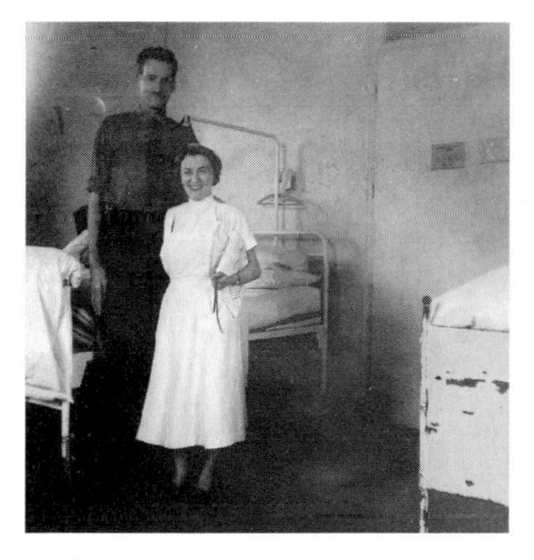

With a patient in the neurology ward of the Hospital Cantonal de Geneve, Switzerland. I was the head nurse of that ward from the fall of 1955 to my departure to the United States in June of 1956.

Hiking in the Alps in the summer of 1955 with, from the left: Cecile and her beloved dog "Nounours" (or little bear) whom I had given to Cecile as a present for New Years in 1951. With us is my future husband, Major L. Cohn.

Major and me shortly after our February 9, 1958, Jewish ceremony under the traditional *Chuppah*, or canopy.

November 1961 with Stephan Jacques (eleven months old) on York Avenue and 72nd Street, New York City, where we lived from 1960 to 1962. I worked then as a nurse anesthetist at New York Hospital while my husband, Major, was on the staff of Sloan-Kettering.

Holding Remi Benjamin (about five months old) with Stephan Jacques (four years old) in Minneapolis in September 1964.

At the Sofitel Hotel in Los Angeles on Bastille Day, July 14, 2000, after the French Consul, Yves Yelda, officially presented the Médaille Militaire to me. From left to right: Major; Remi Benjamin; Consul Yelda; and Stephan Jacques. In front: me and my granddaughter, Anna Regina.

I think of her a lot, but I forbid her to cry. She has to be strong because I want to find her young like before when I come back. I will need her. I am not worried for myself; I have a lot of grief for her. My respects to your parents and for Rosy and my most affectionate kisses for you,

STÉPHANIE

P.S. In the last few moments they tell me that we are going to Metz, where we will be working. No need to dramatize. I will give you news as soon as possible. Let my family know good-bye. Au revoir.

The first letter Jacques sent me after our meeting in Paris was written on the train. He spoke of his inner turmoil at leaving me, and of how much he loved me and prayed for our future happiness. "Please understand," he wrote, "whatever happens, I shall always be your very own Jacques."

Two more letters followed, written in quick succession. As long as they kept coming, I knew he was safe. But the fourth never came. I waited a week, then three more days, but nothing arrived. Flushed, unable to catch my breath, I waited for the mail every morning, but none came. Cecile kept asking me what was the matter. I hadn't told her what Jacques had done, and she didn't understand why I was so upset.

"It's just this stupid German occupation," she told me. "You'll get no letters for ages and then a whole bunch of them will arrive, you'll see."

"I have to find out what's happened to him and why his letters have stopped," I told her distractedly. "I'm going to telephone Poitiers." Cecile reminded me of the risks, but I knew I had no choice.

I went to a public pay phone in a local post office so as not to have the call traced back to Cecile. My hands shaking, I nervously telephoned Jacques's aunt, who lived next door to his parents' house in Poitiers.

"Hello, Madame Marcoux," I said in a voice that belied my fear, "this is Jacqueline Lenôtre. I'm just calling to find out if everything is all right."

In a voice thick with emotion she told me, "No, it's not. It couldn't be worse. He is terribly ill. It's highly infectious. You must be very careful."

The catastrophe I'd so feared must have happened. Walking home from the post office, I fought to retain control of myself. To have broken down in the crowded streets would have aroused suspicion and could have led to my immediate arrest. I barely registered the faces of the people pushing past me. A man in a hurry nearly sent me flying, but I didn't even acknowledge his apology or his attempts to help me to my feet.

Cecile opened the door of her apartment, took one look at my face and quickly understood that something terrible had happened. I was unable to speak.

My nerves frayed, I finally sat her down on the edge of the bed we shared and told her exactly what Jacques had done. I told her of Dr. Guerin and the sabotaged train. Cecile was aghast. For us both. She was also afraid that I'd be linked to Jacques and arrested, too.

"This is awful," she said, her hand to her mouth. Thinking for a moment as she held my hand in both of hers and searched my face, she suddenly jumped up. "Come, Marthe, we have to leave. Immediately."

She took charge completely, grabbing a few of our most indispensable belongings and ushering me out of the apartment. We knew Jacques had a written note of our address somewhere, and we had no way of knowing if he'd had time to destroy it. We took refuge in the apartment of Elise Kirsch, a non-Jewish friend and a former neighbor from Metz with whom Cecile had kept in touch. We remained there for another two weeks before nervously returning to our apartment.

I barely remember completing my training at the pediatric hospital, or returning to Marseille at the end of August. But apparently I did. It's a complete blur. All I remember is that Cecile moved south to take care of me. I don't know what I'd have done without her.

For the French Resistance, Jacques, Marc, and their compatriots had become heroes. His fellow prisoners were his school friends Eloi Rieckert, Jean Gauthier, and Jacques Massias. Their case made national headlines and was reported on the radio across France and in Britain. But nothing could eradicate the cold dread I felt inside.

I was right to be fearful. Jacques and his friends were handed over to the newly appointed and much-feared Section of Political Affairs (SAP). It wasn't until much later, and from his mother, that I learned how badly he'd been treated. These fine young men from respectable middle-class families endured severe and prolonged beatings with leather truncheons while hung from their wrists in chains. When they screamed, their mouths were stuffed with stale bread, and when they passed out, their heads were plunged into buckets of water. Jacques, whom they considered the most vulnerable, was strapped naked to an operating table while the most unspeakable tortures were devised, using electrodes and surgical implements. Every day, under the close supervision of the SS, these young idealists underwent the very worst cruelty imaginable. Not surprisingly, perhaps, they eventually admitted what they'd done, but all insisted that it had been a mistake and that they'd never intended to kill Dr. Guerin.

They first appeared in court in Poitiers on August 16, 1943, and were sent to Paris, amid high security, for a show trial in front of a special tribunal of French judges. Another school friend, Annette Boutin, wrote to me and told me of the unfolding events.

The case opened on September 10 with the prosecution calling immediately for the death penalty. The famous French lawyer Maurice Garçon defended them, having voluntarily taken up their cause. He described the pitiful young men in the dock, broken by torture, as "political prisoners," and claimed that their only crime was that they loved their country too much. He blamed Dr. Guerin's repeated incitements to murder for his "accidental" death, and begged the judges to "take pity on these children whose passion for their country has set them on a wrong path."

The judges took his words to heart and agreed that the murder of Dr. Guerin had never been intended. Instead of the death penalty, four of the five were condemned to exile and hard labor for life, under recently introduced military laws. Jacques was sentenced to twenty years' hard labor rather than life, because he hadn't been directly involved in the killing.

Sitting in my bedroom in Marseille, I was overjoyed when I read of his twenty-year sentence in Annette's latest letter. It was such a relief that he hadn't been condemned to death. "He'll be safe until the end of the war," I told Cecile joyfully, before she returned to Paris. "He won't be able to get into any more trouble." Dancing around the room, the letter my imaginary partner, I felt as if the weight of the world had been lifted from my shoulders.

Under German occupation, being in prison was nothing to be ashamed of; in fact, it was considered a gauge of one's patriotism. What hardships awaited Jacques in the German-supervised forced labor camps, I could hardly bear to contemplate, but I knew that he was young and strong enough to face what lay ahead. I could only pray ever more fervently that the war would soon be over so he could be released, in the same way I sincerely believed Stéphanie would.

Six weeks later, on the morning of October 25, 1943, the first day of my five-day final nurse's examination, I opened the Marseille newspaper as usual and scanned the pages while eating my meager breakfast. The headlines were full of Italy's about-face in declaring war on Germany, and how the Allies were making sweeping advances across the European theater. Hamburg was licking its wounds after saturation bombing, Corsica had fallen to the Resistance—the first corner of France to be liberated—and the Germans were being beaten back in Russia. It seemed that there was room for optimism at last.

A small article on an inside page caught my eye. Its headline read: THE FIVE STUDENTS FROM POITIERS. Putting down my mug of tea and a dry piece of toast, I ran my finger down the text.

> The German war council announces the summary execution of four of the five students of Poitiers, recently tried for the murder of Dr. Guerin. They were handed by the French authorities to the council on September 24, and condemned to death for the sabotage of a train carrying German armaments. One was spared and sentenced to an indefinite term of imprisonment. Five of their communist compatriots have also been executed. Monsieur Maurice Garçon, the defense lawyer who represented them during their Paris trial for the murder of Dr. Guerin, for which they were sentenced to hard labor, was not present at this final hearing.

The newspaper report gave no further details and did not print the name of those who'd been shot or the one who was spared.

I stood up, and to my surprise found that my legs still worked. They walked me to the window and allowed me to stand there for an hour or more, staring out unblinkingly without seeing anything. I thought Jacques must still be alive, that I'd know it in my heart if he were dead. Surely he would be the one who was spared, as he'd only been the lookout at the killing of Dr. Guerin. But this sentence was for the later sabotage of a German supply train, in which Jacques had much more of a hand.

For several hours my head swam and I could barely catch my breath. I had no means of contacting anyone to find out the answers to the question I wasn't even sure I wanted answered. Part of me longed to catch the next train to Poitiers and hammer on the door of his mother's house, knowing that one look at her face would tell me all I needed to know. Common sense told me to stay calm, to hope for the best and wait until there was official confirmation. It might be a propaganda stunt to promote a Resistance reaction. The newspaper might have made a mistake and confused the students from Poitiers with someone else.

The hour of my examination drew closer. With sudden clarity, I recalled Jacques's sheer unbridled enthusiasm for my becoming a nurse and his determination that we'd work together in Indochina. "It'll be wonderful," he'd told me, his eyes bright. "We can save lives side by side."

Still standing at my little window onto the world, I thought, too, of Fred, who'd sacrificed so much to invest in my tuition to get me to this point, the final examination to graduate as Infirmière Diplômée d'État. If I didn't do something to occupy my mind, I knew I'd go mad. I forced myself to gather my things together, walk to the private Red Cross clinic where I was due to report, and make myself do what I'd been trained for. Several people noticed immediately that I'd been crying and asked me what was wrong.

"Something in my eye," I replied, without further explanation.

That night, I sat down and wrote a letter to Annette. I never mentioned Jacques's name, but hidden among several meaningless questions about mutual friends, I wrote: "Please send me any news of the young patient who's been seriously ill since the summer." I walked to the mailbox and went back to my bedroom to wait.

For five days I tried to block out all personal thoughts. Like an automaton, present in body but not in spirit, I took both written and oral examinations, sitting at a desk, focusing so intently on the questions that they burned my eyes. I undertook clinical tests and dealt with patients, bandaging wounds, administering drugs, changing dressings, all supervised by an examiner, biting my bottom lip until it bled. Most of the time I was acutely nauseous, as I fought with all the will I possessed to keep going. Often I felt I was losing my mind. I reran conversations I'd had with Jacques. I agonized over our time in Paris when I hadn't given him my full and unequivocal support. A battle raged within me. One minute I'd convince myself that he was still alive, the next I'd be plunged into despair.

After each examination, I'd walk the streets of Marseille until my feet were too tired and sore to take another step. I barely ate or slept, and sat up reading most of the night. Reading had always been my salvation, the only activity that permitted me to forget my tribulations, although several of the chapters had to be read over and over again before I could begin to take them in. The words just merged on the page.

Annette's letter took three weeks to arrive. For an hour after it came, I sat holding it on my lap, staring at it before I found the courage to open it. Tearing the pale blue envelope, I lifted out the single sheet and unfolded it gingerly.

"I am very sorry to inform you," she wrote, "that the patient you asked about has died."

Standing alongside his nineteen-year-old brother Marc and two others, my brown-eyed Jacques was lined up against a wall at Mont Valerien—the most feared German prison in Paris—and executed by a firing squad. Like thousands before him caught in the volleys of the firing squad, the sputtering candle that had been his life was extinguished without a second thought. At the age of twenty-one, he was buried in an unmarked grave in a suburban cemetery south of Paris. The date of his execution was October 6, a day like any other, that had passed for me without incident, without my even knowing what he was facing.

In the last letter Jacques wrote to his parents, on the morning of his execution, he told them: "Tell 'Jacqueline' that I love her with all my heart. She should marry someone else and not waste her life in mourning." I wasn't to learn of that letter until one year later, but his words would not have been much comfort.

It would be days before I could contact Cecile and the rest of my family and tell them what had happened. I was completely on my own. For a while I couldn't even be alone in a room. I walked aimlessly in the streets for hours just to be among people. I'd sit in a park and bury my nose in a book, pretending to read. Like a robot, I continued going to nursing school each day. No one at school had ever met Jacques or knew that he had any connection with me, so no one knew why I was so listless. Only once did I let my guard slip. A girl in my class approached me one day and, placing an arm around my shoulders, she asked, "Marthe, tell me, why are you so sad?" Breaking down, I held my head in my hands and sobbed until I had no more tears left to cry. When I was finally able to speak, I told her only that my fiancé had been killed. Nothing more.

For a while the pain was too much to bear. I couldn't think of the next day or how I could begin to get through it. Life seemed to be on hold, frozen in time. There was no future, just the past. I tried to make sense of the senseless. Torn by thoughts of how Jacques must have suffered, I cocooned myself in comforting memories of the precious times we'd been able to share—cycling along the riverbank, walking hand in hand through the forest, talking and dreaming of our future together in the Far East, of having lots of children and growing old together.

People had laughed at us, at the difference in our heights, but I didn't care. I was deliriously happy. In the two short years we'd known each other, we'd become so close. A single lifetime would never have been long enough to achieve all our plans. He'd been so full of life, a great athlete, an excellent student, and an unusually caring and gentle human being. I was immensely proud of how courageous he'd been for his country. I knew that over and above any personal patriotism, he'd also been trying to get even for our forced separation. There would never be another like him.

The anger came later, and for a while I was consumed with hatred for the Nazis. They'd denied me so much—the chance of happiness with the man I loved, to bear his children, to continue our future together. They'd even denied Jacques dignity in death. There was no funeral, no wreaths, no public mourning. I couldn't even write to his mother and express my condolences for the loss of her two sons and of her husband, who'd been deported to Buchenwald concentration camp for his own Resistance activities. I'd been denied any succor those who knew and loved him might have been able to give me. The Germans wanted him and his fellow students to be forgotten, without tombstones or memorials. They were nothing to them—just a handful among thousands of brave Resistance members tortured and killed for their beliefs—their bodies tossed into graves like so much discarded rubbish.

In an entirely private and carefully considered decision, I took a solemn vow to God that Jacques would always be remembered. "I will never stop loving him," I said out loud. I wasn't even sure I believed in God by then, but I whispered an oath. "Dear God, I resolve here and now that I shall never marry."

No one else knew. It was between God and me.

I found it difficult to fathom, but when my exam results came through a week later, I'd passed my finals with distinction. I was a qualified nurse. The trouble was, nursing no longer held the same attraction for me. My only thought was to join the Resistance in Marseille and do all I could to undermine the Germans. But they wouldn't have me.

When Fred had come to Marseille with the money to try to free Stéphanie months earlier, he'd introduced me to Armand Kramer, a former lieutenant in the French army, who was very active in the South. "I'm a trained nurse and I can help," I now told the brooding stranger who, Fred had informed me, lost a brother to the Nazis. "Please give me something to do."

Kramer threw back his head and laughed. Looking me up and down, he smiled and patted me on the head. "My organization doesn't ask little girls to risk their lives," he said. "Why don't you stick with nursing?"

Beyond anger, I moved back to Paris to live permanently with Cecile. Maybe the Parisian Resistance groups wouldn't be quite so picky. But first I had to get a job; Cecile couldn't be expected to support both of us. It was too dangerous for me to work in a hospital—they would have checked my papers too rigorously—so I signed on with an agency that found me a job with a wealthy Catholic woman, Madame Matilde Lucas, who needed a nurse for her elderly mother.

Madame Lucas was extremely kind and treated me like a daughter from the outset. Her brother was the chief curator at the Louvre, and she was very well-connected. I never told her I was Jewish, although I think she may have suspected. I worked for her five days a week, caring for her sick mother, and taking all my meals with them. Each night I went home to Cecile, who now lived in a much larger apartment on Avenue de la Bourdonnais.

Life was hard. There was little gas or electricity, blackouts were almost permanent, water shortages were rife, and the bread we waited in line for, along with everything else, tasted like sawdust. We were only allowed one new pair of shoes per year, and they were made of wood, with high platforms, no leather, just some material. They were cheap and ugly. There was no material with which to make clothes—the Germans took everything. We couldn't buy anything without coupons, and what we could buy was very limited. I had no winter coat, and couldn't get one. There was no coal and no heat and such a shortage of gas that we were only allowed to cook during certain hours.

Numb to much of it, still grieving for Jacques, every Sunday I took the Metro to the far south of the city, near the Porte d' Ivry, to visit his simple, unmarked grave.

Cecile was worried. "Be careful, Marthe," she told me, "the Gestapo will almost certainly be watching the cemetery. They'll want to speak to anyone who knew those who were shot."

Reaching for my scarf, I kissed her on both cheeks and left.

I came to find comfort in that weekly Metro journey through the darkness of the underground. It was long and slow and took me twenty minutes at each end to walk to where I was going. My face pressed against the glass, crisscrossed with tape to prevent it from shattering in an explosion, I watched as my breath clouded it then cleared, clouded it and cleared. I had little money and there were rarely any flowers for sale in Paris anymore, but I nearly always managed to find something simple in the blue-collar neighborhood near the cemetery. Clutching a handful of chrysanthemums or a few straggly roses, I'd weave my way through the symmetrical rows of marked graves, with their impressive tombstones, to an unmarked corner of the graveyard.

Here, the caretaker told me on my first visit, were the graves of those who'd been lined up against a wall and shot on the little hill at Mont Valerien. Running his finger down a page, giving me a serial number, he directed me to the low earth mound that marked the final resting place of the vital young man I'd hoped to spend the rest of my life with.

"Take care, mademoiselle," the caretaker had warned me, his fingers yellow with tobacco stains. "There are eyes everywhere."

Reaching Jacques's grave, I'd discard the old flowers that had withered from the previous Sunday. Rearranging my new offering, I'd place a hand on the soft earth and close my eyes. "Hello, *chéri,*" I'd tell him, "it's your little Marthe. I'm here again, as always, my darling. All is well."

I'd lose all track of time, sitting talking to him. Looking around hours later, I'd notice the light fading and the sun setting over the tall buildings to the east. Wearily, I'd gather my coat around me and head back past the tombstones, to the Metro station and into central Paris. By the time I reached Cecile and the welcome of her apartment, I'd be too tired to speak.

We moved regularly, renting apartments from people who never even asked our names, willing to risk their lives for total strangers. There was an extraordinary network of people ready to help those in danger. If we were asked, we always gave the name of Lefevre, Cecile's boyfriend. We moved four or five times in those first months, and when we had to move again, after someone we knew had been arrested, Madame Lucas let us one of her apartments, a beautiful place in rue Felix Potin in Neuilly, without even asking us why we'd had to move. Paris was like that then. Everyone was always running somewhere. We didn't dare stay anywhere too long, in case people who knew we were Jewish were arrested and tortured and told the Gestapo where we were. It wasn't a case of a breach of trust. If someone is tortured long enough and well enough, they'll talk. None of us knows how we'd react under torture, but I suspect most of us would crack. You can be a hero one day and a coward the next. I know. I've been both.

On a day-to-day basis, I barely noticed the extraordinary precautions Cecile and I had to take to avoid being denounced, the constant fear of being caught, avoiding all contact with authority, and trying to make as much money as possible for our family in hiding in the mountains. The Germans were everywhere. They'd taken over all the best mansions and hotels, and were in the restaurants, cinemas, and theaters every night. There was no avoiding them. Sometimes whole groups of Wehrmacht soldiers would stop us in the street and try to talk to us, but we wouldn't have anything to do with them and they'd soon give up.

I believed I had a sixth sense when it came to danger, something that had saved me several times in the past and helped me enormously in Paris. Often I'd be walking somewhere and about to go into the subway when I'd stop abruptly and know that I shouldn't go any farther. It happened several times, right at the entrance to the Metro, and a few minutes later I'd hear the police whistles down below as they arrested all the Jews and "undesirables" in the latest *rafle.* We had many Jewish friends who were arrested in this way and deported. We had to be constantly vigilant.

One Saturday afternoon, as Cecile and I were walking from the Metro on Boulevard Hausmann, near the Opera, my mind was on Jacques, as usual, and my weekly visit to his grave the following day. Looking up as a man emerged from a nearby hotel and almost walked right into us, I was taken aback to find myself recognizing him.

"Hello, Heinrich," I said, without even thinking, pulling Cecile to an abrupt halt in the middle of one of the city's most famous boulevards.

It was our friend from Poitiers, the fine-looking German who'd fled his country and then Poitiers for his communist beliefs. Tall, blond, and handsome, he'd never looked better, and I was genuinely pleased to see him, having often wondered at his fate.

"Hello," he replied. Slowly registering our faces, he threw his arms open in surprise and cried, "Marthe, Cecile! How lovely to see you."

It was only then that I noticed how impeccably dressed he was, with a beautifully cut pinstripe suit, smart briefcase, and shiny leather shoes. He smelled of expensive cigars and aftershave, luxury items I hadn't smelled since long before the war. Looking up, I realized that he'd just emerged from the grand doorway of the Hôtel Ambassadeur, now occupied by the German Kriegsmarine.

"So, what on earth are you two girls doing here in Paris?" Heinrich asked brightly, his manner friendly and relaxed.

"Just up for the day," Cecile answered quickly. "We arrived on the morning train." I looked askance at her momentarily and wondered why she'd lied.

Heinrich looked us up and down carefully, and I could see the muscles in his jaw tighten. "Oh, really?" he replied, his manner altering almost imperceptibly. "Then tell me, why aren't you wearing the yellow star?" He knew that we were Jewish, of course, after so many Sabbath dinners in our home.

My hands suddenly clammy, I found that I couldn't reply, but Cecile, who'd realized the danger long before me, didn't show a single sign that she was afraid. "We just took them off for the train journey," she said with a conspiratorial smile. "You know it makes life so much easier these days."

"I see," Heinrich said, looking around now, as if searching for someone to come to his assistance. "Well, why not let me buy you a drink? For old times' sake? There's a lovely little café just around the corner that I know very well."

"No," Cecile said, too urgently. Softening, she added with a smile, "Thank you, Heinrich, that's terribly sweet, but we really can't. We only came up for the day and, oh, look at the time Marthe, we must hurry or we'll miss our train back home. Lovely to see you, though." She extended a gloved right hand.

We apologized for our rudeness and fled as fast as we could, Cecile dragging me down side streets, doubling back, and going out of her way to make sure we weren't followed. When we finally caught our breath, she rounded on me angrily.

"Why on earth did you say hello?" she asked. "He hadn't even noticed us. Haven't you realized yet that our lives here hang by a very fine thread? How could you have let your guard slip so badly?"

I hung my head in shame. I couldn't answer. I'd just been so surprised to see him, and he'd always been so friendly to us, that I'd acted on impulse. Cecile, with the eye of an experienced fugitive, had instantly figured the situation out. She'd been right never to trust him. Heinrich was working for the German Intelligence Service, a fifth columnist. He always had been, and had probably only been in Poitiers to spy on us all and report back to his German superiors. We'd all been completely taken in.

How we escaped that afternoon in Paris, I don't know. I'm sure he went straight back into the Hôtel Ambassadeur, alerted guards, and phoned the train stations in Paris and Poitiers to have people waiting there to arrest us. We came so close to danger that day, we could almost smell it.

Picking Up the Pieces

Cecile and I remained in Paris, waiting in hope for the Liberation as the Allies pushed their way up through Italy, recaptured Rome, and then succeeded in the Normandy landings of D day in June 1944.

Through the nightly bulletins on the radio we learned of the horrific SS slaughter of nearly seven hundred French innocents at the village of Oradour-sur-Glane; we grieved for Londoners suffering under the new V-1 buzz bombs; and we cheered as the Russian Army advanced on Warsaw. Night after night we listened through the crackling German static fruitlessly designed to jam the broadcasts, waved from the rooftops as the Allied planes flew overhead, jumped at the sound of the antiaircraft guns, and cried bitter tears for every lost pilot.

Despite my hopes to become something in the Resistance, I still seemed unable to get a foot in the door. Time and again I was turned down. One Resistance chief I met in an office in a Paris suburb interviewed me for over an hour only to tell me: "You can't be serious, mademoiselle. You're little more than a child. What good could you possibly do?"

Although I was never allowed to be part of a structured group, I always felt that just surviving each day as a Jew in Paris was resistance in itself. It was a victory for mankind.

As the Allies came closer and closer, the Germans became increasingly belligerent. There was a real sense of desperation about those who'd thought they were invincible. The German Army had been so sure of itself after countless victories, and at first they just thought they'd be able to push the Allies back. The streets were full of German soldiers; every day they marched down the Champs Elysées with great pomp and ceremony, but there was no one there to watch—the French always made themselves scarce, so the Germans goose-stepped to an empty theater.

By August 1944, Cecile and I were living in the apartment on Avenue de la Bourdonnais, the third house on the left up from the Seine, near the Trocadero Bridge. There'd been fighting in Paris for over a week, barricades had been erected, and a lot of people had been killed trying to rout the Germans. I walked to work every day as usual, despite the constant shooting, but I saw many people lying injured in the streets and often had to divert my course to avoid sniper fire. Having seen so many people getting hurt, I made my way to the main Red Cross office and offered my help.

"I'm a registered nurse," I told them. "I'd like to volunteer to help those being wounded on the streets."

"Are you Jewish?" came the cold reply from the young woman on the front desk. "We're not allowed to enlist Jews."

I backed away in horror. It wasn't the first time I was disappointed by the international organization that prided itself on being neutral.

The fighting worsened as the mood among ordinary Parisians lifted. We began to hope that liberation was close at hand. On the evening of August 24, after curfew, we finally heard on the radio that the troops of Colonel Jacques Leclerc and his Second Armored Division were at the gates of Paris. The Americans, who'd led the way until now, had allowed them the courtesy of entering Paris first. I was just back from work and home with Cecile when we heard the momentous news.

Then the bells of Paris, which had been silent for the four years of the occupation, began to ring. "Listen, Cecile!" I said, throwing open the window of our apartment and letting the jubilant peal of bells fill the room. We stood in the window, basking in the early evening sun, and allowed the waves of beautiful music to wash over us.

Everywhere, people did the same. Some climbed out onto rooftops or balconies. Most—like us—leaned out of the windows, tears of happiness streaming down their faces, as it did ours. I can't remember who started it, but further along the street someone sang the first few strains of "La Marseillaise." Impulsively, instinctively, we joined in, as did all the others at the windows and rooftops. Soon the entire street and then, it seemed, the whole of Paris was reverberating to the bells and that most rousing of national anthems.

It was almost unbelievable, the spontaneity of it. We could barely sing for emotion. The Germans in the street below, manning the barricades with their machine guns, raised their heads and looked up at us all singing as loudly and gladly as our hearts would allow, but there was nothing they could do. The Liberation of Paris was the answer to all our prayers; it was what I'd always believed would happen. Of course, I'd been frightened and depressed at times, like everyone, but somehow I always knew the Allies would win because what the Germans were doing was too wrong. "It can't be that this much misery will be allowed," I'd tell Cecile gravely.

Now, after four dark years of German occupation, we were singing directly at the enemy soldiers, some of whom lifted their guns and pointed them at us. They didn't shoot; they were too terrified at the overwhelming reaction all around them. We'd endured their presence until now, avoided them as best we could, lived with their rules and coped with hunger and privations. But the tables had turned. This was their last breath in Paris and they knew it. Only the curfew prevented us from running into the streets and dancing, but as the bells continued to ring out, we were still able to show them how we felt. It was wonderful.

The next morning the sun shone brightly and the gun posts were abandoned; the soldiers had fled in the night. The French stormed into Paris in great numbers, tearing the swastika from the Eiffel Tower and replacing it with a fluttering tricolor. The police went on strike and seized the Ile de la Cité on the Seine. Street fighting broke out as the last few pockets of German or Vichy French resistance were dealt with. Grenades were thrown and snipers were more active than ever.

At midnight an emotional General de Gaulle, the newly appointed commander in chief of the Free French forces, walked through the doors of Notre Dame Cathedral to give thanks. The Resistance seized the radio station from the collaborators who'd been running it throughout the occupation, and finally we were told what was really going on. De Gaulle announced: "I wish simply to say from the bottom of my heart: 'Vive Paris!' "

Early the next morning I called Madame Lucas and told her not to expect me in for work that day. "Isn't it wonderful?" I cried, and she agreed.

"Go out into the streets and enjoy the celebrations," she told me. "I'll take care of my mother today."

I took my bicycle and rode all over Paris to see what was happening. There was still shooting and there were many dead in the streets, but I was so hyped up, I didn't even consider the danger. I wanted to see what was going on, to be a part of history. It's very rare that you live through a moment of history like that. I rode all over the city, ignoring the shooting and pedaling on. I was oblivious to the risks because I was so elated. I was twenty-four years old, and I watched as French patriots rose up against German and Vichy snipers firing from the roofs and the windows and overcame them.

I saw men and women with arms full of flowers and gifts running to the approaching French soldiers, climbing all over their tanks and hugging and kissing them. I felt the same way but I just watched from a distance. The next day the Americans would arrive, in even greater numbers, but the first twenty-four hours it was only French soldiers being welcomed and thanked so profusely. Old men dusted off their best suits, women unpacked the Liberation Day dresses they'd been storing for four years, and barmen popped open their hidden bottles of champagne.

Cecile remained at home. We only had one bicycle, but even if we'd had another, I think she probably would have stayed in the apartment, watching from the windows like so many others. By the time I got home later that night, I was breathless with excitement. "Cecile, it's marvelous!" I told her, my eyes bright. "Paris is saved. The Germans are all leaving. You should see what's happening. The police have to protect the captured soldiers from being lynched."

She sat open-mouthed as I related all that I'd seen, including some of the more ugly scenes. "German soldiers and French collaborators are being taken prisoner, but many are being dragged into the streets and beaten openly," I said, grimacing. "I saw one woman with her head shaved being harangued by a jeering crowd. I'm sure the people doing the beating didn't lift a finger during the war and are only doing this now for show. There were a lot of angry mobs, Cecile. I wanted to intervene, to make them stop, but I couldn't or they'd have called me a German-lover. They were beyond reason."

"So what on earth did you do?" Cecile asked, aghast that I'd been so close to danger.

"I just rode on," I told her, "I pedaled to every arrondissement. I didn't stop until I felt I'd been all over and seen everything. It is the most incredible day!

"I saw military ambulances driven by French women as well as a great number of American women in uniform. Jacques and I had dreamed of joining de Gaulle's army; now I have to do it all by myself. That's what I want for the immediate future, Cecile. At last, I will do my duty for my country."

The Liberation and its immediate aftermath made me so happy, and yet sometimes so unhappy. I was alive and Jacques was dead. As the days passed I became racked with the unfairness of that fact. The elation that had first overwhelmed me became tempered with guilt at having survived. I was still so very fearful for Stéphanie in Metz, a town still very much under German control, and for the rest of my family, whose zone in the Cantal was far from being liberated.

I knew that I had to take charge and do something meaningful to help end the war still raging fiercely across the rest of Europe. Despite the fall of Paris and the loss of so much seized territory, the Nazis were still acting as aggressors, capturing Bucharest, razing Warsaw, and launching their new long-range V-2 bombs. The battle was far from over, and I was determined to play a part in whatever was needed to save France.

The very next day, after Leclerc's triumphal entry into Paris, I approached the regular army about signing up as a nurse. It seemed the most logical step. I was trained for that, after all. When I reached the building I'd been told housed the enlisting offices, I found lines of people outside, on one of the wide boulevards in Paris. I stood in line several days in succession without being seen. Then when I did finally get to talk to someone, I realized it was hopeless. There were too many hoops to jump through.

"What proof do you have that you didn't help the Germans in any way during the occupation?" they asked, after demanding my papers, backed up with my birth certificate, registration documents, and a baffling array of other requirements that, as a refugee with forged papers, I could not fulfill. I understood their reasoning. They were wary of enlisting just anyone, for fear of collaborators wishing to whitewash their shameful past.

"How can I sign up without all that you ask?" I asked a woman officer in exasperation.

"You can't," she said unsmilingly. "Next."

Walking home one evening after caring for Madame Lucas's mother, my mind was busily engaged on what I could do next to help. Stiffening, I heard footsteps behind me on the bridge and looked around to see a very tall man in uniform close behind me. Something about the way he looked frightened me. It was only about seven-thirty at night, but there was no one else about and no cars. We were alone.

Quickening my pace, I hurried along, almost making it to the other side of the bridge, straining all the while to try and see the Avenue de la Bourdonnais and the building where Cecile's apartment was.

He came from behind suddenly, and I spun round. Facing me was a huge American. His breath stank of alcohol. He started to speak to me in slurred English. I couldn't understand a word. Wrestling to break free from his viselike grip, I wriggled in vain. A smirk on his face, he began to drag me down a nearby stone ramp leading to the Seine, where there'd be even less chance of anyone seeing us. He was twice my size, and I knew I'd never be able to fight him off.

Reflexively, I went completely limp, allowing my legs to give way under me as I slumped, a dead weight, to the pavement. It took him completely off guard, and he was so surprised that he let go of my arm. Seizing my chance, I got up and ran across the street to where there were houses.

"Help! Help!" I yelled, hoping someone might hear me. But my assailant soon recovered and ran after me, gaining on me easily with his long legs. In an instant he was grabbing at my clothes and pulling on my French plait. My blouse was torn from the shoulder, revealing my bra. His hands were everywhere and the smell of alcohol was nauseating. I tried to summon up the strength to fight him off, but I couldn't.

I wanted to warn him that I'd scream, but the only English I knew was from songs played on the wireless, so I told him breathlessly: "I'll cry!"

He laughed at me, grappling with me even more ferociously as I pummeled my fists on his chest. "Cry, baby, cry," he laughed.

His intentions were clear as he fumbled with my clothes and his own. Realizing what was about to happen, I was filled with such anger that I pulled myself up to my full height and launched into a venomous verbal tirade.

"You disgust me!" I spat, flicking my head back proudly. "You drunken lout of a soldier. You come to Paris, you claim you've come to save us, but no Boche ever attacked me!"

He was completely taken aback. Registering the word Boche, he suddenly understood that I was comparing him unfavorably to the Germans. Releasing me from his grip, he ran his hands through his hair, staggered a little, and looked suddenly contrite.

His tone changed and he tried to placate me, but I looked at him with utter contempt as I adjusted my torn clothing and pulled my bedraggled hair back into place.

To my surprise, he dropped to his knees and clasped my hand. He seemed to be begging my forgiveness. *"S'il vous plaît,"* he said in poor French, "can't I see you again?"

Looking down at him, I spat the word *"Non!"* and ran off as fast as I could. He called after me for a while, I heard his footsteps, but finally he gave up. I didn't stop running till I reached Cecile's.

The name Delaunay held considerable sway after the death of Jacques and Marc. Anyone who'd died for the cause was now a national hero, and for a family to have lost two sons to the German firing squads gave them near hallowed status. I'd never met Jacques's mother. She'd been in Saigon when I was in Poitiers, and had only returned after we fled.

But as soon as I was able after the Liberation, I traveled to Poitiers to meet her. The train journey there seemed to take forever, and by the time I walked up the front path to the home I'd only ever known as Jacques's, I was ready to drop. Knocking on the door, I waited a few minutes and then almost turned and ran away. But I heard someone approaching and the bolt was drawn back. A woman's face peered out from around the half-open door. Her eyes were ringed with dark and her skin was as pale as alabaster.

"Madame Delaunay?" I said tentatively. "I'm Marthe."

There was silence and no glimmer of recognition.

"You may know me better as Jacqueline," I explained. "Jacqueline Lenôtre."

The door was thrown open and Madame Delaunay pulled me into her bony arms. Our tears mingled as we held each other tightly for several minutes without speaking. When I finally looked up, she held my face in her hands and kissed me tenderly on both cheeks.

"Welcome, Marthe," she said, her voice breaking. "Come in, my child."

For what seemed like hours, we sat side by side in her living room, talking, weeping, and sharing memories. She opened photograph albums and showed me pictures of Jacques and Marc as children. She told me of her few visits to see them in prison, of how they'd been tortured and how hungry they were.

"Especially Jacques," she said, smiling at the memory. "Even as a child, he'd always had such a healthy appetite."

Watching her, listening to her, I realized that Madame Delaunay would have to come back to Paris with me. The loss of her children and her husband—from whom she'd still had no word—had made her weak, and she was physically ill from dysentery she'd contracted in Indochina. Gathering together a few of her things, I brought her back to Cecile's apartment and the two of us cared for her as best we could.

When she was strong enough, I took her on the train to Ivry and the graves of her sons. I stood back as she knelt before them, consumed in grief. "I want to take them home to Poitiers," she told me, her gaunt face wet. "When I'm well enough, I want to take them away from this dreadful place."

De Gaulle came to visit the cemetery to pay his respects to those who'd died. During his brief visit, Madame Delaunay and I stood by the graves of our loved ones, as did the relatives of the dozens of others in the bleak corner of that suburban cemetery, all hoping for a word of comfort from the great leader. But de Gaulle simply arrived, saluted, turned, and walked away. I think that hurt Jacques's mother almost more than anything since their deaths.

"Are my sons' deaths not worth even a brief word?" she asked, her eyes mad with sorrow.

But the Resistance chiefs didn't overlook her. As the mother of two dead, she was afforded every possible respect. When they asked her if there was anything they could do for her, she nodded and replied stiffly, "Yes. You can help Mademoiselle Hoffnung join one of your army units. She was my son Jacques's fiancée, her credentials are impeccable, and she has my full and complete endorsement."

And so it was, with her personal recommendation, that I was finally accepted into the army, with the regimental number 44-758 02236. I was assigned to the 151st Infantry Regiment, a former Resistance unit, under the command of the Parisian resistance hero Colonel Pierre Fabien. He and his men had fought valiantly before and during the Paris insurrection. Fabien was famous for killing the first German soldier in Paris. On the orders of General de Gaulle, they were integrated into the regular French Army, and I was one of their newest recruits.

In November 1944, as Aachen became the first German city to fall to the Allies and the British landed in Greece, I set off for the Alsatian front in a rickety old bus with a group of men returning to the front after a well-deserved leave. I was in civilian clothes, an elegant navy-blue tailored suit and my best blouse. One of the officers on the bus asked me politely, "Are you visiting someone, mademoiselle?"

"No," I replied, smiling happily, "I'm joining up."

The bus kept breaking down every few miles, and the journey

took four or five days through the devastated French countryside. There was no fuel available and we had to stop and steal some from the Americans before we could go any farther.

When we arrived in Alsace, an officer named Michel Gueret, an ugly character in every way, debriefed me. He stood in front of me and peered down his Gallic nose. "Were you in the Resistance?" he asked.

"No, sir," I replied crisply, standing at attention. "I wasn't, but I—"

"How dare you come here when you didn't do anything in the war," he interrupted, his face purple. "I'm sick and tired of cowards trying to gain credibility by signing up now."

"I'm not a coward. I did a lot of things in the war," I told him, smarting. "I just wasn't in any structured group. My fiancé was in the Resistance and he was shot."

Lieutenant Gueret was not impressed. "Even more of a reason to fight the Germans," he said. "Anyway, I'm not talking about your fiancé, mademoiselle, I'm talking about you. Why didn't you just go out and kill Germans wherever you could, regardless of any so-called structure?"

No matter how I tried to tell him of my attempts to join the Resistance, or how my family had been helping people escape across the border, he remained singularly unimpressed. "This is no place for you," he told me sneeringly. "Why don't you go home where you belong?"

"No, sir," I said firmly. "I was sent to your unit by Army Command in Paris and I intend to stay."

As a nurse, I should have automatically been ranked as an officer, but Gueret decided to punish me for my supposed lack of courage and downgraded me to a sergeant instead. When he informed me of his decision, the expression on his face was triumphant.

I shrugged my shoulders, which made him even madder. He then told me that he had plenty of medical staff and that my nursing skills wouldn't even be required. He assigned me instead to the position of a social worker, looking after the welfare of the men. There were no uniforms in my size, and the American khaki one I was issued was so ugly and ill-fitting that it swamped me. I did the best I could with it, but it was the most unstylish and unfeminine thing I'd ever seen.

I was billeted with an Alsatian family in a small village between Colmar and Mulhouse. The village lay in a valley through which ran a narrow section of the Grand Canal d'Alsace, marking the front between our forces and those of Germany. The Germans had only just retreated and were on the other side of the canal, still fighting doggedly. The closer they got to their Fatherland, the fiercer they fought, for fear of what the Allies might do to their homes and families in retribution for what the Germans had done to theirs.

It was the middle of a wind-lashed winter and thick snow blanketed the ground. The temperatures plummeted to well below freezing, and the only consolation of my ungainly uniform was that it was warm. No one seemed to have any idea what my job entailed or where I should go, so on my first day I got up very early and took a brisk walk through the forest and down to the canal to see our soldiers on the front line.

"*Bonjour,*" I said, my breath creating huge white clouds of condensation in the chilly trenches, "I'm Sergeant Hoffnung, your new social worker. Is there anything you need?"

The men were astonished. A tiny blonde in an oversized uniform was the last person they'd expected to drop into their foxhole. In all the years they'd been fighting in the Resistance, they'd never had a social worker before and no one had ever inquired about their welfare. I carefully took down their requests for more blankets and clothing, paper, pens, and extra food and decided to try and drum up some additional supplies in the village.

On my way back through the forest, two officers, one of whom had been on the bus with me, Claude Velley, accompanied me. He told me he was married with two children and had been a ranger in his civilian life. We were walking along, chatting about his family, when we heard a loud whistling noise overhead, and then the earth erupted in a spume of mud and rocks just ahead of us. I was startled at first, but realizing with gratitude that the enemy shell that caused the explosion had missed us by several feet, I just kept walking. It seemed the best thing to do. Before I knew it, I'd been rugby-tackled from behind, crashing to the ground, bruising my knees and tearing a perfectly good pair of silk stockings.

"Are you crazy?" Velley asked, as he released me. "Don't you know that you're supposed to take cover during an artillery bombardment?"

"No, I'm sorry," I said, examining my stockings with considerable dismay. "I didn't know. I've never been in one before."

He and his fellow officer looked at each other and shook their heads. "You're either very brave or very stupid," they said.

It wasn't courage, it was naiveté. The next time I was under bombardment and the sound of heavy shelling tore the air, I was so frightened that I ran into one of the foxholes and refused to come out until the shelling had subsided. That's how brave I was.

I wasn't the only woman at the front. There were several nurses and some woman doctors, too, but we rarely mixed, and I found my position lonely. Doing the best I could, for the three weeks I was there I visited the men daily in their foxholes, crawling in and talking to them and bringing them anything useful that the people in the village had been generous enough to give me.

On my third week I was crossing the little square of the village on a quest for some fruit when I came face-to-face with my commanding officer, Colonel Fabien, whom I'd only seen from afar before. He was slim, dashing, and handsome, with a ready smile. When I saluted him, he stopped and asked my name.

"Sergeant Hoffnung, sir," I replied.

"Well, Sergeant Hoffnung," he said, "would you be kind enough to man my telephone for me during my lunch break? I seem to have mislaid my assistant."

I couldn't possibly have said no. He accompanied me to his office, gave me a pen and paper, and told me to take a message if the phone rang. Just as he was about to leave, he turned with a smile and said, "I'll try not to be too long. I'm sorry there's nothing here for you to read. There are only German books left."

"That's all right, sir," I replied. "I can read German."

Astonished, he closed the door and came back in. Walking toward me, his eyes wide, he asked, "Do you speak it?"

I smiled. "Yes, sir. Fluently. I was raised in Metz. It was the only language my parents spoke."

Colonel Fabien ran his hands through his hair and looked me up and down. "We've been desperately looking for army personnel who speak German," he said, rubbing his chin with his hand. "We particularly need women because they're far less likely to attract attention in a country where the men have all been called up." His expression thoughtful, he added, "Would you be willing to do intelligence work?"

Without considering the consequences, I said brightly, "Yes, sir, I would."

The colonel smiled and left. It was only after he'd closed the door that I slumped on the edge of the desk and wondered what I'd done.

What's wrong with you, Marthe Hoffnung? I chastised myself. What have you let yourself in for now? I thought of the line from Moliere's play, *The Trickeries of Scapin, "Que diable allait-il faire dans cette galère?"* Why in the name of the devil did he go into the galley?

Three days later, Lieutenant Yves Latour, a member of the "antenna" intelligence units of the French First Army commanded by General de Lattre de Tassigny, came to get me. Lieutenant Latour took me to Mulhouse, where his antenna was quartered. Having hidden my background for so long, I decided not to tell my superiors or anyone else of my religious persuasion, for fear that they might not trust me. The words of the priest in St. Secondin still stung.

I was billeted in a large house and given the luxury of my own room, being the only woman. That night, I locked my bedroom door and went to sleep, but I was disturbed with alarming regularity. One by one the amorous men I was to work with knocked, tapped, and sometimes hammered on the door, whispering their intentions as they tried unsuccessfully to gain access to my bedroom. I didn't even answer them; I just sat up in bed, the covers tucked under my chin, and waited for them all to give up.

Launched straight into training, I was given the affectionate nickname "Chichinette" by my chief trainer, Lieutenant Roger Verin, a name I hated but that stuck with me for the duration of the war. It means a fussy girl, and the rumor was that I'd raised a few eyebrows by not sharing my favors with my fellow officers. I raised eyebrows even more when I finally found a local tailor and had my baggy old khaki uniform transformed into a stylish pencil skirt and tailored jacket.

My training was all about memory—I had to memorize German

uniforms, ranks, armaments, munitions, equipment, and anything to do with ground troops. My bedtime reading, as I waited for the nightly knocking at my door to stop, was diagram after diagram of insignia and uniforms, from units such as the Gebirgsjäger, or mountain troops; Waffen SS; Fallschirmjäger, or parachute regiment; and the Grosdeutschland Panzer Corps. Small details such as buttons, collar patches, and shoulder straps all had to be committed to memory, along with helmets and caps, medals, ribbons, and cuff titles. It was harder than being in school.

I was taught how to read a map, signal in Morse, and interpret codes. I studied photographs, charts, and diagrams of anything from a panzer tank to an aerial reconnaissance shot of the area, and learned about the entire German military apparatus. Finally, I was taught to shoot all kinds of weapons, from tommy guns, 9mm weapons, and small pistols, to machine guns that were so heavy I couldn't even lift them.

Taken to the firing ranges, which were just trees in the forest, the cold steel of the weapons sent a shiver down my spine. These were things I'd never seen or wanted to see in my life. They felt strange and unwieldy in my small hands. Raising them and pointing them at the distant cutout figures of men pinned to a tree, I pulled the trigger, trying not to imagine what it would be like to fire a bullet into soft flesh. To my amazement, I hit the target time and again. Little had I known, I was a crack shot.

"You must make up your own story of who you're supposed to be and why you're in German territory," Lieutenant Latour told me. "When you've got it completely straight in your mind, we'll interrogate you and do our best to pick holes in it."

I thought of Heinrich and how plausible he'd been, and I decided to learn from his expertise. He was undoubtedly German, and he almost certainly came from the region he'd spoken so fondly of. I suspected that he really was married to a woman named Martine and that he had small children. His talk of them had been so heartfelt, with such genuine sadness at his wife's alleged divorce when he went to Spain to supposedly fight with the Republicans, that he could only have been telling the truth. With that in mind, I came up with an identity not dissimilar from my own, with virtually the same first name, which would enable me to use my own childhood memories and anecdotes, as he had.

My new identity was Martha Ulrich, a German nurse from Metz, desperately looking for my fiancé Hans, a soldier in a front-line unit. I was an only child whose parents had been killed in an Allied bombing raid, making me doubly patriotic and giving me a deep hatred of the Allies. Hans really did exist and was all I said he was—a German soldier in the infantry whose name had been given to me by the military—only he was currently a prisoner in a French POW camp. Once my story had been finely honed, the hapless Hans was placed under close guard, in solitary confinement, so that if I was ever captured, the Germans couldn't get to him to try to verify my existence. When my superiors grilled me about my story, being as tough as they could, I tried not to imagine how I'd react if they were Gestapo.

"Why did you choose to look for Hans now?" one asked, his face inches from mine.

"Because the war is almost over and I want to find him before it's too late," I responded. "I've lost everyone, I don't want to lose Hans."

"Why did you cross our lines so late at night and in such a remote area?" asked the other interrogator, his expression even more fierce.

"Because I was afraid of the French and what they'd do to me if they found out I was trying to make contact with the German Army."

Memories of what Jacques had gone through under torture sustained me and made me strong. He had endured so much in the name of his country, it was the least I could do to do the same. I thought of Stéphanie and of her cruel interrogation by Hipp in Poitiers. Papa had said she remained defiant and proud throughout. I lifted my chin and tried to be worthy of her. With them both at the forefront of my mind, I passed.

"If you should ever be successful in crossing enemy lines," Lieutenant Latour told me gravely, "you'll automatically be promoted to the rank of lieutenant and will become eligible for a substantial monetary reward."

"Why would I want a reward?" I asked, puzzled.

"It's normal," he explained. "It is a way of compensating you for risking your life."

I shrugged my shoulders. "I'll just take the promotion and the salary, thanks," I told him. "I'm not interested in hiring myself out as a mercenary."

I was eager to start work. I'd had the training, I was all hyped up, and I wanted badly to begin. It felt as if I was living history again. I'd been a little afraid at first, but once I was in the system, I just went ahead and did it. For security purposes within French intelligence, I took on the name Marthe Lenôtre, adopting the surname that Jacques had used when writing to me. Most of the men still thought I was a social worker, which helped keep my real identity secret. As preparation for crossing enemy lines, I wrote a series of short dated letters to my mother, one for every week I was expected to be away, to let her know that I was all right. She knew I'd joined the army but had no idea I was about to embark on something so dangerous. It was my idea, to keep her happy and my secret safe.

"Chère Maman," I wrote, "I'm working in a field hospital near Mulhouse, nursing those wounded in the fighting. We are well back from the front and I'm fine. I'm eating enough and am surrounded by friendly soldiers, so please don't worry about me. Love, Marthe."

With those letters written and my training complete, I felt ready to begin, as Hitler's crucial counteroffensive, the Battle of the Bulge, was being successfully repelled in the Ardennes a few hundred miles north.

An Unlikely Spy

My work as the most unlikely of spies officially began on January 20, 1945. I was assigned to the Commandos d'Afrique, the first French unit to land on the Mediterranean coast. It was a legendary unit, which had fought the Germans throughout North Africa under General Bethouart and had participated in the liberation battles throughout Tunisia, Italy, and France. I was deeply honored.

On a bitingly cold January night when temperatures dropped below zero, Lieutenant Verin took me to Cernay in the Vosges Mountains, where the commandos were holed up in the basement of the abandoned St. André mental hospital after a day of heavy fighting. During the course of that day alone, 189 of their men had been killed and 192 wounded. They were shattered.

Lieutenant Verin, who was in much thicker clothes than I, drove me there in a jeep. The blackout meant that he couldn't use his headlights, so he had to have the windshield down to see the road in the pitch-dark. I was in civilian clothes, with the labels removed for security, half frozen, my little suitcase at my feet. I had no idea where we were heading or whether I'd be going straight across enemy lines. My brain was so numb with cold, I couldn't even produce enough energy to be afraid.

Arriving at the asylum, we stumbled our way down into the huge basement in the dark. Verin had no flashlight, so he struck some matches and picked our way through hundreds of exhausted commandos sleeping on the floor. Waking a few and asking for Major Marcel Rigaud, we were directed to a large man laid out cold on a stretcher. Verin shook him by the shoulder and he sat up and blinked at us.

"I've brought you Mademoiselle Lenôtre," Verin informed the major.

Rigaud looked at me vaguely, said, "Find somewhere to sit," and promptly fell straight back to sleep.

Verin found two metal chairs and we sat side by side, waiting for the morning. I don't think I'd ever been so uncomfortable in my life. There was nowhere to escape the cold. My teeth were chattering and spasms of shivering racked me. I had a bad chest infection and was coughing repeatedly above the cacophony of heavy snoring all around. The chairs were hard, and I wanted nothing more than to lie down. Slowly, in the darkness, I shuffled around and felt a thin mattress on which I put my feet to lift them off the icy floor. Gradually, as I became increasingly tired, I shuffled nearer and nearer to the mattress, until I was so exhausted I just slid off my chair and lay down upon it.

I knew there had to be a soldier asleep on the rest of the mattress somewhere in the darkness, but I didn't care. I put my head where his feet were and my feet where his head was and I lay there, shivering. With my numb fingers I reached out and found that he also had a thin horsehair blanket over him. Very slowly, inch by inch, I tugged at it until it was covering me. I didn't sleep all night, I just lay there praying for morning and some sort of warmth.

At dawn the soldier stirred and rolled over, his hand touching one of my stockinged legs.

"Nom de Dieu, une femme!" he said, sitting upright and staring at me in disbelief.

I jumped up, too, and we both sat facing each other in the half-light. I think I was as startled as he. Taking one look at my blue hands and chattering teeth, however, he cried, "But you're frozen!" Before I could say anything, he'd slipped off my shoes and, tired as he was, rubbed my feet and legs so I didn't get frostbite. I was so grateful to feel the circulation flowing again.

Later that morning we introduced ourselves properly. My "mattress mate," as he called me ever after, was Lieutenant Neu, who'd joined the commandos as a volunteer after their landings in the South of France. He was a beautiful-looking man, married with children, and someone I became very fond of.

I was taken to headquarters that afternoon and introduced to Colonel Georges Bouvet, the commanding officer.

"Welcome to the commandos," Colonel Bouvet said, shaking me warmly by the hand. "My, but you're cold, come and sit by the fire." Having learned a little about me and my skills as an interpreter, the colonel decided that my services could best be put to use in interrogations.

"Have you ever interrogated anyone before?" he asked.

"No sir," I replied in all honesty.

"Just let them know who's boss" was the only advice he gave me.

I cut my teeth on the Alsatian civilians, the men and women who'd been under German occupation until a few days earlier and who could tell me a great deal about the strengths and positions of the enemy forces in the area. I was nervous at first, unaccustomed to questioning people from a position of authority, but I soon found my way and they seemed happy to help. Many were French patriots whose sons and fathers had been conscripted into the German Army against their will and sent to the Russian front. They'd celebrated when France was liberated and were eager to talk.

When the first German POWs were brought to me, I resolved to appear completely in control from the outset. Sitting behind a huge desk, I hastily rearranged my hair, tugged on my jacket, and told the guards to bring them in.

One by one the German officers were marched in and formed a

neat line in front of me, standing at attention in their gray uniforms. Two armed guards stood by the door. I watched silently as each prisoner registered his surprise at who they were to be interrogated by. Glancing askance at each other, there was laughter in their eyes. Contempt even.

I rose slowly to my feet and walked toward them, standing very close, so they could see exactly how small I was. Craning my neck, I paraded back and forth in front of them many times, staring them directly in the eyes without saying a word. Finally, I resumed my seat behind my desk, took out a pen and notepad.

"*Guten Tag,*" I said, in German so indistinguishable from their own that I could see them wondering if I was German or French. "You must now give me your names, ranks, and roll numbers." This, they were allowed to give, and they duly did so before being split up and ushered back in to me individually.

"Now, before this interrogation begins," I told each of them, "I'd like to remind you that Germany is losing this war. You will be treated according to the Hague Convention but should bear in mind the brutal crimes against humanity that your Wehrmacht has committed in France and elsewhere. There's no denying that the SS and the Gestapo were too often assisted by the regular army such as yourselves, so there's no use blaming others. It'll get you nowhere. If, however, you feel able to tell me anything that will facilitate the end of this long and bloody conflict, then I shall see to it that you receive better treatment in custody and are repatriated back to your loved ones as soon as possible. It may also mean that word can be sent to the Allied troops in your home areas, informing them to treat your families well."

The smirks soon disappeared from their faces as I took each of them very strictly through their paces, asking which unit they belonged to, how many of their men were left in the woods, villages, and plains east of the front, and what plans there were for ambushes, attacks, and retreating troop movements. The higher their rank, the stricter I was, barking questions at them in quick succession. Before long they'd all but forgotten who I was and what I looked like. Sometimes sitting, sometimes standing, I was relentless in my quest for information until, tired and hungry, they'd crack.

I had one rule that was strictly enforced. Not a single German was ever allowed to sit or lean against the walls. They had to stand rigidly at attention at all times. If they grew tired or slumped, I barked at them, gripping my side of the desk.

"Stand up straight! Straight, I say!"

If I ever saw any of them clutching their side of the desk with exhaustion, I'd go crazy. None of them ever understood why.

Colonel Bouvet's own chauffeur, a thin Moroccan called Ya-Ya Ben Bouvet, which meant "son of Bouvet," drove me around the area close to the front lines. He spoke French and called me "Madame" and was very sweet.

"I'm holding you completely responsible for her," Bouvet had warned him. "You'd better treat her as if she were me." From that day on, he considered me his baby.

Because of the proximity to the front, we drove at night with our lights off and the windshield down in order to see where we were going. Ya-Ya would wrap my entire head and body in blankets so that only my eyes were showing. It was my only protection against the Siberianlike weather and icy winds.

"I look like a mummy, Ya-Ya," I told him, laughing through the layers.

"Yes, madame, but a warm mummy," he replied, his open mouth revealing two rows of bright white teeth.

In between interrogations, I monitored the constant radio reports about the progress of the war elsewhere. The Russians were said to be less than a hundred miles from Berlin, and there was independent testimony of the widespread retreat of German soldiers across Europe. The radio announcers made it sound as if the war was all but won, but as I listened, I watched from a window of HQ as Moroccan soldiers tried to break through impenetrable German lines just across a huge field during the siege of Cernay. It was the first time I'd ever seen a real battle, and there was certainly no sign of enemy retreat.

Standing alongside a distraught Colonel Bouvet, his teeth clenched, I listened as he told his staff: "Whoever gave the order to attack is a criminal!" Together we watched the men from the Sixth Regiment of Moroccan Infantry being mercilessly strafed with machine guns, cut down as they waded through thick snow across an open field in full view of a series of impregnable German machine gun positions.

The men lay injured or dying where they fell, unable to be rescued by their comrades or treated by medical staff because of their exposed position. It was sheer carnage and something I hoped never to witness again. As with the deportation of the Jews in Aubagne, all I could do was watch helplessly.

The next day, Colonel Bouvet's headquarters were relocated to the home of a butcher in Thann, where I lived side by side with the leading commando officers. There was one office and two bedrooms, occupied by Bouvet and his second in command, Commandant Jean Ruyssen. My bed was the office sofa and my sleep was more often than not interrupted by important phone calls, messengers from the front, and battle-planning meetings, to which I was always privy.

As Colonel Bouvet was given the orders that evening to attack again on the outskirts of Cernay, he grabbed the telephone. "If you really insist on implementing this strategy, then you are a murderer!" he thundered into the telephone at an officer of the Troisieme Bureau. "It's completely irrational and will cause the unnecessary deaths of a great number of my men." Despite his protestations, the orders were not rescinded.

On an afternoon late in January, at a meeting attended by several of his commanding officers, Colonel Bouvet, who was a tall, slim man with a prominent chin, turned to me, the muscle in his jaw twitching. "Chichinette," he said, "are you ready to go on your first mission into enemy territory?"

"Yes, sir," I replied without hesitation.

Colonel Bouvet explained. "Since the fiasco around Cernay, the Germany Army has pushed back our forces in that entire Alsatian area, clinging to our soil. It's their last desperate attempt to prevent us from spreading war into Germany. We need you to infiltrate enemy lines on the Amselkopf Mountain, where they're strongly entrenched, and find out the strength of the troops we're facing, and as much as possible of their plans."

Captain Mollat de Jourdin began to explain what had been planned. To take pressure off the German troops in the Battle of the Bulge, in which 600,000 U.S. and Allied troops had only just managed to halt the massive German counteroffensive in Belgium, the enemy had launched Operation Nordwind to try and trap seven American divisions along the Rhine and recapture Strasbourg. The Germans were halted at the last bridge short of the city and were now slowly retreating.

"Firsthand intelligence is urgently required," the captain told me. "They're fighting fiercely. We need you to report back to us as often as possible, and follow the retreating Germans as you do so."

He introduced me to Lieutenant Charles Sautier, an Alsatian who knew the area well and who was to act as my guide. Sautier showed me various charts of the numerous paths that crisscrossed the Amselkopf, all of which I had to memorize because I couldn't risk carrying a map.

"I'll be in charge," Captain Mollat informed me. "Myself, Captain Ligouzat, Neu, Sautier, and a group of twenty commandos will escort you to an exact point. Before daybreak you'll have to make your own way alone through a small valley and, once on the Amselkopf, climb to a path that leads eastward to the German post."

Colonel Bouvet interrupted. "As I have told you, this is a very dangerous area. The Germans are there in strength. We haven't been able to make much progress, and we desperately need to know what we're up against on the other side. It's a highly sensitive mission." I knew that he'd grown very fond of me, in a fatherly way, and could see his reluctance at giving me such a task.

I nodded. Deep snow, freezing temperatures, pitch-darkness, surrounded by trigger-happy Germans, female, unarmed, and Jewish: It was going to be a long night.

I'd never seen Colonel Bouvet so restless. He stayed up until very late that night to ensure that nothing had been overlooked, and came to talk to me just before I departed. He'd often told me that, having a daughter the same age as me, he felt especially responsible for my survival.

"If when you reach the German post you feel that you're in any danger whatsoever," he told me, taking me firmly by the shoulders, "then you should scream and shout as loud as you can. I've instructed a group of my men to watch out and intervene if necessary. They're commandos, remember, and would love to rescue you, so you're not to be afraid. I want you to return safely from this mission." He kissed me good-bye on both cheeks and tears welled in his eyes. He turned away in the hope that I hadn't seen them. Somehow, his fear allayed mine.

I spent those final few hours bracing myself for what was about to happen. There wasn't any time to be frightened, I had so much to do. The butcher's wife, who served us food and drink, had given me some leather ski boots that belonged to one of her children. "Here, mademoiselle," she said. "These should fit you and will be more appropriate to the weather than those you're wearing." I glanced down at the leather court shoes, which had so suited Paris, and thanked her.

Around midnight I left with the four officers and twenty heavily armed commandos. In the intense dark and cold, we marched more than four miles through deep snowdrifts in complete silence. At the edge of a small valley my military escort left me and I carried on, alone in a hostile world but for my wits.

Forcing myself forward, I spotted two German soldiers camouflaged in the valley, but continued walking, pretending not to have seen them. Then a soldier sprang out from behind a tree just below me, a rifle with a bayonet pointed straight at me.

Looking around me intensely for the first time in the half-light, I saw several soldiers dead on the ground nearby, their blood seeping into the snow.

"Halte, qui vive?" whispered another soldier nearby.

"Don't shoot!" I cried, my hands up defensively against their weapons.

There was an interminable silence as the soldier blinked at me, the point of the bayonet a few inches from my chest.

In the low gray light creeping over the mountain, I stood with my hands in the air. Gradually focusing on the uniforms before me, I realized, with some stupefaction, that the soldiers pointing their guns at me were Moroccan, and part of the First French Army.

Before I could say a word, one of the soldiers spat on the ground next to my feet and began to insult me in French.

"You dirty German spy," he whispered between clenched teeth, "what are you doing here in the mountains? We should shoot you."

Having exhausted his limited vocabulary, he launched into Arabic, softly but vehemently hurling more insults at me that I was glad I couldn't understand.

Ten more soldiers suddenly appeared from nowhere, emerging from trees and bushes, all heavily armed, closing in on me. I was completely surrounded and felt certain that any minute I'd end up as a corpse on the forest floor with what I could now see were dead Germans, my life's blood mingling with theirs in the snow.

"We're going to teach you, filthy whore, a lesson," said one in the patrol, his Arab accent thick. "We're going to beat you, then shoot you."

Pulling myself up to my full height and adopting the imperious tone I'd used with the German POWs, I said, with great sangfroid: "Don't shoot and don't you dare touch me! Don't you even come near me. Just call your senior officer and bring him to me. Immediately!"

My words literally stopped them in their tracks. Each looked at the other and hesitated. Seizing my chance, I repeated my demand, shaking an accusatory finger at them and adopting the most indignant expression I could muster.

After some deliberation, they reluctantly dispatched one of their number into the forest. A young lieutenant was eventually brought forward. Taking him to one side, I told him I needed to talk to him privately. With his men guarding us closely, we walked a few paces to a small clearing behind some trees.

"I'm about to recite a telephone number to you," I told him under my breath, "which I want you to call immediately." I gave him the number and watched his surprise.

He stared at me, startled. "How do you know that number?" he asked suspiciously.

"Don't ask questions!" I responded. "I cannot explain anything. Just call it."

"I want to know how you know this number," he persisted. "This is the number of the commando HQ."

"I cannot tell you," I repeated, shaking my head. "Just call it."

"But that's the colonel's direct line," he said, scratching his head. "How do you know him?"

When I refused to answer once more, he clapped his hand to his forehead. "Oh my God," he said. "Are you the 'shadow' we were supposed to be watching for? They never said it would be a woman, and anyway, you weren't supposed to be on this path, but the next path up. We'd never have stopped you if you'd been on the right path!"

I stared back at him with equal shock, and realized that he was from the group Bouvet had stationed near the German post to safeguard me. The soldiers dead on the ground all around us had been killed for my benefit.

"I was on the right path and I need to carry on," I told him, through clenched teeth. "I've come here to do a job and I have to finish it. I must be less than a hundred yards from my destination, so please let me go."

But the lieutenant grabbed my arm and shook his head. "That's impossible, mademoiselle," he said sadly. "The Germans are everywhere and they'll have seen everything. If they don't see us arrest you and take you back, they'll know you're with us and that will be the end of you."

Having reported to Colonel Bouvet over the telephone, he ordered two of his men to escort me unharmed back to headquarters. At my request, and to keep any future missions safe, I asked him not to tell the escorts that I was the "shadow." Since our division had successfully advanced toward the Amselkopf earlier that morning, my two armed guards escorted me back to Thann on a much shorter though still arduous route, due to the deep snowdrifts. It was no easier, knowing that I was returning empty-handed. My feet felt leaden in the snow. Along the way we passed several hundred North African soldiers who'd swarmed into the area to reinforce it early that morning. Seeing a young civilian woman being led back to HQ, they assumed I was a German spy, like their predecessors.

They showered me with insults and spittle as I walked past them, and delighted in telling me I was going to be shot. My Moroccan guards, who clearly shared their view, urged the hecklers on. The Africans hated Germans more than most not only because of the Nazi racism and dislike of dark skin, but because their warmongering had brought them to the snow and the cold, which was anathema to them.

I hung my head low so no one could clearly identify me or recognize me in the future, and shuffled along between my guards, looking as guilty as they clearly believed me to be.

Back at HQ, Bouvet was thrilled to see me and embraced me warmly. The next day he received a communiqué that the night after my aborted mission, there had been a massive German operation in the mountains, retracing the route the commandos and I had taken. The Germans would have found my small footprints next to the giant footprints of the commandos and instantly deduced that I was a French agent. Had I proceeded and crossed enemy lines, they'd have shot me as coldly as they'd shot Jacques.

Furthermore, when Lieutenant Neu took a patrol back a few days later, using the same route in daylight, he discovered that the path I'd taken alone had been heavily mined. The combination of the deep snow and my slight weight—about 94 pounds—had prevented the mines from exploding beneath my feet. I'd been blissfully unaware of the peril.

When I'd had some rest, Captain Mollat debriefed me at HQ in front of the top brass: Colonel Bouvet, Commandant Ruyssen, Lieutenant Neu, and Captain Ligouzat. Mollat was an excellent officer but a perfectionist who couldn't tolerate the fact that his mission had failed.

"I think you were afraid," he told me in front of his superior officers. "You got scared and that's why you didn't complete your mission." I was bitter with indignation and so mad I almost killed him.

"How dare you!" I told him, my face coloring at the accusation. "I did everything I could to get across enemy lines. I even told the officer who arrested me that I wanted to carry on."

Mollat scoffed loudly. "I doubt that very much," he said.

"Well, ask him!" I protested, rounding on him. "Ask anyone who was there. I admit I was frightened, but I was never so afraid that I couldn't carry on. The only reason my mission failed was because your guide told me to take the wrong path."

Mollat began berating me again. "I think it's far more likely, Sergeant, that you misunderstood him and took the wrong path," he said, "or you did so deliberately to abort the mission."

Colonel Bouvet grabbed me to keep me from flying at Mollat in a rage. "There's only one way to find out the truth, Captain," he said. "Call for Sautier."

The guide was summoned and, telling Mollat and me to keep silent, Bouvet asked him to show us exactly which path he'd instructed me to take. The map was laid out on the table and Sautier examined it closely. "That one," he said finally, pointing to the path he'd shown me both at HQ and in the forest.

"And is that the correct path?" Bouvet asked him. "The one we'd agreed in the planning stages?"

Sautier frowned and examined the map still closer. Raising his head, he looked at the colonel guiltily. "*Non, mon colonel,*" he said, hanging his head. "I think I may have made a mistake. The correct path was the third, not the second, *n'est-ce-pas?*"

Mollat was horrified, both at my audacity in challenging him so publicly and at his guide's serious error. The captain hated my guts after that. He stormed from the room, his face purple.

Bouvet told me afterward that I was absolutely right to defend my integrity so vehemently. "Never let anyone get the better of you, Chichinette," he said with a smile. "Although I somehow doubt they could."

The next few months were filled with similar frustrations. I made no less than thirteen attempts to cross enemy lines in all, most of the time at night, always in the snow, each one more daring than the last. I had never objected to any plans, but at the suggestion of one impossible undertaking I finally had to protest. It was made by the chief of our antenna, Captain Zimmerman, a blond Alsatian who only seemed interested in glory for himself and didn't seem to care if it killed me. At Zimmerman's suggestion, I was expected to swim across the icy Rhine, fully clothed, in the middle of winter. I queried the plan privately with my fellow officers, Lieutenants Verin and Latour, and they thankfully questioned the order on the grounds that I would almost certainly die of hypothermia.

"Even if she were to survive," they told Zimmerman, "no one would believe she'd do such a thing just to search for her fiancé." Fortunately, the plan was jettisoned.

Mostly, my missions failed due to rapid shifts at the front and difficulties in interpreting the intelligence reports in such constantly fluctuating conditions. Often, the Germans had either fled from the village I'd carefully made my way to or were there in such huge numbers that the mission had to be aborted for fear of discovery. Each time, I'd get hyped up, ready to go, driven somewhere in the dead of night, and then something would happen for the mission to be called off.

On one such occasion, on the night of February 4, Captain Ligouzat and I were dispatched with the first squadron of the Moroccan Spahis to an isolated forest road. On one side was a vast field, several hundred acres across and covered in snow, and beyond it, on the far horizon, the village of Gundolsheim, which had been garrisoned by the Germans. The buildings were in darkness; a blackout was in force. But to prevent our troops from advancing, the Germans were barraging the field in front of them with a constant stream of tracer fire and live bullets. It was like an awesome display of fireworks, mounted from a position in the woods behind Gundolsheim.

My mission was to cross the field in the dark, enter the village, mix with the Germans, assess their strength, and follow them to their eventual retreat. The snow was not as deep as before, just up to my ankles, and the going wouldn't be quite so tough. With the tracer fire as my guide, I was quietly confident of succeeding this time.

At midnight I took off, heading straight into the noise and the incoming tracer fire. The bullets whizzed straight over my head. I could hear them whistling past a few feet above my ears. I wasn't afraid; there was no time to be, and anyway, the tracer fire was beautiful, all different shades of green, red, and yellow. I had no map and no compass and there was no moon. My instructions were just to head for Gundolsheim, but once I was in the field I could no longer see it because of the lay of the land. It was so dark I couldn't even see my hand in front of my face.

My only guide was the tracer fire, but a few minutes after I'd set off, the firing became more sporadic and then abruptly stopped. My colorful beacons had disappeared. I continued walking, stumbling in the pitch-dark until I heard German voices and the staccato barking of dogs in the distance. They were all I had to go on. Creeping forward, I moved very slowly in case I was shot at. After a while I couldn't even hear voices anymore. Inexplicably, they seemed to have become fainter.

Confused, I stumbled on, straining my ears for sound and my eyes for the slightest sign of light. I walked and walked, expecting to come across the sleeping Gundolsheim at any minute, but the journey seemed without end.

Then my footing gave way beneath me and I plunged feet first through thin ice into a canal. The ice was covered in snow and was indistinguishable from the rest of the terrain. I went completely under, breaking through before bobbing back up, gasping for air. It was such a shock—both the very fact of the canal and the iciness of it. The water was as cold as death.

I knew that if I stayed in the water, I'd die. There was no one around, and even if there had been, I couldn't possibly have called for help. I was soaked to the skin and my clothes now weighed twice as much. Kicking out, trying to keep my legs moving, I splashed my way to the bank. The sides of the canal were sheer. There was virtually nothing to hold on to, just a thin concrete ledge and some frozen tufts of grass. My clothes were so heavy they pulled me back each time I tried to hoist myself out.

Come on, Marthe, keep trying, I told myself angrily. You've got to keep moving. The temptation to give up and sink back into the water was becoming greater and greater. My fingers scratched at the concrete ledge until they bled, and I felt impossibly tired. Kicking out again, moving along, I found some larger tufts of grass and a slightly deeper ledge. With supreme effort, I managed to lift myself up onto my elbows and fall facedown into the deep powdery snow at the water's edge. Snow thrust into my mouth and up my nostrils, making me cough and almost lose my grip. Closing my eyes, head down, I gave myself one final push on my arms and collapsed on my side into a drift.

For a while I just lay on my back, staring up at the stars and catching my breath. My teeth chattering, I got to my knees and hugged myself, squeezing the excess water out of my clothes and hair. Standing unsteadily, I began to jump up and down, water squelching from my little ankle boots, trying desperately to get warm.

Completely disorientated, I stumbled on, careful to avoid the rest of the canal I'd never been warned about by the guide, still heading for what I hoped was the village. All sounds had ended, there weren't even dogs barking anymore. I was in such a state of nervous tension, I didn't even notice the cold and wet after a while.

As dawn broke I could see my own footprints in the snow, and realized that in my confusion I'd been walking around and around in huge circles. I was cold and tired beyond belief. All I wanted was to get warm and dry and find somewhere to sleep. Part of me wanted just to lie down in the snow, but I knew if I did, I'd almost certainly never wake up. I now suspected (and learned later) that when the Germans stopped firing, they'd retreated east, which is why I could no longer hear them. Had I known, I'd have tried to follow them and report back. But it was all too late. Day was breaking, so I headed wearily back for the road I'd first arrived on, dreading Mollat's gloating response when he heard I'd failed yet again.

"See," he'd tell Bouvet, "she really doesn't have the guts to go through with it."

I knew that the Spahis and Captain Ligouzat would be long gone. I just hoped that someone else would be patrolling the area who could at least escort me back to HQ. As the first hesitant rays of light began to illuminate the valley, I saw a whole unit of tanks surrounded by infantry advancing along a road. Squinting, I tried to focus on the uniforms.

Germans.

Perhaps my mission wouldn't be aborted after all.

My head held high, I marched purposefully toward them, eager to resume and complete my task, my story ready in my mind. But as I drew nearer I hesitated. They weren't Germans at all, they were French soldiers leading a long line of German POWs. Disappointment and then relief washed over me, but I shouldn't have been so relieved. They were Moroccans again, this time an entire armored division. They took one look at me and rounded on me, as before.

"What are you doing here, you Nazi?" one spat. "Do you know what we do to women like you?" Once again I was surrounded and more than a little frightened, only so terribly tired and cold after my night's exertions that my priority was to get somewhere warm.

As before, I refused to answer questions or let them lay a finger on me. In the most authoritative tone of voice I could muster in the circumstances, I demanded to see a superior officer. He took one look at me and laughed out loud.

"Well, what have we here?" he cried, as his men joined in his laughter. "A drowned rat?"

Angry, I told him, "I must talk with you alone." At some distance from his men, I told him I was from the headquarters of the First Army. Steam rose from me as I spoke.

The senior officer eventually believed me but said he couldn't do anything for me, he had his own orders to obey. He had no spare transportation to take me such a distance, but agreed to keep me with them until someone could be sent to fetch me.

"Find the lady some clothes," he barked at his men, who were still standing around laughing. "Take them from one of the POWs." Looking back at me with a half smile, he added, "Find the smallest German you can."

The uniform they brought me was massive. The sleeves of the greatcoat scraped the ground and the trousers were enormous, like a clown's. Having been taken for a Nazi spy, I was now walking around in an oversized Wehrmacht uniform. But at least I was warm and dry. I couldn't have cared less how I looked. I rolled up the trousers and the sleeves and wrapped myself up in it as best I could.

"Can you speak German?" the officer asked me once he'd established that I must be with French intelligence.

"Of course," I replied, my teeth still chattering as I cradled my hands around a welcome tin cup of Moroccan mint tea.

"Then I'd be grateful if you would interrogate some of these prisoners for me, while you're waiting," he said with a smile, "and tell me what they know."

I was shown into a room in an isolated house and placed behind a low table. A group of about eleven German officers were ushered in to see me, including several of high rank—colonels, majors, and captains. They took one look at me—a short, damp, blonde woman with blue eyes and fair skin, swamped in a German private's uniform—and were stunned. Their bewilderment was so palpable that I could hardly control the urge to burst out laughing. The officers addressed me haughtily, as if I were the lowest of subordinates. They simply couldn't believe that I had any right to interview them.

My voice as strident as possible, I pounded the table and barked orders at them in German, like a senior officer would. I told them to stand at attention, which soon wiped the smirks off their faces. More deferential now, they each answered my preliminary questions, giving their names, ranks, and regiments. I then questioned each of them individually, and their arrogance soon disappeared. Whenever they were uncooperative, I tried to shame them into responding by reminding them of the brutalities perpetrated by the German Army in France.

Despite my extraordinary appearance, they were to learn that I was not someone to be trifled with. Under a barrage of questions several cracked, giving me invaluable information.

Recrossing the Line

Early one February morning Captain Ligouzat escorted me to the outskirts of a small Alsatian town northeast of Thann and handed me over to a French tank unit. After a succinct briefing about my next mission, I was assigned to ride inside an armored personnel carrier, *une voiture blindée.* I'd never suffered from claustrophobia before, but it was dark and close inside, the air stale with sweat and fear and fuel. There were two soldiers—the driver and a gunner—and me. I sat next to the driver in the semidarkness, shifting in my seat. In front of us were two Sherman tanks, and behind us were more armored vehicles and some troop carriers. We were wedged in like sardines in a tin.

The plan was to enter the heavily occupied town at dawn and engage the enemy. In the heat of the battle, I was expected to slip from the personnel carrier, hide somewhere, and infiltrate the enemy. Simple as that. Though our intelligence had correctly placed a large contingent of German infantry in that town, the appearance of our tanks, armored cars, and strong infantry support was supposed to be so overwhelming that it would send the enemy running for its life, me with them.

After a few minutes the orders were given to move and the driver started up the noisy engine. Jerkily, we set off, the racket deafening. Our only view of the outside world in the gray, misty morning light was through little gun ports all around us at eye level, whose armored covers or flaps were raised to provide us a limited view. Nothing was said, no words were spoken, among the three of us trapped inside. We did as instructed and followed the two leading tanks, trundling toward the main street of the town. My hands were so clammy I had to sit on them.

Almost as soon as we arrived at the first row of houses, the Germans opened fire. All hell broke loose, with enemy soldiers everywhere. Through the gun ports I caught glimpses of gray uniforms, distinctive helmets, and flashes of Wehrmacht insignia. Men were darting left to right, right to left, shooting at the French infantry around and behind us. The man with the machine gun in the seat behind mine began firing indiscriminately. Bullets hit our vehicle with alarming regularity, their tinny noise jarring every nerve.

A hundred feet ahead of us the first tank reached the crossroads at the corner of the town square. Just as it arrived, out of nowhere came an almighty rushing noise followed by the most enormous explosion. The blast rocked our vehicle as an incoming shell hit the first tank. Acrid black smoke poured from its gun turret and out of its hatch. Pieces of burning metal showered us.

The man to my right cursed aloud. The gunner stopped firing and leaned forward to see what had happened. The tank directly in front of us mostly blocked our view, but we could still see the flames leaping high into the air and imagine the terrible fate of the occupants.

This is where you're going to die, a little voice in my head suddenly said. *In this vehicle, in this place, squashed between two complete strangers. You're going to be burned alive.*

On impulse, I snapped shut every little flap around me so I could no longer see the billowing black smoke. With even less light, I was seized with a desperate panic at being trapped. I stared longingly at the sealed door through which I'd come a few minutes earlier, but my limbs were frozen. I seemed to be paralyzed. I couldn't make myself small enough in my seat. I closed my eyes and tried to imagine myself shrinking into the tiniest, most invisible speck, miraculously out of range of whatever it was that had hit the tank so close to where I crouched.

But at the same time, my pride got the better of me. Even stronger than my desire to escape was my determination that my fellow soldiers shouldn't see how frightened I was. Looking into their pale faces, I suspected they were trying to do the same. I resolved never again to pronounce judgment on other people's response to fear. In that moment I realized that courage or cowardice depends entirely on circumstance and one's state of mind.

The tank was by now completely ablaze and burning fiercely. The French soldiers had all been killed, incinerated within its fiery furnace. For a while we just sat there, immobile, silent, watching, like sitting ducks. The second tank had stopped, too, its crew unable to move it forward or back. There was an entire line of trucks and vehicles behind us, so we couldn't back up. I was still curled up into a little ball in my seat, head down, the smell of my fear mingling with that of those with me. I knew I'd never be able to climb out of the personnel carrier and continue my mission now. All I could hope for was that we'd somehow manage to escape from the village alive.

To my great relief, the carrier's radio hissed into life and I heard the order from command to abort the mission. This seemed to jerk everyone into action, and the ground troops somehow disabled the panzer that had hit the French tank. A fierce battle once again ensued, during which we were buffeted and knocked, hit and shot at, but after much confusion we were finally able to retreat, our limbs still attached. Once again I was thankful. My name meant hope and good luck, and often it was sheer luck that saw me through.

A few days later Colonel Bouvet moved his HQ from Thann to Lützelhof and I moved with him. Soon after our arrival, he summoned me to his office. His eyes looked weary of war.

"My men have picked up a German deserter at the front," he told me with a sigh. "They're bringing him here now. He claims to have been forcibly enlisted into the Wehrmacht and wants to defect to us. He may have some important information for us, or he may not. I'd like you to question him in my presence, but I don't want you to translate what he says immediately. Make him think he can trust you, that you're on his side. You know what to do."

The soldier was brought in, flanked by two Moroccan guards. He looked frightened and kept twisting his cap in his hands as his eyes darted back and forth between the colonel and me.

"*Guten Tag,*" I said, smiling and stepping a few paces forward.

"*Guten Tag,*" he replied.

"*Parlez-vous français?*" I asked.

"*Oui,*" he replied. "*Je suis un Alsacien.*" His French was fluent and the accent indistinguishable between that of an Alsatian or a German.

Reverting back to German, I asked him his name, rank, and serial number, which he gave me. Colonel Bouvet's assistant wrote it down. He repeated his story that he'd been conscripted into the German Army and said he'd tried many times to escape.

"And where do you come from in Alsace?" I asked.

"Haguenau, in the northeast," he replied. "It hasn't been liberated yet."

"I know it well," I lied, "but surely your family will be punished for your desertion. Aren't you worried for them?"

"Very," he said, wringing his cap still tighter. "I'd be grateful for anything you can do. My mother, my wife, and two children are all at risk."

"And isn't it unusual for an Alsatian to be in this part of the theater of war?" I asked. "I thought all the men from this region were sent to the Russian front, for fear that they'd desert back to their homes?"

The story of the *malgré-nous,* or soldiers against their will, was well known. More than 140,000 Alsatian men, citizens of France, had been forcibly conscripted, many to be used as human minesweepers on the Russian front.

"Er, yes, they were," he replied, a thin film of sweat appearing on his top lip. "But a few of us managed to slip through the net."

"Tell me," I asked, still smiling, "what did you do in the German Army? What was your role?"

"Infantry," he replied, pointing to his insignia. It was the correct badge for what he claimed to be.

"And what action did you see?"

"A great deal."

"Tell me about it."

My interrogation lasted for over an hour as he talked me through his experiences and his repeated attempts to desert. Colonel Bouvet, who knew only a little German, sat silently watching and listening throughout.

By the time I'd asked my final few questions, the prisoner looked distinctly uncomfortable. When I asked him again about his family, he seemed inconsistent. "I'm terrified for them," he said again, "my wife and children."

"And what about both your parents?" I asked.

"Yes, and them, too," he added hastily.

"What are your children's names?" I asked.

There was a pause, so slight as almost not to be noticed. "Freida and Gottlieb," he replied. Smiling broadly, he added, "They're beautiful kids."

Looking at my watch, I apologized to the colonel and pretended I had to leave shortly for a prior engagement. "We'll have another talk later on," I promised the prisoner with a smile before the guards led him out.

Colonel Bouvet waited until the door was closed. "Well?" he asked.

"He's a spy," I said.

The colonel frowned. "How can you tell?"

"If he were an Alsatian, he'd almost certainly be on the Russian front, not this one. What's more, he mentioned his mother only first and then—when I spoke of his parents—he concurred. Furthermore, he didn't tell me the names of his children quickly enough. I think he made them up when I asked, which is why he hesitated."

"Anything else?"

"Yes. There'd be no reason for him to desert now, knowing that the end is nearly in sight. His family would be taken out and shot for his crime, and yet he only mentioned it when I brought it up. I think he's in German intelligence, sent to spy on us."

"Thank you, Chichinette," the colonel said, smiling. "That'll be all."

I never saw the prisoner again, but the following day the colonel confirmed my suspicions. "You were right," he said. "He cracked under further interrogation. He admitted he was an agent sent by the Germans to see what he could find out about our strategy. I've delivered him to the counterintelligence group. We won't be having any more trouble from him."

I almost felt sorry for the man.

Bouvet was an excellent commander and a great man, and I had nothing but respect for him. During my time in HQ, living alongside him and his finest officers, I learned a great deal. The colonel seemed to trust me implicitly and openly introduced me to a variety of people at our meals.

I was saddened, however, to discover that Bouvet was unable to completely remove himself from the prejudicial influences of the army. Lieutenant Neu, my "mattress mate," was sent on a dangerous reconnaissance mission near enemy lines. He was gone for a day and a night and I was very worried for him. I shouldn't have been. A consummate professional, he returned to us safe and well, with a great deal of valuable information. I was party to his debriefing and felt terribly proud of what he'd managed to achieve.

"Go and get some rest now," the colonel told him warmly, patting him on the back. "And well done."

Neu had only just left the room when the colonel turned to Commandant Ruyssen and, in the presence of Captain Ligouzat, said, "Neu did bloody well for a Jew, didn't he?" It was an off-the-cuff remark, not intended to offend, but it shook me to the core. Making an excuse to leave the room, I went for a walk to get some air, grateful that I'd never revealed my religion to the colonel or the rest of my comrades in the unit.

A few days later I was sent with Captain Ligouzat to a dam across the western branch of the Rhine at Kembs, just south of Mulhouse. Our instructions were to undertake a reconnaissance on how commandos could cross the river south of the dam without alerting the Germans waiting just across the water near the village of Istein. Ligouzat and I were supposed to be army logistics personnel checking on security.

On reaching the heavily defended dam, we asked to be shown to the officer in charge. Ushered along a corridor, we were led to a closed door. The nameplate said CAPTAIN GRANDIDIER, the same surname as the teenage boy who'd stalked me all those years before in Metz—the street urchin who'd sent me a postcard and so upset my father. Opening the door and walking in, I froze in my tracks as the young man inside stood up to greet us. It was the same Grandidier I'd known.

Worst of all, he recognized me. "Marthe!" he cried. "Marthe Hoffnung!"

I knew how dangerous it could be for me, both professionally and personally, if my secret got out, and I wanted nothing more than to get away from the intense scrutiny of this young man. Shaking my head at him, as if confused, I said: "Sorry? My name is Lenôtre."

But Grandidier wasn't buying it. He laughed and wagged his finger at me. "I'd know you anywhere," he said. "I even know your address; it's four rue Marechal Pétain, Metz. I was terribly in love with you as a young boy. Surely you remember me?"

Seeing the confusion on Captain Ligouzat's face, I shook my head once more. "No," I said. "My name's Lenôtre and I lived on Avenue de Nancy."

Ligouzat tried to intervene. "Her name is Lenôtre. Sergeant Marthe Lenôtre," he said crossly. He clearly wanted to get to the business at hand.

"No it isn't," a bemused Grandidier continued, "it's Hoffnung. I know her. I used to follow her everywhere, even to the synagogue."

My face coloring, I swallowed hard. "You're completely mistaken," I said. "It's not me. I've never met you before in my life."

Grandidier looked askance at me and said nothing. "I could have sworn it was you," he said finally, frowning. "You look so much like her."

"Well, I'm very sorry to disappoint you," I said, forcing a smile. "Now may we please discuss why we're here?"

We spent almost an hour at the dam, being shown around by my former suitor, checking out possible vantage points for the commandos. Out of the corner of my eye I studied the dashing young captain and marveled at how handsome he'd become. I'd have hardly recognized him from the rough boy who used to follow my footsteps so doggedly. In different times, I mused, it might have been nice to make his acquaintance.

As we were leaving he grabbed my arm and pulled me to one side. "I don't care what you say, it's wonderful to see you again, Marthe," he whispered. "I was in the Catholic seminary, but I left because of you."

"I told you," I said, pulling my arm firmly away. "I'm not who you think I am. Good-bye."

"Au revoir," he replied, blowing me a kiss.

A few days later, through Captain Zimmerman, whose antenna was based at St. Louis, I met some senior officers from Swiss intelligence, with whom the captain had become very friendly. The Swiss were meant to be neutral, but their neutrality was often compromised—first by the Germans and later by the Allies. The impetuous Zimmerman invited me to dinner one day and introduced me to three officers from Swiss intelligence, all based in Basle.

Their chief was Colonel Reinhart, a very impressive, tall middle-age blond man who seemed to take an instant shine to me.

"Delighted to meet you," Reinhart said, taking my hand and kissing it. "I've heard very good things about you from Captain Zimmerman, mademoiselle, and if ever you need my services, I am at your command." He bowed deeply.

Deciding to take Reinhart up on his offer a few weeks later, Zimmerman sent me to Switzerland with Lieutenant Tallichet, in order to arrange my crossing into Germany via Switzerland. This would be my fifteenth attempt to infiltrate the enemy, but my first directly into German territory. It was April 11, 1945.

Basle was a complete shock to the system. Lieutenant Tallichet took me to lunch at a wonderful restaurant, and I was overwhelmed by the choices offered on the menu. In the end I opted for a cheese fondue, the first I'd ever tasted. Everything seemed so normal. People dressed in the sort of clothes I hadn't seen since before the war. The shops were open and full of luxury items like chocolate and furs.

There were no blackouts and cars roamed the streets freely, with no apparent restrictions on fuel. After lunch Tallichet took me to a patisserie shop. "Choose anything you like," he said, smiling. He was very patient. The selection was so bewildering, it took me ten minutes to choose. My face pressed against the glass, I wanted them all.

More satiated than I'd been in years, dazzled by the sights and sounds and smells of life in a country not at war, I sat beneath the spring blossoms eating the stickiest pastry I could find. There wasn't a single indication that mayhem raged all around in Europe or that people were dying in the streets in neighboring countries. There were no shortages, and Swiss life seemed to be frozen in a time I barely remembered.

"Well, I suppose we'd better go and see these intelligence people," I told Tallichet, still heady with the day's events. "Then at least I can get my feet back on the ground."

He took me to their HQ, where Colonel Reinhart received me warmly. "So, you want to cross into Germany?" he said. "I think we can arrange that. Call for Georges Lemaire."

Monsieur Lemaire was an intelligence officer, a tall, slim man in his mid-fifties with a small mustache and piercing brown eyes. He examined me as if I were a specimen under a microscope as he was told to take me to Schaffhausen, an enclave of Switzerland that jutted into Germany west of the Bodensee. From there I could walk to Singen, an industrial border town with strategic importance.

"We'll leave right away," he said, looking at his watch. "You'll be able to cross before dusk."

Quelling my sudden bout of indigestion, I bid Colonel Reinhart and Lieutenant Tallichet farewell, picked up the small suitcase containing my few belongings, and left the building with the guide. Basle soon slipped from view from the window of his car as we headed forty miles east.

Our journey took less than two hours, during which time Lemaire sat in near silence next to me as I prepared myself mentally for what I was about to attempt. It felt different, somehow, crossing into Germany. I hadn't previously realized quite how much of a comfort the security of remaining on French soil had been. I went over and over my story in my mind. There had been a slight change in my story, due to an unexpected offer of help by a French Alsatian doctor, Christophe Mueller, who'd recently escaped from Germany and who I was supposed to have worked for. He'd been automatically enlisted in the German Army during the war and had befriended families in Singen and in Freiburg-im-Breisgau, "capital" of the Black Forest. Having been wounded on the Russian front, he was sent to work in a clinic in Konstanz and had escaped back to Alsace as soon as it had been liberated. His German friends still believed him to be in Konstanz.

Though I'd never met him, I'd been shown a photograph and given a detailed description of his personality and history, his relationship to each German family, and of my supposed friendship with him. He was a man very much loved by his patients and staff. He was now back in France, working for the French Army, and had said through the intelligence service that if I said he'd sent me, the people he'd known would almost certainly be kind to me. I certainly hoped so. The alternative was too unpalatable to contemplate.

Martha Ulrich, I repeated to myself, Martha Ulrich. I'm a nurse working in Konstanz and I'm looking for my fiancé. I'll be fine.

Reaching Schaffhausen all too quickly, we left the car on the edge of a wood and walked in silence for half an hour through the trees. The birds were singing noisily and the sunlight filtered down through the branches in great shafts. Signaling me to crouch, Lemaire led the way as we neared the road that marked the border.

"There," he whispered, pointing through the trees. "There's the road, and those are the border guards."

Blinking, I stared at the narrow road that divided neutral Switzerland from Nazi Germany, and watched its two rhythmically patrolling soldiers as they met and crossed, marched several hundred yards in the opposite direction, turned and marched back again.

"Now," Lemaire said, flopping to the ground and leaning his back against a tree, "we wait."

Watching and waiting, my heart was pounding in time to the constant, muffled grinding noise that filled the air. It sounded like hundreds of tanks all going somewhere.

Lemaire explained. "Ball bearings," he said. "Huge factories buried deep underground, manned by forced labor, making armaments for the Third Reich." I wondered if Stéphanie could be somewhere beneath me under the forest floor, slaving away on a production line, oblivious to how close I was.

Brooding, Lemaire had lit a cigarette and turned to me with a smile. "Tonight," he said softly, blowing a smoke ring high into the dank forest air, "you may well die." I glared at him, trying not to think of what he was saying. "So," he added, leaning forward conspiratorially, a glint in his eye, "why not have a good time first?"

I had no intention of dying and even less of sleeping with such a cold, calculating man. "Thank you, but I don't have affairs with married men," I said flatly, smoothing down the plain skirt I was wearing and rechecking my forged papers again. I had indispensable items like German coupons for food and clothing, a *carnet,* or notebook, for traveling, and a photograph and letters from my "fiancé" Hans.

Reaching into my suitcase, I pulled out a pair of white socks and slipped them over my silk stockings to protect them from the rough ground. Ready for my mission, I sat in silence waiting until just before dusk.

"Now!" Lemaire said suddenly, stubbing out his cigarette and breaking my contemplation. "Go now. The guards have just parted."

Rising to my knees in readiness, I took a deep breath.

"Remember," Lemaire whispered in my ear, his hand cupped over it, "I'll be waiting until you go."

It took more than twenty minutes to crawl on my hands and knees through the scrubby undergrowth to a position close to the road. Never taking my eyes off the guards, I finally reached the point Lemaire had suggested, next to a scrawny thornbush.

"Wait until they cross and have their backs to you, then get up and walk toward the road as quickly as you can," he'd told me. "Head east and you'll meet the guard to the right when he turns. Carry on walking, as if you've come from the west. He'll stop you and ask for your papers, so don't panic, just smile and do as he asks. The main thing is to get past him and on your way before he meets up with the other guard."

I watched and waited, saw the guards approaching and knew the moment of my bid for the border was imminent. I knew the drill, I'd been watching them long enough. Trembling, I saw them cross—my signal to get up and walk as casually as possible into Nazi Germany.

My brain told my legs to move and make me stand, but the muscles in my legs disobeyed orders.

Fear pinned me to the ground. Facedown in the undergrowth, I flattened myself as much as possible as the border guards marched away a few feet from where I lay. Pressed into the soft earth, I cursed myself for wearing socks, which I now feared stood out whiter than white in the dusk for the whole German Army to see. Lifting my head a few inches, I peered through the undergrowth and watched the guards meet, cross over and part once more, but still I couldn't move.

Nobody had the right to expect so much of me, I reasoned silently in my head. Nobody. Hadn't I done enough? Couldn't I just creep back to Lemaire and tell him I'd changed my mind?

Though he told me that if there were any trouble he'd use his pistol, I hadn't been convinced. It would have sparked an international incident at a time when Switzerland was, at least outwardly, struggling to maintain its neutrality. My antenna had assured me, in no uncertain terms, that nobody would ever come to my rescue.

Every bone in my body seemed to ache. My throat was so dry I licked the sweat from my top lip. I could see the guards coming back again, a few minutes away from crossing over and turning once more. The light was fading and I knew that the longer I lingered, the more dangerous it would be for me to arrive after nightfall at the town of Singen.

Nearly an hour passed and the guards crossed and recrossed several times. What must Lemaire be thinking? I wondered. He must have realized that I'd lost my nerve. The thought of such an accusation drained the color from my cheeks. An image of Captain Mollat flooded my brain. I was filled with dread at the thought of what he would say if I returned empty-handed from this assignment, Lemaire a silent witness to my cowardice.

Looking up in the twilight, I saw that the guards had parted and were about halfway to their farthest point.

"There will be times when you have to reach deep within you to find courage," Colonel Bouvet had once told me. I thought of Jacques and the courage he'd shown in the face of torture, his trial, and, ultimately, a firing squad. I remembered Stéphanie and her refusal to betray the farmers, her determination to stay in the camp and help others, and her last letter to Dedé, in which she wrote: "You know that for the great ordeals I'm always very strong." Well, this was my great ordeal, my baptism of fire, and I was being less than strong.

My resolve suddenly bolstered, I reached for my suitcase and stood up, brushing myself down. Before I could change my mind, I forced myself to put one foot in front of the other and walk toward the road. It was too late to run away. I was walking toward the guard in the failing light, my suitcase gripped firmly in my left hand.

I watched him turn, register my presence and march toward me. He must have been sixty years old. He walked with a slight limp, as if his feet or arthritic hips were paining him.

"Heil Hitler!" I said, raising my right arm in the customary salute as he approached.

"Heil Hitler!" he replied, raising his automatically. "Where have you come from?"

"Gottmadingen," I said with a smile, giving him the name of a village to the west.

"Where are you going?" he asked, clearly surprised by the sight of a young woman so late in the day at such an isolated spot.

"Singen," I replied. "I'm visiting some friends."

"Let me see your papers," he barked gruffly, determined to at least appear efficient. I retrieved them from my pocket, and he examined them closely, squinting in the low light. I prayed now that the month-old pieces of paper, with their rubber-stamped dates in different faded inks deliberately put on at an angle, looked authentic enough to fool him.

He studied them for a moment, chewing his bottom lip as he considered whether he should question me further. I could almost hear the mechanism of his brain working as he tried to decide if he should wait to corroborate my story with his fellow guard. But it was dusk, he was probably due to be relieved from duty imminently, and I sensed, as I stood smiling up at him, my body rigid, that he just wanted to get back to his post and put his feet up.

"Go on your way," he said, handing my papers back to me after what seemed like an age. As I folded them neatly and put them in my pocket, I was grateful that he had neither the training nor the drive of some of his younger colleagues.

Smiling, I nodded and set off, walking just fast enough to be out of sight by the time he met up with his fellow guard, but not so fast as to arouse suspicion. The hairs tingling on the back of my neck, I resisted the urge to turn and look back.

Walking east and parallel with the field in which I'd lain for so long, after a few hundred yards I was almost at the spot where Lemaire had told me he'd be waiting. I wondered if he was still there somewhere, watching out for me, as he'd promised he would be.

I didn't have to wonder long. From behind the Swiss enclave, where a wrought-iron fence bordered the road, I heard a low sound, a song emerging from my Swiss guide's lips. It was a familiar tune, a drinking song, but he'd added his own words. *"Grus Gott,"* he sang liltingly in Switzerdeutsch. (God keep you, but meaning "Good day.") Picking up his tune, I reached the point where I knew he must be very close and sang back softly: *"Grus Gott."* (And good day to you.)

Was I mistaken, or did I hear Lemaire chuckle? I can't have been because, just before turning and heading back into Switzerland to report on my safe delivery into German territory, he used the same tune to sing the wry line: "I—never—thought—you'd—do—it."

Blushing, I didn't dare reply. Inwardly, I was smiling, immensely proud of myself for overcoming my dread. There had been several dark moments lying in that field for so long when all courage had abandoned me. Now here I was, a young French soldier and a Jew, walking straight into the mouth of the beast, and I don't think I'd ever felt more free.

The Mouth of the Beast

Less than ten minutes into Germany, I heard footsteps behind me in the dark and a man's voice call out.

"Hey you!"

I turned to see a German soldier marching purposefully toward me.

In the few seconds it took him to reach me, I played out an imaginary scenario in my mind in which the border guards had met as they crossed over and the one I'd seen said to the other, "She was a pretty little thing," or something similar, and the other guard replied, "Who?" Then my guard laughed and said, "The little blonde from Gottmadingen," and that's when the other guard would have told him that no such person had passed him on the road.

It would only have taken a quick call to Singen on their field telephone to alert them to my arrival, and the Gestapo would have been waiting for me, or perhaps they'd sent this soldier after me now. There were plenty of holes in my story, I'd realized as I lay sweating in that field. It wouldn't have taken long to find me out. For example, I'd realized that I knew absolutely nothing about Konstanz on the Swiss-German border, and yet—in my latest incarnation—I was supposed to have worked there for a doctor who was now helping French intelligence.

I'd have to rely on my wits. If I were ever caught, my antenna probably wouldn't even find out what had happened to me. I had nothing to identify me either as Marthe Lenôtre or Marthe Hoffnung. It was my fervent hope that I'd never be arrested, so nobody could ever discover my weaknesses. I'd rather have killed myself than be put through the agony of hostile interrogation. But there were no cyanide pills in my suitcase. It hadn't been thought necessary by HQ.

My only means of communication with my service was through farmers at an address I'd memorized in the tiny village of Laufenburg along the Swiss border, between Schaffhausen and Basle, not far from the Rhine. The farmers were Catholic and anti-Hitler. One of their daughters was married to an Alsatian in the French intelligence service who secretly met his wife at the border at regular intervals. I'd been told which days he came, twice a week, so I could get letters to him. My only other instructions if I got into trouble were to make my way back to Switzerland. Colonel Reinhart had told me that if I ever needed help, I should tell the border guards I was one of his agents.

There was no point running now that I'd been spotted. The approaching soldier would soon outrun me. My head pounding so hard it was enough to drown out the continuous grating of the underground factories, I stood waiting for my fate to be decided for me. Looking down at my stockinged legs in the fading light, I was grateful that I'd discarded my white socks soon after crossing the border. For some reason, I'd come to associate them with being found out.

"*Guten Abend,*" the soldier said, smiling. "I saw you walking there and thought you might like some company. Where are you going at this time of night?"

"Singen," I replied warily.

"What are you doing there?" he asked, curious. As he drew

closer, I realized he was almost as old as the border guard and I felt somewhat more at ease.

"Looking up some friends of a friend," I said with a half smile. He seemed to believe me, and we strolled on, chatting about the way the war was going, until we reached the edge of the town, where I was very relieved when he went one way and I went another.

Unsure of exactly where I was going, I headed straight for the center of town, looking for the address I'd been given by the Alsatian doctor, Christophe Mueller. Singen was a small town in a valley full of blue-collar workers, and it had been heavily bombed by the Allies because of its surrounding armaments factories. Many buildings had been completely destroyed, and huge craters pockmarked the roads. The eerie shell of a burned-out building towered over me as I entered the main square; its gaping windows seemed to be watching me. A blackout was in force and I could hardly see where I was going. I had no flashlight; I hadn't even thought to bring one.

After stumbling around in the dark trying to orient myself, I finally came upon the center square, where two men with rifles were sitting at the edge of a large crater, talking softly. I watched them from the shadows for a long time, debating whether I should approach. I knew it was risky for me to be walking around alone at night; I could easily be arrested and questioned by the German police. I needed to get to the address I'd been given, but at the same time I was afraid to tell anyone where I was going, because if they were asked about me later, they could say exactly which way I'd gone.

Hesitating, I eventually decided the safer option would be to get to my destination quickly. I approached the two men very cautiously so as not to startle them and have them shoot me out of fright. I made little coughing noises as I neared and when I reached them they shone their flashlights into my face and shouted: "*Wer sind sie?*"

As I drew nearer I noticed from their armbands that they were members of the Civil Defense team on lookout duties for enemy airplanes. In my best German I asked them to direct me to the street I was looking for.

"It's not far, *mädchen,*" they told me with a smile, and pointed the way. It was about ten P.M.

Finding the address, I wearily climbed the stairs to a flat on the second floor. Standing in front of the door, my throat dry, I rang the bell.

The door opened slightly and a tall, slim woman in her late twenties wearing a bathrobe regarded me suspiciously through the crack.

"*Ja?*" she said, pulling her robe more tightly around her. "What do you want?"

"*Guten Abend.* I'm terribly sorry to disturb you, Frau Schmidt," I began, smiling broadly, "but Dr. Mueller sent me. He said you'd be kind enough to take care of me if ever I needed a room for the night."

Upon hearing the doctor's name, the woman's face immediately lit up and she threw the door wide open to usher me inside. I showed her a letter of recommendation from the doctor and gave her recent news of him. With hardly a question, she gave me some food to eat and made up a bed for me to sleep in. Her name was Ilse Schmidt and her husband was a soldier somewhere on the Russian front. She'd had no news of him in a very long time. She lived with her father and her child, who was about a year old. They didn't have much food but they weren't starving, either, and they graciously shared with me what they had, some bread and a bowl of hearty stew. I was extremely tired and slept surprisingly well that night, relieved that I'd finally made it into Germany and managed to survive my first few hours.

The next morning I woke early and, having washed and dressed, wandered into the kitchen. Ilse was clothed and chopping vegetables noisily with a knife, her jaw set. Seeing me enter, she turned to me and, waving the knife at me as she spoke, she said coldly, "Last night, I couldn't help noticing that your stockings were torn. We've been warned time and again to watch out for strangers, and I've been thinking about it all night." Wiping her hands on her apron, she took a few steps closer. "We hear frequent reports of enemy agents being arrested in and around Singen, because we're so close to the border. I can't help wondering if you tore your stockings crawling in from Switzerland. Tell me, fräulein, are you a spy?"

With a laugh I replied, "Look at me, Frau Schmidt! Do I look like a spy?"

Ilse stopped for a moment, looked me up and down and laughed, her head thrown back, hands on her ample hips. "No, no, you don't," she agreed, and nothing more was ever said. From that moment on she and her family believed me to be a true patriot.

Ilse and her father couldn't have been more helpful in the two days I spent with them. I told them I was en route to Freiburg and that I was looking for my fiancé, Hans. I showed them his picture and his letters, and she empathized entirely with my fears for him, having her own man somewhere at the front.

"God willing, they shall be returned to us," she said, making the sign of the cross. She was very kind; she took me shopping, and in return I helped with the baby. She even took me to the train station and helped me reserve a ticket to Freiburg for the following night; the trains didn't run in the daytime because of the constant Allied bombardments. It was fortunate I had her help because I didn't have a clue how to do that. Serious gaps in my training, I was learning, required instant improvisation or I could so easily have been caught.

I have to confess I did sometimes feel uncomfortable about how much I was deceiving this kind family, letting them believe that I was a good German while spying on their fellow countrymen. But imbued by the importance of my work, I recognized that my fleeting guilt was something I'd just have to deal with. And anyway, some of their fellow Germans had perpetrated many crimes against us—I had to remember that and keep sight of my ultimate goal. If I ever had any lingering doubts, I'd just summon the image of Wilhelm Hipp in my mind, and everything I did seemed entirely justified.

My mission was my foremost concern. I was absolutely determined to do as good a job as I could now that I'd actually made it behind enemy lines. If I was going to risk my life, I wanted it to be for something really worthwhile. I couldn't bear the idea of returning to Colonel Bouvet and Captain Mollat without having discovered anything important.

The next evening Ilse walked me to the station and put me on a train. "*Auf Wiedersehen,* Martha," she said, handing me a small parcel of provisions for the journey. "Good luck. I hope you find your Hans." I waved good-bye with a heavy heart. From now on I was on my own.

The train was packed with German soldiers and civilians, most of them trying to get some sleep. In the dim half-light within the train, I managed to find somewhere to sit, but the corridors were filled with people smoking and coughing. It was completely blacked out and we had to pull onto a siding each time the Allied planes flew low overhead. Despite the crush, there were dozens of heavily armed policemen on board, checking papers; looking for spies, escaped prisoners, or foreign workers.

"Papiere, bitte!" they announced as they slid open the door of my compartment and scanned the faces of everyone inside. One by one we rummaged for our documents and handed them over for close scrutiny. Anyone sleeping was rudely awoken. I wondered if any of my fellow passengers had cause to be as frightened as I. The *polizei* checked my papers many times, shining a flashlight directly onto the forged documents as they examined them, looking for clues. On every occasion, I sat there smiling up at them, but was secretly quaking inside. I made a mental note never to take a train again unless I couldn't help it.

The journey was about 150 miles through heavily wooded forest and the almost inaccessible Hollental, or Hell Valley Gorge, built eighty years earlier using a spectacular network of viaducts and tunnels cut through living rock. Despite wave after wave of Allied bombers flying overhead, we somehow arrived intact the following morning at the Hauptbahnhof in central Freiburg, a once-beautiful old city on the western slopes of the Rhine Valley with an impressive thirteenth-century cathedral. I picked my way through the narrow streets and deep medieval drainage troughs and found the address I'd been given.

Like Ilse before her, once I mentioned Dr. Mueller's name, the woman I'd been told to visit immediately invited me in and accepted me warmly into her home. Her name was Gertrud Schröeder and she lived in the small apartment with her boyfriend, a blue-collar worker. I stayed with her for several days, and she even took me to see a matinee at the cinema one afternoon. It was a film about Leni Rosenthal, Hitler's personal cinematographer. Gertrud was thrilled to see it and assumed, as a German, that I would be, too. I couldn't possibly have refused. I wasn't particularly interested in the topic or the endless footage of the Führer, but I found being a French spectator in a German cinema in the middle of a war enthralling.

Later that afternoon, while Gertrud and I were alone in her flat, a friend of hers came to call. "Gertrud tells me you work as a nurse in Konstanz," the buxom hausfrau said pleasantly, looking straight at me. "I know Konstanz very well. Tell me, what's the name of the clinic where you work?"

I didn't have the faintest idea, and so I said the first thing that came into my head. "Bodensee Klinik," I replied without thinking.

"That sounds more like a hotel or a restaurant," she said, her eyes narrowing.

Quick as a flash I replied, "That's because it was, before it was turned into a clinic. You have no idea what they can do with an old building these days. More tea?"

The woman became highly suspicious of me and made me very nervous, but Gertrud could see I was uncomfortable in her presence so she quickly changed the subject and refused to let her friend question me any more.

Freiburg was bristling with armed Germans and police, but I swallowed my fear and did what I'd come to do—gather information. I'd been given the name and address of a Dr. Charles Schaeffer, who lived on the outskirts of town. He was from Alsace and his parents still lived there, but he'd married a German doctor and moved to Freiburg before the war. His parents had contacted the French Army and said they wanted their son to come home. "Please," they'd said, "do what you can to get him out of Germany." The only way he'd be allowed to return to France, having voluntarily remained in Germany throughout the war, would be if he helped me now.

I was quietly confident that he would. His parents had sent him a letter that I was to deliver to him, telling him to offer me "every assistance." I found his office in the suburbs of Freiburg and told his receptionist I needed to see the doctor. "It's personal," I said, and refused to give any more information.

I was ushered in and asked to sit down. "What can I do for you, Fräulein Ulrich?" he asked.

I reached into my pocket for the letter I'd been secretly carrying since crossing into Germany and handed it to him. "This is from your parents, Dr. Schaeffer," I told him in French. "They sent me to you."

He read the brief letter and studied me for a moment. "And what is it that you want me to help you with?" he asked, puzzled.

"I am with French intelligence," I told him bluntly. "You're very well established here and you'll have access to all sorts of information I require. I need you to help me get information on troop movements and defense plans. If you do this, the French Army will provide you and your family with the special passes you'll need to go back to France when the war is over."

Instead of gratefully accepting my proposition, the doctor leaped to his feet. "How can you ask me such a thing!" he cried, his face florid. "My wife is German!"

Realizing the danger, I too jumped up and waved my hands at him to calm him down. "Very well," I said, trying to speak softly so as not to alert his receptionist. "If that's how you feel, that's fine, I understand." I picked up my bag and headed for the door.

"It's outrageous to ask such a thing of me!" Dr. Schaeffer continued, coming after me. "This is my home. I've lived here for many years. My patients are all German. My wife's family are all here. How could I possibly betray them?"

I never wanted to be away from a place as much as I did then. Cornered by the indignant Alsatian, I placated him as much as possible and told him I had to leave. His parents had vouched for him, but clearly hadn't realized how pro-German he'd become. I'd completely exposed my identity to him, and he seemed so upset that I feared he might well summon the authorities and turn me in. The longer I stayed with him, the more I was at risk.

"Where are you staying?" he asked me suddenly, his eyes darkening.

"I'm not staying here," I told him, "I'm moving on today."

"But where can I reach you if I need you?"

"You can't," I replied. Grabbing the door handle, I pulled it open. *"Auf Wiedersehen,* Herr Doktor," I said, and fled before he had time to ask me any more awkward questions.

I spent the rest of that day on the run, taking detours and doubling back, in case I was being followed. I didn't return to Frau Schröeder's until later that evening. Crawling into bed, I fell asleep before my head even hit the pillow.

I spent the next two days wandering around the city, looking for people who could give me any information. Walking past two young women in army uniform on a city street, I heard them whispering to each other in French.

"Are you French?" I asked in German.

"Yes," one of them replied, wary. Her companion had recently been crying.

"What are you doing here?" I asked, this time in French.

"We were forcibly enlisted into the Germany Army," she told me. The one with red-rimmed eyes broke down and added, "We miss our homes and families terribly."

I comforted her as best I could and told her not to worry. "You'll be home sooner than you think," I said quietly, "sooner still if you can help me. I'm with French intelligence, what can you tell me about the unit you're with?"

Astonished, the two girls stared at me, wondering whether to believe me. "Really?" one finally said.

"Really," I replied. "Now tell me everything you know."

Between them, as we stood talking by the side of the road, they were able to fill me in on troop movements in the area and the strength and location of their unit. "We're based in a barracks on the outskirts of the city," one explained, drawing me a map with her finger in the dust. "There's a battalion of men, a company of infantry, and about a hundred POWs."

Making a mental note of all they'd told me, I arranged to meet them at the same spot the next day, when they promised they'd be able to tell me even more. "We're so happy to be helping," one of the women enthused. "It feels like we're finally doing something positive for France."

German civilians were often inadvertently helpful. Talking to them enabled me to assess the local morale and to see what they knew. Usually by then their spirits were pretty low. They knew that the tide had turned and that their army was on the run. A few remained defiant, however.

"The Führer has a secret *wunder waffen,*" several told me conspiratorially. "He'll wait for the Allied armies to penetrate deep into our territory before he'll use it. It is a weapon capable of destroying whole cities, you know."

I found myself wondering, with some discomfort, if the stories were true.

Putting that from my mind, I decided to visit a friend of Captain Ligouzat, a German who'd been a fellow student at the Sorbonne. Though badly burned by my experience with Dr. Schaeffer, I went to visit Herr Greenwald and his wife in a village farther north. Their home wasn't far from the Westwall, better known in Allied circles as the Siegfried Line, a series of near-impregnable fortifications along Germany's western frontier from Holland to Switzerland, following the Belgian, Luxembourg, and French borders, which Hitler had insisted be held at all costs. The line was three miles deep in places and contained thousands of pyramid-shaped concrete obstacles known as "dragon's teeth," and more than nine thousand heavy concrete pillboxes set into the ground and carefully camouflaged with interlocking trenches. Beneath the surface lay massive underground bunkers that housed troops and armaments brought to the surface by hydraulic lifts.

A few months earlier, following the biggest air assault of the war, in which more than two thousand bombers had saturated the Siegfried Line farther north, the American army had broken through and into some of Germany's most heavily defended fortress towns. Freiburg was just six miles from the part of the Westwall that was still unassailed.

There were always people walking to and from towns, both in Germany and France. There was little transport during the war apart from military vehicles, and though one could sometimes hitch a ride, they were usually full of troops. Unable to find any going my way, I fell in with a group of about seven people, mostly women, leaving Freiburg to visit friends and family. One woman was pushing an empty wheelbarrow along in front of her. Among them was a noncommissioned SS officer who reminded me of Hipp—small, ugly, and mad. My jaw clenched when I spotted the familiar silver flash on his collar.

His name was Sergeant Major Helmut Werner. He was a braggart and a bully and spent the entire journey ranting and raving and boasting of how many people he'd killed.

"I was in Poland when we cleared the ghettos," he said, smiling broadly to reveal yellowing teeth. "You should have heard those Jews scream!" The women around him laughed. Encouraged, he continued. "I can smell a Jew a mile away. They disgust me."

Trying to change the subject, I asked him why he walked as if he were in pain. "I was wounded in the stomach," he said. "I've been in the hospital for four weeks. I'm going back to the Westwall now to return to duty." My ears pricked up immediately and I wondered how I could question him more closely.

Impressed that he'd been hurt fighting for the Fatherland, one woman asked, "Were you shot?"

"Yes, on the Russian front," he said. "A shrapnel wound. Those damn Bolsheviks!"

It was a warm spring day and the sun was high in the sky. Walking briskly and keeping pace with the rest of the group was tiring. Sergeant Major Werner went quiet for a while and then suddenly collapsed, folding across the empty barrow being wheeled along next to him. Hot and exerting himself after his spell in hospital, he'd fainted.

"I'm a nurse," I said, pushing my way through to where he lay. "Please, I can take care of him." We laid him on the road and I loosened his belt and the tight collar of his tunic and shirt. I fanned his face with my hand until he gradually recovered his senses. His eyes flickered open and he looked up into my face.

"Wh-what happened?" he asked weakly.

"You fainted," I said. "Lie there for a moment and get your bearings. I'm a nurse."

"What is your name?" he asked.

"Martha, Martha Ulrich," I said.

"Thank you, Fräulein Ulrich." He smiled.

I waited with him for a few minutes until the others tired of watching us and went on their way. Helping him to his feet, I told him to lean on me and we carried on much more slowly.

"Where are you going, Martha Ulrich?" he asked.

"To visit friends," I said, stopping to let him catch his breath. "And I'm looking for my fiancé, Hans. He's in the German Army and

I've learned that he may be in this area. I'm desperate to find him. Can you help?"

I reached into my pocket and pulled out a photograph of Hans.

"He's a lucky man," the SS officer said. "Of course I can help. I'd like to after what you've done for me. Why don't you come to the Westwall in a few days when I've settled back in and I'll see if any of my men know your Hans?" he said. "I can even give you a guided tour if you like."

His sense of smell must have been failing him.

After I'd left him at the entrance to the Westwall, I had a good look around. There was little outward indication of the underground bunkers, and the impenetrable dragon's teeth, or antitank barriers, were a few miles farther west. I'd half expected to hear the grinding noises I'd heard in Schaffhausen, indicating great activity beneath the surface, but all was quiet. The only evidence on the surface was the series of low concrete pillboxes dotted all around, and the extraordinarily high number of German soldiers milling about.

Having undertaken a reconnaissance, I went on to the home of Herr Greenwald, only to be told by his maid that he and his wife were out for the day. As it was midday, she offered me a much needed lunch before I returned to Freiburg. On the way back, I decided to leave for the Swiss border almost immediately to send a coded message to my unit concerning all that I'd discovered so far. There would be time enough to go back to the Westwall and see Sergeant Major Werner on my return.

Unwilling to take another train journey, I resolved to hitchhike back to the border. It was intensely cold that night, and my clothes did little to keep it from penetrating to my bones. Shivering, I found an open-back truck already loaded with soldiers and several other civilians. The driver told me he was heading for the southern edge of the Black Forest. The truck offered little protection against the weather and the wind, and it was deeply uncomfortable in the back, as people shuffled to make room for me and my suitcase, but we huddled together as best we could.

"Where have you come from, fräulein?" a young blonde woman with an upturned nose asked. "You're not from around here."

"I'm from Lorraine originally," I told her, blowing onto my fingers. "I lost my entire family in an American air raid. I'm completely alone in the world apart from my fiancé, Hans. He's with an infantry unit, which is supposed to be in this area. Here, I have his picture. Please, have any of you seen him?"

None had but they were all very sympathetic and wished me well. Above the grinding din of the truck's engine and the bumping along on the poor roads, each of them imparted their own stories of loss and sorrow, of sons, brothers, or husbands they hadn't heard from in years, and of the ongoing hardships of war.

"My family died in an air raid, too," one middle-age woman said, her hand to her face at the memory. "I lost everyone, even my little granddaughter. She was only two years old."

I squeezed her hand and told her I was sorry.

At daybreak the driver finally stopped and dropped us at an isolated crossroads. "You can pick up your next lift here," he said gruffly before moving on.

Lowering my aching bones from the truck, I was stunned to discover from a road sign that I was in an area called Wüertenberg, northeast of Baden, and even farther away from the Swiss border than Freiburg had been. I couldn't understand why the driver had so misled me as to his destination, but I was not in any position to complain. Dispirited, cold, and exhausted, I slumped by the side of the road under a tree with the other passengers, still clustered together for warmth because there were no blankets. I had no choice but to wait there until another vehicle came along and took me back to where I needed to go.

I hadn't slept all night because of the bumpy ride and the cold, and I soon drifted into a deep but uncomfortable sleep, my neck and shoulders stiff. My dreams were dark and full of sudden jolts as my body reran the unpleasant journey in my head. I must have been at my deepest point of unconsciousness when someone suddenly shook me awake violently.

"Fräulein! Fräulein!" I heard a voice say through the swirling fog in my head. "*Volle deckung!*" Somebody, somewhere, was warning me to take cover.

Still dazed, desperately unwilling to emerge from my slumber, I grunted and turned away from the voice grumpily. A huge hand grabbed my shoulder and shook me violently as the voice repeated, this time much louder, *"Aufwachen! Volle deckung!"*

Half squinting into the morning light, I yawned sleepily and inquired, *"Pourquoi? Que se passe-il?"*

There was no reply and I sighed and half slumped once more. But something about the sudden silence troubled me. Rubbing the sleep from my eyes and yawning noisily again, I looked up to find that my fellow travelers had gathered all around and were glaring down at me, open hostility on their faces. Blinking hard, forcing myself to think, I realized in a sudden rush of adrenaline that I'd accidentally spoken to them in French.

Jumping up in such a hurry that I felt giddy, I brushed myself down. Picking imaginary specks from my clothing, I tried to pretend that nothing untoward had happened.

"Sorry, I was asleep. Is there an air raid?" I asked in German, looking skyward as casually as I could. "I can hear the planes, but I can't see them."

No one spoke. They just stood, stock-still, eyeing me suspiciously. The Allied planes were flying ever closer and yet none of them looked up or took cover. Instead, they were shuffling still closer.

Smiling, I said quickly, "Air raid or no, I have to relieve myself. My bladder is fit to burst!" Picking up my suitcase, I scurried off into some thick bushes.

Think, Marthe, think! I told myself, looking around frantically from behind the scrub. In the distance, through some trees, I could see a road, and on it a milk wagon, being pulled at a fair pace by a huge black and white carthorse. Taking a deep breath, and not looking back, I bent double and ran as fast as I could through the undergrowth until I reached the second road.

Running in front of the approaching wagon, I raised my hand and flagged it down.

"Bitte, can you give me a lift to the next city?" I asked breathlessly.

"Ja," the driver nodded, and I gratefully climbed up onto the seat next to him.

The Art of Subterfuge

The city the milkman drove me to was still smoldering when we arrived, having become the latest target of the Allied pilots who'd flown in so low overhead. As sirens sounded the all clear, people wandered around in a daze, checking for damage. Several buildings were ablaze, and the overstretched fire crews and medical personnel were doing what they could with the dead and injured.

Tired, cold, and hungry, I barely took in the devastation all around me. All I knew was that I'd have to stop awhile and try and find something to eat before embarking on my long walk to the border, but I was wary of where I should go. It was extremely dangerous for me to go to restaurants, which were usually full of either German soldiers or nosy civilians. Even though I carried the relevant coupons, I avoided public places as much as possible, trying instead to eat with ordinary people in their homes. The fewer people who questioned me, the better. Worse, with everyone tending to those affected by the air raid, there'd be few restaurants open and my presence might be scrutinized even more closely.

As I walked on, considering my options, a skinny old woman shuffled out into the street in front of me, her spine curved with age.

"Fräulein!" she barked, "Come here at once and help me home. I'm too old and too tired to carry on alone and I want to see if my house is still standing."

I did as I was told, grateful to have the distraction of something to do. Helping her into her small house off a side street, I was pleasantly surprised to find it welcoming and full of charm. A fire burned merrily in the grate, and a waft of something cooking on the stove made my mouth water. Spotting a bubbling pot of stew and a loaf of bread on the side, I suddenly realized just how hungry I was.

"Is there anything else I can do for you?" I asked wearily.

"Yes, help me unpack this," she said, pointing to her basket full of basic provisions such as candles and salt. As I did so, she sat down in a large wooden chair by the fire and studied what she could see of me more closely. "Who are you, anyway?" she asked, her tone still gruff.

"I'm a nurse," I replied, unpacking her bag. "My name is Martha and I'm from Lorraine. I'm searching for my fiancé, a soldier in our army."

The old woman's voice softened considerably. "I have a son in the army," she told me. "I haven't seen him for five years. The last I heard he was in Russia." Her bottom lip trembling, she dabbed at her eyes with a lace handkerchief and abruptly stood up. "Now, young lady," she said, "when did you last eat?"

My hunger sated, I bade the old woman farewell and continued on my way. I found myself hoping that the Allied bombs would miss her cozy little home again next time.

Catching a bus to the outskirts of the city, I settled myself down among a group of women and a single man, who was a noncommissioned Wehrmacht officer. To my great dismay, just like Sergeant Major Werner, he spent the entire journey regaling us with stories of how many people he'd killed in Russia and Poland.

"We'd take them from their villages, men, women, and children, and march them to a nearby forest or clearing, where they had to dig their own graves," he said, his eyes quite mad. "Then we'd line them all up and open fire. You should have seen them run as we strafed them with bullets. Like little mice!"

His stubby fingers did little running movements and he made a squeaking noise with his mouth. All the women in the bus laughed openly as the officer threw his head back and roared at the memory. I felt sick to the stomach. My recent meal threatened to reappear but, clutching my belly as if in mirth, I joined in the laughter as convincingly as I could.

I couldn't wait to get away from that man. Every moment with him seemed like an eternity. The stench of his guilt as he continued telling his appalling tales made me retch several times. Images of Stéphanie and Jacques made my head swim.

"Are you ill?" one of the women asked, concerned.

"A little," I replied. "I think it may be something I've eaten." I was very thin from not eating regular meals, and looked suitably under the weather.

I got off the bus as soon as I could and began walking toward the mountains. As I got farther from the Wehrmacht NCO and his stomach-churning tales, I felt a little better. After a few hours I'd managed to almost completely banish him from my mind.

The weather helped. After such an unseasonable cold spell, it was a beautiful day. The atmosphere was so clear and bright as I climbed up a mountain and started down the other side, I couldn't help but feel happy. My moments of real happiness had been few and far between since Stéphanie's incarceration and Jacques's death and were often accompanied by overwhelming feelings of guilt. How could I possibly smile when Jacques was dead and Steph was suffering untold miseries somewhere? But despite such pangs, the sunshine that day lifted my spirits, and I carried on with my journey.

Looking down into the valley deep in the Black Forest, I stopped in my tracks. There below me on the plains, spread out like a vast toy army, was a huge military encampment with men and trucks and armor all openly on display.

"Mon Dieu!" I whispered under my breath before running for cover behind a tree in case anyone should see me on the hill. Peering

out from behind the trunk, I watched, open-mouthed, as the machinery of war in front of me geared itself for action.

It was a strange feeling, being all alone, solely responsible for relaying the whereabouts of such a strategically important camp to my countrymen, without a map or grid reference and unable to write anything down. Fortunately, I had a near-photographic memory and could retain a vision of it in my mind. Looking all around, I memorized the nearest landmarks such as specific peaks, roads, types of forestation, and any unusual rocks. When I felt sure that I'd seen and remembered everything, I pressed on, the adrenaline pushing me faster toward my destination with the now urgent need to alert the Allies.

It took me two days to walk to Laufenburg at the Swiss border. Nearby was the farm whose address I'd been given, where I could report to my unit at last. My mind was buzzing with all I had to tell them. As well as the military encampment, I'd memorized infantry units, numbers, strengths, and positions. I had details of train times from Singen, defense posts in and around Freiburg, and the exact location of the best entrances to the Westwall.

I reached the small farmhouse at dusk the next day and knocked gingerly on the door. A young woman opened it and stared at me suspiciously. "*Ja?*" she asked.

"I'm Martha," I said. "Martha Ulrich."

Her face lit up and, grabbing me, she pulled me quickly inside, calling to the rest of her family, "*Mutter, Vater,* it's Martha. She's come, she's come at last."

Their welcome was overwhelming. Susanna, the girl who'd let me in, had a warm smile and an open face. Her eyes shone like dark pieces of green glass. She was the younger sister of Greta—the young wife of the Alsatian intelligence agent working for my antenna.

"We've been so worried," she said. "We thought you might have been arrested. There'd been no word and we expected you much sooner. We were beginning to consider fleeing."

I realized then, with some humility, that the lives of these good, simple people depended on my freedom. If I were ever arrested and tortured, one of the many things I could have told my interrogators under duress was the name and address of this German family. Hence their genuine relief when they saw me walk in unscathed.

Susanna led me to a small bedroom in the attic in which there was a comfortable bed made up with crisp linen, and a jug and basin. I washed up and lay down for a few minutes to rest before starting to write my intelligence report. I desperately wanted to sleep but knew I had to stay awake for a while longer and complete my mission. Part of my training had been how to write in code, and I'd learned how to use key letters from a familiar piece of poetry or prose to convey a message. The piece I had chosen for my mission was "Les Fleurs de mal" by Baudelaire, a favorite poem, which includes the lines: "The air is filled with the shiver of things which flee away," and "I have more memories than if I had lived for a thousand years." Using a coding system far more complicated than the one Stéphanie had used to convey her feelings to us, I carefully compiled my report.

Greta came to my room later that night. "I'm meeting my husband tomorrow at dawn," she said, her eyes bright at the thought. "I'll take your letter to him then."

"Thank you," I said, feeling sorry for this young woman whose love affair had been so horribly interrupted by war. She was not much older than I, and I remembered the blissful encounters I'd had with Jacques in Marseille and in the mountains of Vic-sur-Cère and how much I'd looked forward to seeing him. I also knew the bitter pain at parting, never knowing when we might meet again.

"Don't worry," I told her gently, "soon you'll be able to spend all your time together. With your help, the end of this war is within sight."

She smiled. "I hope so. I love Pierre very much. We want to have a family and grow old together on our farm."

Turning away so she couldn't see my eyes, I folded the coded letter in two and handed it to her. "There you are," I said, too briskly. "I'll be leaving first thing. I'll see you again next time I come."

"Very well," Greta said, her expression confused. She had no idea why her words had upset me. Stepping forward nervously, she handed me a long green skirt with an embroidered hem. "I—I thought you might like to try this on," she said.

Taking the roughly made garment, I wrinkled my nose at it slightly. "Well, thank you," I said, wondering how to reject it politely, "but I don't think it's really for me."

"That's the whole point," she said, her eyes twinkling at my obvious disdain. "It's what Martha Ulrich would wear."

"Not this?" I said with surprise, staring down at the plain serge skirt and jacket I'd been wearing ever since I crossed into Germany. It had been the most dowdy I could find among the clothes I'd brought from Paris.

Greta laughed. "No," she said. "That's not at all what a German nurse would wear. It's far too . . . well, far too . . ."

"Far too what?" I asked.

"French," she finally decided, folding her arms with great satisfaction across her chest.

I hated that German skirt. The material was so rough it scratched my skin with every step I took on the long walk back to Freiburg. But I knew Greta was right as soon as I put it on. My old clothes were too French, but oh how I loathed looking like a frump.

Walking toward Freiburg, I came upon more French men and women, this time forcibly deported from France into the compulsory labor service in 1943 and sent to work on farms in place of fighting men. Like the two young women I had met in Freiburg, they were homesick and only too eager to help, promising to watch the roads for any major military movements and agreeing to report on what they knew. With their assistance, I was quickly able to establish an extensive network of displaced French civilians who could give me vital information about the feverish activity for the defense of Freiburg.

With every group I came across, I always scanned their faces, in the hope that Stéphanie might one day be among them. Although her last letter had said she was being sent to Metz, I felt that she could easily have been moved to another area by those desperate for workers. But none of the faces ever matched that of Steph, whose image still haunted my dreams.

Gertrud Schröeder very kindly put me up again as I busied myself finding out everything I could from the French men and women still living and working around the city. In the short time that I was gone, there had been much activity, they told me. This part of Germany was almost surrounded. The French, Americans, and English were getting closer by the day, and the ordinary German people had started to panic. More and more soldiers were pouring into the city, and there was an air of desperation as the residents of Freiburg began to hoard food and secure their homes and businesses with sheets of metal or planks of wood.

Then I heard on the German radio that the French First Army under General de Lattre de Tassigny had crossed the border eighteen miles away and was breaking through.

With the French so close, I saw my opportunity to call in the favor I'd done the SS NCO I'd nursed after he'd collapsed. It was time to pay a visit to my "friend" Sergeant Major Werner with the poor sense of smell. It took me more than two hours to walk to the Westwall, and when I got there I was immediately struck by the difference since my last visit. There seemed to be nobody around now; the scores of German soldiers I'd seen earlier had all vanished. Near where I'd left Werner, I came across two young soldiers walking toward me along the road, each with a heavy backpack. They'd just emerged from what looked like the entrance to a large concrete pillbox.

"*Entschuldigung,*" I called, gaining their attention. "Please can you tell me where I can find Hauptfeldwebel Helmut Werner who was recently injured? He's a friend of mine. This is his telephone number; he said to give it to the switchboard operator, who would tell him I was here."

"He's gone," the older of the two soldiers said, as I noticed four more men in uniform emerge from the pillbox behind them. "So have the switchboard operators. We're among the last left."

"I'm sorry, I don't understand," I said, shaking my head. "He lives here. Am I in the right place? Is this the entrance to the Westwall?"

"Yes, fräulein, it is," the other soldier replied, a bemused expression on his face. "But as my colleague just explained, everyone has gone. We've had orders to abandon the Westwall in this area. I'm afraid your boyfriend was one of the first to leave, along with all the other ranked and petty officers."

Not disabusing them of the relationship they'd assumed between my "boyfriend" and me, I feigned great distress and pressed them further: "But that's impossible. He told me himself that the Führer gave orders that the Westwall be defended to the death. He can't have gone. He'd have said good-bye." I reached into my pocket for a handkerchief and pretended to be close to tears.

"The orders only came through this morning," the first soldier said, pity on his face. "There wouldn't have been time to say good-bye. This whole part of the Westwall is now empty. You won't find him here, fräulein. I'm sorry."

I thanked them and watched them march off. Waiting, watching the pillbox, I approached two more small groups of soldiers who emerged with their backpacks and told me the same thing. My heart raced at their news. I knew how crucial this information would be to the approaching French Army and I quickly rushed back to Freiburg.

Along the way, at the outskirts and in the center of the city, I came across several groups of soldiers manning machine gun emplacements. Their orders were to stay and stop the Allied tanks with bazookas.

"How brave you are!" I told them admiringly. "I've just come back from the Westwall and found it completely deserted. All the officers and men have fled southeast. You're the only ones left between the French Army and the rest of Germany. Please stay and defend us or we'll all be doomed."

I went on a short distance, turned, and saw that one by one they all got up and ran away.

In Freiburg there was chaos. Civilians were panicking, running to their homes to hide. "The French are coming! The French are coming!" people screamed as they hurried past, clutching children and possessions.

I nodded and continued walking.

Reaching the main boulevard, I found it eerily deserted. Shutters were tightly shut, doors and windows bolted, and not a soul was about. A stiff breeze blew litter toward me. Somewhere close by I could hear the distinctive squeaking of tank tracks. A few hundred feet ahead of me a French tank suddenly turned into the boulevard and came trundling toward me. Taking up every inch of its exterior were German POWs, clinging to it, placed there by the French to prevent German guns from firing upon it.

Inhaling deeply, I stood in the center of the boulevard, directly in the path of the tank. The POWs, thinking I was a foolhardy German, waved frantically at me to get out of the way. The tank trundled closer, its tracks squealing against the asphalt and jarring my nerves.

Raising my right hand, I spread my fingers and gave the V for Victory salute. The tank didn't slow. Some of the POWs started banging on its roof to alert the driver that I stood in its path.

"Achtung! Achtung!" they shouted, worried for me. They believed me to be a good if somewhat crazy German citizen.

Standing firm, despite the proximity of the heavily armed beast approaching me, I held my arm even higher. Holding my breath, my head was filled with the noise of its engine and its tracks as it inched toward me. Finally, the tank was so close I could smell its diesel fumes and feel the heat of its engine. The squeaking finally stopped. It had ground to a halt less than three feet from where I stood. The huge barrel of its 75mm gun loomed out over my head.

The tank hatch opened and a man's head appeared. It was a bemused Frenchman. "I must talk to the officer in charge," I said in French.

I arrived at French headquarters in that tank, much to the amusement of several officers who watched as I inelegantly dismounted. The HQ had been set up in an old mansion in the center of town, and I was ushered in to see Commandant Petit of the Second Zouave Battalion.

The major was a tall, elegant man in his late thirties. He'd been in intelligence himself, and initially was extremely wary of me. "Why on earth should I believe you?" he asked me coldly when I told him all that I'd learned, including the news from the Westwall. "This could be a trick."

"Call this number," I said, scribbling on a pad on his desk. "It is the number of First Army HQ. They'll vouch for me," I added, standing ramrod straight.

The major frowned and dialed the number. "I have a Martha Ulrich here who says she can help me with information," he said to someone at my antenna. "Can you vouch for her?"

Clearly impressed by the response, he put down the phone and studied me for a moment. "Are you absolutely sure about this information?" he asked. "Our biggest headache is the Siegfried Line. Our entire purpose has been to avoid it around Freiburg, but if what you say is true, then this is incredible."

Having assured him that it was so, he sent a patrol to check, and within a few hours they'd confirmed that my information was accurate. "The Westwall is completely empty in this sector, sir," a junior officer reported on the radio. "The Boches have all run away."

Major Petit looked at me and a huge grin broke across his face. Armed with this information, the entire attack plan for the whole area could be revised, and the thrust into the south of Germany accelerated. He invited me to dinner as his special guest that night and placed me on his immediate right. I was enthralled by the splendor of the dining room and the delicious meal, beautifully served.

"So now," Major Petit said with a smile after refilling his wineglass, "you'd like to be returned to your antenna, I expect? They must be somewhere back in France. I'll make some calls."

"No, please, don't!" I responded, aghast. "I don't want to go back yet, sir. There's still a great deal of work to do. My mission is far from over."

The major looked at me with an expression of fatherly concern. "Don't you think you've done enough already, young lady?" he asked. "There's still a war on, you know. These Germans aren't giving us any quarter. Don't push your luck."

When I assured him that I was determined to carry on until the bitter end, he finally conceded. "Very well," he said. "Tell me what you need."

"A bicycle," I said, flashing him a huge smile.

After dinner Major Petit had a message for me. "There's someone here to see you," he said. "He's a French doctor, a Dr. Schaeffer. He asked for you by the name of Martha Ulrich and claims you'll help him and his family get back to France."

My face coloring with anger, I shook my head vehemently. "No, I won't," I told the major. "This man did nothing to help me when I needed him. Offer him no such assistance and tell him I refuse to see him. Let him see how he fares now in an occupied Germany."

The following morning, before I left Freiburg, I made a personal call. Returning to the only "home" I'd known in the city, I knocked on the door of Gertrud Schröeder.

"Oh, Martha!" she cried when she opened the door. "Where have you been? I was so worried when you didn't come home last night."

"I'm sorry, Frau Schröeder," I said, stepping inside and closing the door softly behind me. "I should have sent word. I stayed with some friends." Before she could respond, I reached into my jacket pocket. "I'll be leaving today," I added, "but before I go I want you to have this." I handed her a folded document.

"What is it?" she asked, opening it and shaking her head at the incomprehensible French wording.

"It's a letter of protection from the French Army," I explained. "It's signed by Commandant Petit, the officer in charge of this sector, and will help you if you are ever in any difficulties with the occupying forces."

Gertrud was still shaking her head. "I don't understand," she said. "How did you get this?"

"Let's just say I have some friends who were able to help," I said. Silently, she followed me into my room where I collected my few belongings and headed for the door.

"But Martha . . ." she said, still trying to reason everything out in her head.

"Thank you for your hospitality," I said, extending my hand with a warm smile.

"Auf Wiedersehen," she said, still unsure what it all meant.

"Au revoir," I replied, and turned on my heel.

Armed with my new two-wheeler, I crossed enemy lines again that morning as the battle for Germany raged all around me. Hundreds of Allied bombers flew overhead and pulverized the last remaining pockets of resistance. Wehrmacht soldiers, retreating home from the four corners of Europe, became ever more desperate to save their own from Allied invasion and continued to fight bitterly. There was a new expression on the faces of most of the ordinary Germans I met. It was panic.

Leaving Freiburg, I came across a group of heavily armed German soldiers at the southern edge of the city. Stopping, out of breath, I told them how glad I was to see them. "You must stay and defend us," I said breathlessly. "Freiburg is completely overrun. There's a huge column of French tanks and a swarm of Arab and black soldiers, many of whom are raping the women. I fled just in time."

The men expressed their admiration for my patriotism, but as I prepared to leave, they began arguing about whether they should stay and face the French war machine or disband. I left them to their arguing, but turning after I'd pedaled a short distance, I saw that the argument to disband had won.

I must have ridden for hundreds of miles across southern Germany, garnering information and spreading propaganda wherever I could. In my role as Martha Ulrich, I became accomplished in the art of subterfuge. It felt so normal to me by then—lying to everyone I met about who I was and where I'd come from—I didn't feel at all guilty, not one little bit. It was as if I had two different personalities, and when I slipped into that of Martha Ulrich, I was so convincing, I almost believed my own stories.

The bicycle was a godsend, although it was very hard to push up mountains sometimes. Fortunately for me, there were always plenty of young German soldiers around, eager to push it for me. We'd walk companionably together as I made up my elaborate stories of the French military strength and tell them how terribly afraid I was of the dark-skinned soldiers. Scores of young men would gather around, their mouths open with horror at the graphic descriptions I gave them of what was happening in Freiburg.

Mostly, these young men were in complete chaos. Many of their officers and best soldiers had either been taken prisoner by the Allies or been summoned to Berlin to form a ring of steel around it to protect it from the expected assault. The remnants of both the Nineteenth German Army and the Eighteenth SS Armee Korps were concentrated in a compact block in the southern part of the Black Forest. Their intention was to break through our front to reach either the Bavarian or Austrian Alps, or find refuge in Switzerland. For those left behind, there was little cohesion or structure. They'd been ordered to stay and defend Germany until their dying breath, but the majority seemed to be fleeing south in the hope that Switzerland would accept them. None of them had vehicles or fuel, and most had walked for miles to get there.

Cycling down a steep descent on the southern edge of the Black Forest, I came across a vast convoy of German ambulances parked on one side of the road. I was surprised to come across so many vehicles with fuel in such a well-organized group. Repeating my sad story of having escaped and of my elusive search for Hans, I told of my sorrow at seeing the German Army defeated and having lost the will to fight for our Fatherland.

One of the senior medical officers in charge of the ambulances took pity on me. "Where are you heading, fräulein?" he asked.

"To seek refuge with a family down in the plain," I replied sadly. "They were the best friends of my dear departed father and mother, killed in bombardments of Metz by the monstrous Americans."

"You poor child," he said with a sigh. "The war's been very hard on you, but don't worry, it's not over yet."

I was dying to ask what he was doing there but knew better than to question him directly. So I continued to tell of my fruitless quest for Hans and regale him with horrific tales of the scenes in Freiburg.

Finally, unable to keep his secret from me any longer, he looked around conspiratorially and said, "We're heading for Switzerland. The Swiss have authorized our safe transit through, from where we'll cross to Austria. But there's a little surprise awaiting the French in the Black Forest." He winked at me knowingly.

"Ah!" I said, grinning at him and nodding my compliance. "A little surprise. I like surprises."

"It's not so little, actually," he added, delighted with my giggling response. "A bloody great big one!"

"Ah, a big surprise! How marvelous!" I cried. "Do tell me more." Privately, I feared that he might be referring to Hitler's much vaunted *wunder waffen,* and I wondered how quickly I could alert the authorities.

The colonel beamed at me, happy for the distraction of a young female audience. "An entire armored division supported by a great deal of infantry," he whispered triumphantly, "waiting in a massive ambush in the Black Forest." Unsolicited, he then told me the exact location. I thought back to the huge military camp I'd seen a few days earlier and wondered if it was one and the same.

With a firm handshake in genuine gratitude, I thanked him and pedaled off as casually as I could. As far as I could estimate, I was a good ninety miles from the nearest French unit and about fifty miles from Greta's farm on the border, where I could make contact with my antenna. It was mid-afternoon and I'd have to cycle very hard to get there before nightfall the following day. Bracing myself for a long hard ride, I headed southwest as quickly as I could without arousing suspicion.

After five hours I'd been cycling nonstop and still seemed no nearer my destination. I'd barely paused for a drink or a rest and had eaten nothing since breakfast with Major Petit and his staff. I was absolutely shattered. When I chanced upon a remote forest restaurant I knew, I had to stop. Resting my bike against the front wall, I gingerly pushed open the door. Peering cautiously inside, I wondered whether it was safe to enter, but my hunger made me risk it. There were no other diners, just the owner and his family eating at a table at the back of the room.

The husband, at least six feet three inches tall, heavyset, with a thick neck and a small mustache, stood up to greet me. As he did so I saw that he had a highly polished Nazi party pin in his lapel.

"Heil Hitler!" he said, raising his arm in salute.

"Heil Hitler," I responded, doing likewise.

"Where have you sprung from?" he asked suspiciously.

"Freiburg," I replied quickly. "I'm very hungry. Do you have any soup?"

Having grunted that he did, he turned as if to go toward the kitchen. I noticed that he had a pronounced limp, with his bad leg scraping along the ground. It was an injury that had presumably saved him from the front. Stopping at the table at which his family was seated, he said to his wife in a loud whisper, "You mark my words, that young girl's mighty suspicious. She may be an escaped foreign worker who's trying to seek refuge in Switzerland. I'm going to try and find out some more about her."

His wife, a large, square-set woman with blonde hair plaited intricately around her head, stared at me fiercely the entire time her husband was in the kitchen, heating my supper. Her three plump children did likewise. Every now and again her husband's head would appear over the wooden half-doors to the kitchen and he'd watch me closely, too.

My teeth chattering with fear and my jaw aching, I mulled over the choices in my head. I could get up and run out of the restaurant, jump on my bicycle and resume cycling, with almost no hope of outrunning any pursuers. Or I could sit it out and hope to fool them. Ultimately, there was no choice.

I heard his loping gait approach and braved myself for what was to follow. As he neared with my meal, I felt like a helpless spectator watching events unfold.

The soup smelled so good. Steam rose from the huge bowl of fresh vegetables and barley and a great hunk of bread sat invitingly next to it. My stomach rumbled noisily as it was set down in front of me, and I could hardly wait to start. I dipped the spoon in and sipped at the piping hot liquid, burning the tip of my tongue.

I was aware of the restaurateur standing close by, looking down at me. Ignoring him, hunched over my bowl, I carried on rhythmically stirring my soup. Without warning, he pulled up a heavy oak chair and sat down opposite me.

"Now, tell me, fräulein," he said, his gray eyes piercing. "Exactly who are you and what are you doing here?"

Still stirring the soup to cool it, I broke off a hunk of bread and slotted it quickly between my lips. With my mouth full, I had a good excuse not to answer immediately and to prepare myself mentally. Taking a deep breath, I swallowed the bread and began talking very fast, looking him straight in the face.

"My name is Martha Ulrich," I said. "I'm a nurse from Lorraine. I was staying with friends in Freiburg when the French Army arrived. The next morning I escaped, but I'm still terribly afraid."

"Why?" the man asked, his eyes searching for mine.

"There are so many soldiers, guns, and tanks," I said, gulping down my soup hurriedly. "And you should see all the black soldiers they have, with their white teeth and thick lips; I heard that they were raping every woman in town, and me a good Aryan girl."

I'd never eaten so fast in my life and my stomach felt stretched as I wiped the last piece of bread around the bowl. Pushing the empty plate away, with a tremulous voice I told my host how my parents had been killed in an Allied bombardment of Metz.

"I have no one left apart from my fiancé, Hans, who's a soldier, and he's missing," I wailed. I reached into my pocket and pulled out Hans's picture and his well-worn letters. "Do you think I'll ever see him again?" I asked, a convincing tremor in my voice.

The faithful party member patted my arm. "Yes, of course you will, my dear," he replied with surprising gentleness. "The might of the Führer and his armies is insuperable. There has been a setback, but Hitler will rise again and so will the Fatherland. Your Hans will be safe and well somewhere. You'll be reunited with him very soon, I feel sure."

The chair was pushed back and he limped off, wandering back to his wife and children. I reached for my jacket, unfolded some food coupons and money, and stood to leave as I heard him tell her, "She's perfectly all right, poor child. She's had a very rough time."

A few minutes later he returned to my table to inform me that there was a whole convoy of German soldiers with assorted wagons and carts heading south on a road just west of his restaurant. "I'll take you there," he offered. "I'm sure one of them will give you a ride."

True to his word, he did. He escorted me to the road, hailed an officer, and helped lift me and my bicycle onto the back of an old pig wagon.

"Auf Wiedersehen, fräulein," he said, waving me good-bye. *"Gut Glück."*

It was dark when I arrived in the next town and found myself in the small square. Sitting on a bench for a moment to rest, I was suddenly filled with the urge to stay in the town. It was about ten o'clock. Hearing footsteps, I considered hiding, but was too tired to move. An old man approached out of the shadows and asked me what I was doing there.

"I've escaped from Freiburg," I said wearily. "I'm on my way to friends, but I thought I might stop here for a while."

"Very wise, my dear," he said. "There's a huge roadblock out on the other side of the town, full of military policemen with nothing better to do than stop an old man, search his papers, and make a damn nuisance of themselves. My advice to you is not to go anywhere near it."

My lips white at the thought, I asked him if he knew anywhere I could find shelter overnight. "Certainly I do," he said. Pointing to a large town house on the opposite side of the square, he said, "See that house there? In it live the kindest ladies in town. Knock on their door and ask for their help, and they'll be sure to give it."

The man was right. The two sisters, both in their thirties, were kindness itself. They invited me in and gave me a bed for the night. Their husbands were both in the army and had disappeared. They had several children between them and shared the house. My story about Hans seemed to touch a nerve.

The checkpoint had disappeared the next morning, and it took me most of the next day to reach the rustic little farm near Laufenburg that had become my haven. Knocking on the door, I was greeted warmly and with open arms by the family I'd grown so fond of. Greta smiled when she noticed I was still wearing the rough green skirt she'd given me.

"I have a very important report to send," I told her as she ushered me inside. "When is your husband coming next?"

"Not for two more days," Greta replied, her face crestfallen. "He was here only this morning."

I'd missed him by a few hours, and yet it was vital that I pass my information to the French authorities as quickly as I could. I remembered the Swiss intelligence chief, Colonel Reinhart, telling me what to do if I ever needed help.

"I have to go to the border crossing at first light," I told my hosts. "I'll have to hand my information over to one of the border guards."

Their faces fell in unison. They tried to dissuade me from my plan, telling me it would be extremely dangerous. The German and the Swiss posts were not far apart, and the Germans watched for agents all the time. They had orders to shoot anyone suspicious on sight.

"Nevertheless, I must go," I told them firmly, thinking of the murderous ambush awaiting my unsuspecting compatriots in the Black Forest. "Now please fetch me a pen and paper."

Seeing they could not sway me, they did as I'd asked. I sat up all night writing out all that I'd learned in Germany, including the most important news about the ambush. There was no time to write it in code. I'd have to hand it over unencoded and hope that only the right people saw it. Sealing the envelope and placing it in a jacket pocket, I wrapped a scarf around my head and left the farm at dawn with Greta and her sister.

We crept out into the little lane leading from their farm and headed for the border crossing less than a mile away. There was only the eerie glow of the gray morning light as the first strains of the dawn chorus struck up all around us. As we neared the heavy barbed-wire fence that surrounded the post, we crouched behind a large conifer and listened for patrolling Germans. Hearing nothing, Greta pointed to a small hill.

"There," she whispered. "If you climb that hill on the other side of the wire, you'll reach a road, and then you'll find the Swiss customs house on your left. The one on the other side is German, so be very careful."

Shuffling forward with me, she and her sister lifted the coiled wire, so I could crawl underneath it. With her spare hand she quickly made the sign of the cross as I squeezed her hand. Lying flat on my belly, I wriggled under the wire until I'd reached the other side without snagging my clothes. Standing, I bent over slightly as I hurried forward, concentrating hard on my destination. My left hand was in my pocket, tightly clasping the unencoded letter, which would undoubtedly cost me my life if it were ever to get into the wrong hands.

The building was dimly lit as I approached, and there was no sound. It was still dark as I reached the glass door and tapped gently on it. Standing back, looking around me constantly, I waited a few moments, but to my surprise no one answered. The Swiss are so efficient and regimented that I'd expected an answer immediately. Peering through the glass, my nose pressed against it, I quickly scanned the room, which was lit by a bare bulb hanging in the middle of the ceiling. There was no one immediately evident, but its contents made me gasp and stagger back and out of the light.

A large framed photograph of Adolf Hitler glared menacingly at me from the opposite wall. On either side of it were draped the distinctive red and black Nazi flags, bearing the swastika. Three German caps lay on the table where their owners had recently thrown them. This wasn't the Swiss post at all. It was the German one. I had inadvertently stumbled upon it, my own death warrant signed and clasped in my left hand.

Retreating, I turned and fled before the sleeping Germans awoke and discovered me there. Running back toward the road, my breath making huge clouds of steam, I saw, about a quarter mile in front of me, a very tall man step out from behind a large tree and wave his arm frantically. He was clearly signaling me to come to him. My head pounding, I hurried across to him as fast as I could and virtually fell into his arms, whereupon he pulled me quickly behind the tree.

"Maidl!" the huge soldier cried, speaking Swiss German. "What were you thinking? I saw you crawl under the wire and head for the German post instead of ours. Were they sleeping?"

Unable to speak, I nodded.

"How lucky can you get?" he exclaimed. "What on earth made you go there?"

Catching my breath, I replied, "I was misinformed by someone who obviously can't tell her right from her left."

The Swiss guard nodded. "Now," he said, "you'd better tell me why you've risked so much to come here."

Swallowing hard, trying to compose myself, I finally answered, "I'm a Swiss agent," as Colonel Reinhart had told me to say. Retrieving the letter from my pocket, I handed it to my savior. "This has to be delivered this morning before eleven A.M. to Colonel Reinhart in Basle. It is a matter of the utmost urgency. Please see that it gets there."

He took the letter and nodded. "It will be done, I can assure you of that," he said. Something about the way he thrust it deep into his breast pocket was deeply reassuring. "Now, where do you need to get to?" he asked. "Can I fetch you an escort?" For the first time I noticed he had very blue eyes.

"I have to go back," I told him. "My work isn't yet done. Thank you for your help."

To my very great surprise, this huge bear of a man clicked his heels together and snapped his hand crisply to his forehead.

"I salute you, fräulein," he told me, towering a good thirteen inches over me.

With a quick flick of my right hand, I acknowledged his salute and headed back to the barbed wire.

The Beginning of the End

Greta was horrified to learn of her mistake when I returned to the other side of the barbed wire. "She has always had problems with her rights and lefts," her sister Susanna told me. "When she was younger, we used to have to check her shoes to make sure she had the correct ones on."

I assured Greta that no harm had befallen me because of her error and that I was fine. Inside, I was still trembling.

My plan was to remain at the farm to explore the border area. I was soon able to join in the family celebrations when Greta's eldest brother, Günther, returned to them from the eastern front, having been conscripted, like all young German males. A well-informed young man, he was able to tell me a great deal about the unit he'd been with and their dismal retreat westward. They were now based only a few miles from where his family lived, and were dejected and broken as a unit.

"You're a German soldier," I said to him as we pored over some maps at the kitchen table just before I was due to depart. "Your family is German. Why are you helping me?"

Günther pointed to a large wooden crucifix on the wall. "There's your reason," he said. "My family are devout Catholics and are restricted under Hitler from practicing our religion. Until this country is rid of him, we can never be free. If he remains, then the Catholics will be the next to be openly persecuted."

I nodded my understanding and resisted the temptation to tell him my own tales of life as a Jew under German occupation. It had been so long since I'd been to temple, so many years since I'd recited the Hebrew prayers my mother taught me, it felt like another life. Suddenly homesick, I longed to see my own family again, to walk with my sisters and my friend Sophie along the banks of the Moselle River, wearing one of the hats made by Cecile, or to laugh with them and my mother. I thought of our apartment in Metz, my parents' business, our friends and family scattered all over now. My eyes filling with tears, I tried to find the words to thank Günther and his family for their courage, but before I could, a demanding voice broke into my thoughts.

"Who's she?"

Turning around uneasily, I found myself face-to-face with a woman in her late thirties, hands on her hips, glaring at me.

Günther quickly stepped in front of the maps we'd been looking at and answered, as nonchalantly as he could, "A friend of Greta's."

"What sort of friend?" the woman inquired, her expression still hostile. She had long red hair and she flicked it back angrily.

"No one you need worry about, Monika," Günther replied, a fixed smile on his face.

Monika was a neighbor, the wife of a soldier at the front and the mother of six children. Clearly, she was interested in Günther. Having arrived unannounced at the farm when she heard he'd returned, she was put out to discover a strange young woman leaning over a table with him.

"What were you studying so intently?" she asked, stepping forward and pushing him aside. Seeing the maps, she frowned and turned to me. "Who are you?" she asked.

I told her my name and that I'd escaped from Freiburg, but that didn't satisfy her. Greta and Susanna came into the house then, and were upset to find Monika there. Greta did everything she could to get rid of her, but Monika's suspicions were aroused and she simply wouldn't go. Deliberately delaying my own departure, I sat with them all for a while, drinking and eating and pretending to be part of the family, until Monika finally stood up to leave.

"This isn't right," she said, eyeing me. "Something isn't right." Grabbing her shawl, she left in a great flurry of skirt and hair.

Greta jumped to her feet. "You must leave immediately, Martha," she said. "Monika's extremely dangerous. Her brother's in the police. She'll be back with him in no time, I'm sure."

"But what about you?" I asked them all, as this brave German family sat staring up at me, their eyes wide. "What will happen if she does?"

"Nothing," Günther said, abruptly standing to usher me out. "We'll be fine. Save yourself."

Within a few minutes I'd grabbed my bicycle and was on the main road heading east. Constantly vigilant, looking around for any patrols, I rode for all I was worth.

I didn't stop for about six miles, not even to catch my breath. Meanwhile, I worried about my friends back at the farm. If Monika had returned with the police, as they feared, how would Günther explain my presence and the fact that we'd been poring over maps together? I couldn't bear the thought of the happy family celebrations in his honor turning to grief for his arrest and imprisonment. I resolved to return as soon as I reasonably could to find out what had happened to them.

I finally stopped, near the small town of Waldshut, when I saw large wrought-iron gates, behind which a long drive led to a huge German villa. Standing sentinel was a German soldier, very spic-and-span, not at all disheveled and wild-eyed, like most I'd seen recently. Pulling my bicycle to the side of the road, I watched for two minutes or so and was surprised to see vehicles moving around within the complex, in addition to a large number of military personnel that projected a sense of purpose and structure. This was the most organized and regimented group of Germans I'd seen lately, and their presence bothered me.

Wheeling my bicycle slowly toward the gates, I stopped and smiled when the guard bid me good day.

"*Guten Tag,*" I said, beaming at him shyly. "*Wie geht es?*"

It had obviously been a while since he'd seen a young woman. "Where have you sprung from?" he asked, his eyes twinkling.

"I've just escaped from Freiburg," I told him, my demeanor suddenly sad. I gave him the usual spiel about the might of the French forces, my search for Hans, and my sad former life. Pulling out Hans's photo, I asked if he knew him. Fortunately, he didn't.

"What are you doing here?" I asked, as innocently as I could. "Are you preparing to take on the Allies?"

"Sadly, no," he said. "We're part of an entire German division pushed south by the enemy and tonight we'll be crossing the Swiss border and surrendering. Our intelligence tells us that the French are coming in great numbers east along this road and that another column is heading south on the road that joins this one over there"—he pointed to a crossroads a few hundred meters away—"and should be here tomorrow. We're outnumbered three to one, and we have orders not to allow our weapons and vehicles to fall into enemy hands. None of us want to become POWs."

"But who will save us if you leave?" I asked, feigning fear.

"Don't worry, fräulein," he said. "God and the Führer are on our side."

"Let's hope so," I said. "*Auf Wiedersehen.*"

Pedaling fast, I knew I had to find the nearby French forces and pass the information on. The capture of an entire German division would be quite a prize. Heading back the way I came, but farther west than the farm where my friends lived, I came upon a village close to a main road leading from the Swiss border to Freiburg. White sheets of surrender hung from every window.

Reaching the town square, I came across a dejected huddle of German men standing in a corner.

"What's going on?" I asked.

"The French are here," one of them told me, pointing to a French jeep parked outside a bakery in the northeastern corner of the square. "Don't go near, fräulein." They huddled around me, looking fearful and tense.

As they spoke I saw the jeep, a tricolor fluttering merrily from its hood. Moving to the edge of the fearful group, I noticed that the jeep held an officer and two heavily armed men. It appeared that this might be my best chance.

Making a dash for it with my bicycle, I shot out of the crowd and ran toward the jeep. Behind me, I heard the crowd baying for my blood as soon as they realized who I was. I didn't look back.

"Please take me to your headquarters immediately," I told the officer breathlessly. "I have some vital information for your commanding officer." The officer nodded and told one of his men to help me into the jeep with my bicycle. The insults stopped. We drove west, the Germans staring daggers at me but silenced by fear.

Sighing with relief, I noticed for the first time the insignia on the officer's sleeve. "Are you with the Second Zouaves?" I asked hopefully.

"Yes I am. But what do you know about the Second Zouaves?" he said, surprised that I'd recognized his badge.

"A great deal," I said, smiling. "Please take me to Commandant Petit."

Petit was delighted to see me. When I met him on the road, he opened his arms and embraced me warmly, just as Colonel Bouvet used to.

"Well, my little firecracker," he said affectionately, "I was wondering when you'd show up. Now what can you tell me?"

I told Petit about the enemy half division at the villa and how they were planning to escape that night. "There are hundreds of them," I said, "all very organized. I suspect they're hoarding a great deal of ammunition and equipment which could be very useful to you, sir."

His eyes bright, he said, "Wonderful. Wait till the general hears of this." He ordered one of his men to use the field telephone to call his commanding officer, but then, his eyes sparkling, he rescinded the order. "Better still," he said, "why don't you go and tell him yourself?"

Accompanied by a captain, I was driven several miles to General René de Hesdin, who was briefing his officers in a small clearing by the side of a road. He was of the old school of military men, and had only one arm after a skirmish in the First World War. His empty left sleeve hung loose at his side.

I had to wait several minutes before he even acknowledged my presence. Finally, looking me up and down in my dowdy civilian clothes, he said coldly, "Yes?"

"Major Petit sent her, sir," the captain said, saluting. "She's one of our intelligence agents and she has some information on the enemy, sir."

General de Hesdin sighed. A formidable array of medals decorated his chest. "Very well," he said wearily. "What is it?"

I told him all that I'd seen and heard and gave him the precise location of the German villa. "There's at least half a division there, sir," I said, showing him on a map. "They plan to escape to Switzerland during the night. They said there was a French column moving south on another main road toward Waldshut and they'd be trapped."

The general shook his head. "I have no knowledge of any such column," he said, and turned back to his staff, ignoring us both. The captain and I glanced at each other in puzzlement but neither of us knew what to do. I'd heard that the general was identified by the phrase *"Il n'y a pas de Boche"*—there is no German there—which he was known to utter prior to any engagements of his troops.

I had no choice but to leave, knowing that he either didn't believe me or didn't care. Returning to Petit, I told him what had happened, and he just shook his head and sighed. "He can be very difficult," was all he said. Later that afternoon the general ordered the Second Zouaves to kick the Germans out of the villa. Several of our soldiers were killed or seriously injured in the ensuing skirmish. That night the German contingent disappeared, unchallenged, into Switzerland.

The next morning Major Petit summoned me to his office. "The Swiss have made contact," he said, his eyes twinkling. "They accepted the surrender of that German division last night and now they want to hand them over as prisoners of war. We're to go to the border and supervise."

He and I drove there and stood on the side of the road as the dejected German soldiers were marched back into Germany as POWs. There seemed an endless stream of unarmed men—generals as well as regular soldiers—all marching past in complete silence, their heads hung low.

One prisoner was an exception. I heard him before I saw him, and when I saw him, I couldn't help but smile. He was the only one marching proudly, his head held high as he screamed abuse at his officers.

"This army is a disgrace to the nation!" he yelled in German as he marched along. "We've been victorious throughout the war but now we surrender like little children. The Führer would be ashamed of us. Our officers have let him down, as they have let down every countryman of our once proud nation. They should all be shot."

I listened to his ranting and knew that much of what he said was true. There had been tremendous respect for the German Army from all quarters. They had seemed unstoppable. Men of great valor had fought for what they believed in as they methodically cut a swathe through Europe and across North Africa. This was the first German I'd met who had the courage of his convictions. Not for him a dejected defeat. He would never have surrendered willingly.

Stepping forward, I stopped the winding snake of marching men by raising my hand. The vociferous soldier stood a few feet in front of me, temporarily silenced. His fellow soldiers, his superior officers, the Swiss border guards, and Petit all looked up to see what I would do. Extending my right hand, I shook his.

"I do not agree with you," I told him in German, "but I admire your conviction. You're the first German who openly professes his allegiance to Hitler. Few Germans now admit their Nazi past."

As a bemused Major Petit looked on, I waved the row of men on.

On the way back from the border in his jeep, the major said something that surprised me. "I'm putting you up for a medal," he told me. "For all you've done in Freiburg and here in the south of Germany. The Croix de Guerre. Here's the citation." He handed me a copy, and as I read it, my eyes filled with tears. I hadn't become a spy for the glory. I'd only wanted to follow in Stéphanie's and Jacques's footsteps and do what I could to help my country. To be thanked for my efforts so publicly was something I hadn't expected.

"Thank you, sir," I said, the words on the page blurring. "Thank you."

But the one-armed general had other ideas. He had to endorse the nomination first, and when it came to him from the major's office, he refused. "Sergent Lenôtre is not with the Second Zouaves" was his terse reply. "Therefore she doesn't qualify." So, the only the recognition I got was a copy of a citation that was never enacted. In a strange way, it meant more to me than a medal.

Major Petit asked me what I'd like to do next: "Are you ready to return to your antenna yet?"

"No, sir," I told him firmly. "I still have much to do." Asking for a jeep and a driver, I hurried back to the border farm where Greta, Günther, and their family lived. The French had occupied the area the day before, and the family were no longer in fear for their lives. They were delighted to see me.

"What happened after I left?" I asked Günther. "Did Monika return?"

"Yes," he said. "She and the police missed you by minutes. They questioned us all and arrested me and threw me in prison. But then the French arrived and I was released back to my family. Monika has fled."

"And you, Greta?" I asked with a smile. "Have you seen your Pierre?"

Greta beamed at me happily. "Yes, Martha, or whatever your name really is," she said. "He came back yesterday and has been assigned chief administrator of this region by the French Army. From now on, we can be together all the time."

"I'm glad," I said. Shaking each of them warmly by the hand, I thanked them for their help and their courage. "It's been a privilege to know you," I told them, before leaving in my jeep and returning to the temporary headquarters of the Second Zouaves at the Swiss border.

The events of the next few days were the stuff of history. News filtered through of the execution of Mussolini and then, astonishingly, the suicide of Adolf Hitler. On May 8, 1945, I was still with Commandant Petit and his men in the southern part of the French sector when we heard news of the German surrender.

I could hardly believe the war was over. People around me were dancing and singing and cheering and hugging each other. There was shooting and fireworks and celebrations everywhere. But my initial reaction was total shock; I felt numb inside. Yes, of course, it was marvelous that the fighting was over and the killing had stopped. I was relieved to still be alive, and glad that I'd done something meaningful to help. But inside, I was tormented by guilt at having survived. Jacques had relinquished his life for this war. A bullet through his heart had snuffed him out. My family was scattered to the four winds and I had no idea how they'd fared. Stéphanie, deported three years earlier, was still missing, along with Uncle Leon and dozens of others.

I dutifully joined in the celebrations with the regiment, listened to the fine speeches and the congratulatory telegrams, but inside I felt dazed, as if I were a spectator to it all and not a participant. In six long years of war, I'd grown from a naive teenager from a devout Jewish family in Metz to an independently minded intelligence officer who'd taken a vow of spinsterhood in memory of the fiancé she'd lost. I was twenty-five years old but felt very much older. Each year of war had seemed like a decade. Now that it was over, I felt vulnerable and isolated, afraid of what I would find when I looked for my family again, fearful of being alone.

But at first there was no time to dwell on such matters. There was chaos in Europe as the Allies jockeyed for position. Whole sections of Germany were being carved up into sectors, and it was first come, first served. The French were scrambling for a piece of the action, too.

Major Petit called me to his office. "Can you drive?" he asked.

"No, sir," I said. My family had never owned a car and I'd never had the need.

"Well, you'd better learn fast," he said, handing me some car keys. "We're leaving tonight. Our orders are to increase our spread and prevent the English and the Americans from taking control of the northern Rhineland sector."

Outside his office was a gleaming beige BMW, recently requisitioned from a private German citizen. One of his drivers gave me a one-hour lesson on the basics of driving, and several hours later I was behind the steering wheel driving in an all-night convoy north of the Black Forest with orders to occupy a Rhineland sector. I was fine until the truck carrying a cannon in front of me slowed suddenly on a hill and I crashed into the back of it in the pitch-dark. The BMW stalled and I had no idea how to start it on a hill, so one of the drivers had to teach me.

It was the hardest driving lesson I ever had in my life, driving all night, staring into the darkness, covering 180 miles. I thought of my father and the two or three driving lessons he'd had in Metz when I was a child. In exasperation, the driving instructor had told him he could do no more. "You are the father of seven children," the instructor pleaded, "please don't ever try to drive again."

When we arrived at our destination, I remained with Major Petit and his unit, still unsure of where my antenna was. For a few weeks I acted as his scout, doing all kinds of intelligence work, such as economic reconnaissance. Driven all over the region in a jeep, I took inventories from factories and businesses, trying to reclaim items that had been stolen from France. It was interesting and important work and my job took me all over the French northern sector.

Within a few days of the war ending I began to come across strange groups of people in the towns and villages, men and women—little more than skeletons—barefoot or in rough wooden clogs and grimy striped pajamas. Most of them wore funny little round hats and had open sores and a sour smell. Their bodies were wasted, unclean, and unshaved, and their dark-rimmed eyes peered out of their gray faces blankly, as if they'd forgotten how to focus. Huge ragged groups of them gathered in the squares of towns and villages, huddled together. The local people, still unable to feel any compassion for the deported they'd been brainwashed into considering as *untermensch* or subhuman, would shoo them away and throw stones at them.

Telling my driver to stop in one town square where the locals were particularly hostile, I got out and approached the third group we'd come across.

"Who are you people?" I asked in German, as they cowered from the insults of the locals. "Where have you come from?"

"The camps," several said at once, their eyes sunk deep into their sockets.

"Which camps?" I asked. "The labor camps?" I thought immediately of Stéphanie and quickly scanned their gaunt faces for any recognizable sign of her.

"Concentration camps," they replied, their voices at a whisper.

"The death factories," said a man in French who was probably not much older than me but who looked ancient. "The places where they exterminate Jews."

One by one they began to tell me the stories of the camps. I listened in a daze. To begin with, I simply couldn't believe it. It was unconscionable. I thought they were telling tales, that maybe they were inmates from a liberated lunatic asylum with crazy fantasies. But there were just too many of them for that. As they shuffled pathetically closer, eager to speak of the agonies they'd endured, I became increasingly distraught.

Of course, I'd been aware that there were camps. I even knew the names—Dachau, Belsen, Auschwitz-Birkenau, Treblinka, Ravensbrück, Buchenwald—though the names meant little to me then, or to history. They were camps designed to hold in "protective custody" those the Germans deemed dangerous—communists, Jews, homosexuals, Catholics. I hadn't exactly expected the Germans to treat them particularly well, but I'd thought that they'd at least treat them as human beings. After all, the Germans were our next-door neighbors. We had so much in common; some of us even spoke the same language. Their inventors, scientists, musicians, doctors, and philosophers had made enormous contributions to the world. Theirs was the land of Beethoven, Mozart, Einstein, Freud, Heine. Their nobility had married into some of the greatest royal households in Europe. They weren't far-off barbarians, oblivious to culture or knowledge or morality.

News had begun to trickle through about some of the appalling conditions the liberating soldiers were discovering, but working undercover right up to the armistice, and without access to a radio, I'd missed much of it. But as I came across more of these unfortunate souls on the roads of Germany, I began to comprehend the true scale of the deportations, and feared for the first time that my Steph might well not have survived. Stopping almost every group I came across, I searched for her among those harrowed faces.

A group of German civilians came to our headquarters to complain about the refugees from the camps. I was assigned as their interpreter. "These ex-prisoners are very aggressive toward us," the mayor told a middle-age major who was second in command. "They break into our homes and demand food and shelter. They claim we owe them. There have been some very ugly scenes, and the tension is rising daily. If you're not careful, there'll be riots in the streets."

The officer was most alarmed by the news. "Come with me," he told me. "I need you to translate." We drove to the center of town, where one group of refugees had gathered. Once again I was struck by their hollow expressions and sad eyes.

Jumping from his vehicle to confront them, the major stood before the group. "Tell them if they bother any more German civilians, they'll be shot," he said over his shoulder to me. "Tell them we won't have any more break-ins or trouble in our sector."

I stood silently staring at him, unable to speak.

"Go on," he said, glaring at me.

"Don't you know what these people have been through?" I asked him incredulously. "How can you even suggest such a thing?"

"I don't care what they've been through, I won't have civil disorder in our area. Now kindly do as I say and translate."

I did translate for the major, but not in the tone or the style he suggested. "The officer says you must try not to trouble the civilian population," I told the gaunt-eyed group. "He says he'll do what he can to find you food and shelter, but he's afraid some of you will get hurt if you carry on in this way."

The refugees crowded around me, some speaking Yiddish, some German, some French, many in languages I didn't know. "But we have nowhere to live, we have nothing to eat," they cried. "The people won't help us. What are we supposed to do?"

My sympathies were entirely with them. We had plenty of food and rations in HQ, but when I suggested to the major that we distribute some of it to them, he was appalled. It took some time to organize, but the Allies eventually set up holding camps for these displaced people, which meant a return to the barracks and conditions they'd fled. Without identity papers, belongings, or money, they were once again placed behind barbed wire and herded together like unwanted animals. It was terrible to witness.

Summoned back by Captain Zimmerman, I reluctantly bid goodbye to Commandant Petit and his staff and rejoined my antenna in Konstanz, the place with which—as the nurse Martha Ulrich—I was meant to have been so familiar. Major Petit allowed me to keep the gleaming BMW as a token of his appreciation.

"It's yours," he said magnanimously. "Keep it." He even gave me an official military requisition slip, entitling me to gasoline.

My colleagues were much impressed when I arrived in it. Even the civilians of Konstanz looked twice. There was very little traffic on the autobahns, and the roads were long and straight and tremendous to drive along. I was becoming a natural.

Captain Zimmerman, my commanding officer, ushered me into his office. "Congratulations," he told me. "I'm proposing you for a Croix de Guerre with Silver Star, as HQ wouldn't award you the Gold Star. You've also become eligible for a substantial financial reward for your work for intelligence in Germany. I'm authorized to give you a sum of 25,000 francs."

"Thank you for the citation, but I don't want the monetary reward, sir," I told him, staring straight into his ice-blue eyes.

"But you're entitled to it!" he cried, clearly shocked.

"I don't care, sir, I don't want it. I don't want to make money out of what happened. It would be wrong to accept. It would turn me into a mercenary, a professional spy, and that was never my intention."

Nothing he could say would dissuade me. I sat across his desk waiting to hear that I was also to be promoted to lieutenant, as I'd always been led to believe. But the promotion never came, and I never raised the issue. I learned much later that when I received the Croix de Guerre with Silver Star, he received the same medal, but with a Gold Star, just for sending me.

Konstanz lies at the southernmost shore of the great lake after which it is named, in a part of Germany surrounded by Swiss territory. The Rhine flows east to west through the lake and on into Germany. It was a beautiful city, full of lovely villas, and I was quartered in one of them with the other members of my unit. Colonel Bouvet was in headquarters, quite close.

A few days later I was reunited with him and his African Commandos.

"Chichinette!" he cried excitedly when he set eyes on me. "There you are!"

I stood to attention and saluted him, but he shook his head at me. "You don't need to salute," he said. "Just smile."

I discovered that the colonel had also awarded me the Croix de Guerre with Silver Star for having found out invaluable information for him during the war. The citation praised my "rare courage well beyond the ordinary, and astonishing physical resistance." Later, in the name of General de Gaulle, I received a much-prized additional star to my Croix de Guerre. The citation, signed by General Juin, described me as a "young Frenchwoman of exceptional courage who was able over several days to start a network of informants which provided for the intelligence services military information of the greatest importance, which facilitated to an extraordinary extent the success of the last operations of the French Army in the Black Forest."

I hid my ribbons away in a drawer, but Colonel Bouvet insisted I pin them to my uniform. "You've earned them, Chichinette," he told me. "Wear them with pride." It was a far cry from the yellow star I'd last had to wear proudly.

Until I found Stéphanie, I knew I couldn't rest. Knowing that she could be held somewhere, waiting for us to find her, I was determined to search for her in earnest. I asked the Red Cross if they could help me, but the answer was resoundingly negative. "We are not in the business of tracing lost Jews," a severe woman told me.

Colonel Bouvet was sympathetic to my quest and allowed Captain Ligouzat some time off to help me. With him at my side, I toured camps and hospitals, talking to the desperately emaciated and the dying to see if anyone could remember my little sister.

"Stéphanie Hoffnung," I must have repeated a hundred times. "Stéphanie Hoffnung. She'd be twenty-three years old. A beautiful, dark-haired girl. Please, do you remember her?" But they just shook their heads and closed their eyes.

I visited hushed room after hushed room full of these unfortunates. Little more than skin and bone, their huge eyes peered out at me from ravaged faces. I wasn't the only one touring the wards searching for loved ones, but they were patient enough to give me a few minutes of their precious time and tell me their appalling tales. In one clinic, a terminal patient from Buchenwald told us how his entire family had been exterminated. I shivered at the thought of Jacques's father, a man I'd never met, who'd also been sent to Buchenwald.

"They're all gone," the dying man said, his eyes beyond tears. "Marie, Alain, Renée, Pierre, and little Brigitte. I watched as they were marched to the fields and shot. I was on the detail sent to get rid of their remains. With my bare hands, I buried my wife and four children, and I didn't even cry. What sort of a monster does that make me?"

Ligouzat, standing a few feet behind me, let out a rasping sob and buried his face in his hands. His body racked with spasms, he couldn't listen to another word.

Turning to him, I pushed him roughly from the room. "Pull yourself together," I told him angrily in the corridor. "This man doesn't want your sympathy." But later that night I cried myself to sleep at the pity of it all.

Fred, now back in de Lattre's army, wrote to me from his billet: "The rest of the family are well and have survived, but I have some bad news. I've discovered that Stéphanie, Uncle Leon, and Pavel were all sent to Auschwitz along with Rabbi Elie Bloch and scores of others we know."

Auschwitz. I read the word and my head swam. When the Russian Red Army had liberated it in January 1945, their tanks battering down the gates, they found that most of the surviving inmates had been marched off in the direction of Germany. Only five thousand people had been found alive, all of them near death from starvation and disease. Huge mounds of corpses had been discovered. The news had been so grim that, to begin with, it couldn't be fully reported. But in the months since the gates had been wrenched off their hinges, the name Auschwitz had gradually become synonymous with hell on earth.

"Is there any chance of you getting to Auschwitz or to any of the Allied hospitals nearby?" Fred wrote. "Maman is desperate that you try. Please, Marthe, do all you can to find our sister. Without her, our lives cannot be complete."

Carefully folding his letter in two, I vowed that I would.

Truth and Consequences

My fears for Stéphanie were quickly overtaken by anger. While trying to decide what to do, I studied the map of our sector and found the name of the town in the Rhineland I'd been searching for. It was the home of Wilhelm Hipp, the self-styled "King of the Jews" in Poitiers, the man responsible for sending Stéphanie to her fate. I remembered hearing him talk of it with pride when he came to our house one day. I also knew, from Rabbi Elie Bloch, that he was a married man with two small sons.

Colonel Bouvet listened to my request in silence.

"I need two armed men," I told him. "I have the home address of an SS officer who was personally responsible for war crimes in France."

The colonel looked up at me. "Was this someone you knew, Chichinette?" he asked softly.

"Yes, sir," I replied, trying not to blink. "I hold him personally responsible for the deportation of my sister and hundreds of others."

"And what will you do with him when you find him?" he asked, his eyes fixed on mine.

"Arrest him, sir, hand him over to the authorities, and take his two children into care."

Bouvet flinched at the mention of the children. "Why are you so concerned about the children?" he asked.

"I want to seize them and take them away from him, as he has taken so many children from their mothers."

The colonel studied me for a few minutes in silence. "Very well," he said. "I'll sign your travel permits. Do what you have to do, but have Captain Ligouzat accompany you."

I felt unusually nervous as I entered the town and began looking for the address I'd carefully written down. Hipp represented so much that was monstrous to me, I wasn't sure if I'd be able to contain my emotions when I set eyes on him again.

He lived on the second floor of a three-story apartment building. When we pulled to a halt outside, the lace curtains in the neighboring apartments twitched. Taking a deep breath, I climbed the stairs, found his front door, and knocked loudly. Captain Ligouzat and one of the guards flanked me, and a second guard was watching the rear of the building.

Hammering a second time, as Hipp had hammered on our door so often in Poitiers, I tried to quell all thoughts of revenge. It was not something that sat well with me, but I had been unable to resist the temptation to hurt him as he had hurt us. I'd resolved not to harm his children, simply to take them away. I'd arranged with the French social services for them to be taken into care and raised as French citizens somewhere in France.

It soon became apparent there was nobody at home. Knocking on the neighbors' doors, I smiled and asked in German. "Herr Hipp? Is he in town? He was so helpful to me in France and I came here to thank him."

"Nein," they all said warily. "He and his family fled to the Russian sector. He's not here."

Biting my bottom lip, I thanked them for their help and backed away. It was a bitter pill to swallow, but I was too late. Hipp had slipped from my grasp, and I had no choice but to give up the chase. The Russian sector now held the two people I sought most—Hipp and Stéphanie.

When Colonel Bouvet told me he was going to Paris for the July 14 victory parade and asked me if I'd like to go with him, I jumped at the chance. The Russian embassy was in Paris, and a pass for the Russian sector could only be obtained by a direct application.

"Don't expect too much of the Russians," Bouvet warned me. "They don't trust anyone."

Despite his news, I was still hopeful I'd be granted my wish. But when I arrived, dressed in my uniform, I was told that the consul only spoke Russian and I couldn't see him without an interpreter. Luckily, I found a man in the waiting room who spoke French and Russian and who agreed to help me.

We were ushered into his ornate office and sat down in leather chairs facing a small wooden desk. My initial impression was that the consul was a Jew. He was of mid-size height, slim, and appeared bored. Through the auspices of the interpreter, I told him I was in the French Army and needed a pass into the Russian sector to try to find out what had happened to my sister, uncle, and cousins who'd been deported by the Germans from France to Auschwitz.

"Please," I said, smiling. "I need your help. There's a good chance that my sister is still alive somewhere, but I need to find her."

To every sentence I spoke, the consul leaned back in his chair and replied, imperturbably: "*Nyet.*" When I tried to explain, he repeated his refusal flatly. After several minutes I turned to the interpreter, annoyed.

"I don't believe for one minute that he doesn't speak French," I said, wagging my finger at the consul. "Most educated Russians speak perfect French. I think he understood every word I said and is just being difficult." I knew I had nothing to lose, but the consul showed not the slightest flicker of an expression at my outburst. He was like a robot sitting there, unmoved by my story and refusing me permission to even go and look for my relatives. Having given him the name of Wilhelm Hipp and a brief résumé of his crimes against humanity in Poitiers, I left the Russian embassy angry and frustrated.

Reunited once again with Cecile in Paris, we spent a long summer evening in her apartment discussing what we could do.

"Do you think Steph is still alive, Marthe?" Cecile asked me.

"I don't know," I said, unable to meet her gaze.

"But there is still a chance?" she asked, reaching out to take my hand.

"Yes, of course," I replied, looking up finally. "Of course there is."

After my brief reunion with her, I headed south to visit the rest of my family in Vic-sur-Cère, for which Colonel Bouvet loaned me a jeep and a driver. En route, I decided to detour through Poitiers.

Walking down rue Gambetta, I pondered how little Poitiers had changed since we'd fled—a period of three years that had changed me beyond recognition. When I'd lived here, I was a young girl, engaged to Jacques. Now I was a decorated member of the armed forces, an experienced intelligence officer who'd been robbed of my happiness and plunged into the world of war and danger in a way I could never possibly have imagined.

Lost in my thoughts, I was brought back to my senses by the sound of a man's voice calling my name.

"Mademoiselle Hoffnung!"

Looking up, I was delighted to recognize a man across the street on the arm of an attractive woman, a young boy at their side.

"Monsieur Charpentier!" I cried, rushing over to where he stood with his wife and son. "How wonderful to see you!" Shaking his hand warmly with both of mine, I grinned up at him in gratitude and joy. "I was hoping to find you, and now I've bumped into you. It's a blessing."

Charpentier blushed at the warmth of my greeting and introduced me to his wife. "Do you have any idea who I am?" I asked her, shaking her hand just as enthusiastically.

She shook her head speechlessly.

"Well, I'm one of the people your husband saved from certain death at tremendous risk to himself," I said softly. "He provided me and my entire family with false papers so we could escape from occupied France. Were it not for him, we wouldn't have survived. I have no idea how many others he helped. He's the most marvelous person. We owe him a great deal."

My savior reddened further and shook his head. "I was only doing what I thought was right," he countered. "It was nothing."

"It was everything!" I persisted. "Without those documents, we would never have made it. They saved each of us countless times, monsieur. I can't thank you enough."

His wife nodded and smiled up at her husband with pride. It was clear from her expression that she not only knew what he had done for us and others, but fully endorsed it. I was so happy to have found him, to let him know we'd survived and to thank him in this way. "If there is ever anything I can do for you in return," I told him solemnly, before bidding him adieu, "please don't hesitate to ask."

My next port of call was going to be just as emotional. Jacques's mother, Madame Delaunay, was back in residence, and her husband Georges—a man I'd never met—had finally returned from Buchenwald. He'd survived chiefly because his close friends in the camp, knowing that Jacques and Marc had been shot, kept the news from him. He only discovered the truth when he was reunited with his wife in Paris after the Liberation.

The Delaunays had been warmly embraced by the people of Poitiers for their double sacrifice. Madame Delaunay had been elected mayor, and her husband was appointed Deputy of Liberation in Poitiers and was already an important and influential figure. Their street was renamed rue Georges Delaunay in his honor. We'd corresponded by mail since his release, and I'd found the tone of his letters both comforting and warm. Knowing how fond Jacques was of him, I was eager to meet him at last.

After a brief emotional reunion with Jacques's mother, I went to see his father at his office in the prefecture.

"Monsieur Delaunay, please," I told the receptionist.

"I'm afraid he's in a meeting," she replied.

"Then please ask him to come out. My name is Marthe Hoffnung."

As he walked toward me down a long corridor, I could tell that he was not in the best of health. But as he neared, I was caught completely off guard. Those dark brown eyes, that half smile—always used to cheeky effect, in Jacques's case—were almost identical.

"Marthe," he whispered, his eyes glistening. He opened his arms and invited me into them. Burying my face in his chest, I held on to him tightly. There was so much of Jacques in him, I never wanted to let him go.

Both Jacques's parents were very pleased that I'd returned, and they made me most welcome. They each filled me in on events, and I told them of my experiences. Madame Delaunay had told her husband how Cecile and I had taken her in when she was so unwell, and how much that had helped. She also told me she'd found a bundle of letters hidden between the beams in the attic. They were mine to Jacques; one-half of the hundreds of love letters we'd exchanged from the day I'd escaped from Poitiers. I couldn't bear to see them.

I spent a few hours with the Delaunays. "Are you going to visit Jacques now?" Madame Delaunay asked as she led me to the door. She'd had him and Marc reinterred in Poitiers and buried in the local cemetery during a flower-decked funeral with full honors.

"Yes," I said, nodding. Kissing the people who would have been my parents-in-law on both cheeks, I bid them adieu.

It had been almost a year since I'd laid flowers on Jacques's grave. Buying some from a florist now and walking slowly to the place where he was buried, I reflected on how much had happened in the interim. He was no longer in the shabby corner of a Paris graveyard with an unmarked grave. Now the two brothers lay side by side with identical tombstones chiseled with their names.

I had no more tears left to cry, so I sat dry-eyed at his graveside, telling him all that had happened in my life since my last visit, and of my plans for the future. Over an hour passed and I was still talking.

"I'm going to have to go now, Jacques," I said softly. "I'm going to see Maman, Papa, and the rest of the family in Vic-sur-Cère. You were with me the last time I was there. I know you'll be with me again now, my darling. *Au revoir.*"

Leaving Poitiers with a heavy heart, I traveled to the mountains of the Cantal to check on the rest of my family. It had been over two years since I'd last seen them. They were all thinner, older, and wiser, but they were at least alive. They'd survived on the fruit and vegetables grown by Fred and Arnold, and milk, butter, and cheese for which they had bartered their crops. They'd had no kosher meat, and all but my parents and grandmother had eaten what meat was available. One day, my father gave in and agreed to eat the meat after all, but he was as sick as a dog after just one morsel.

"Papa truly believed the sky would open up and fall on him for what he had done," Rosy told me with a smile.

It was thanks to Fred that the family had survived. He'd organized an entire network of Jewish refugees and resistance groups to outwit the Germans in the mountains, with people watching the only two roads into Vic-sur-Cère night and day. Whenever German cars and trucks were spotted, they'd all flee higher up into the mountains. My little nephew Maurice was just eighteen months old at the time and he didn't understand much, but knew enough.

"I hate Germans," he'd tell his mother angrily. "They do not let me sleep in my little bed." As the German incursions into Vic-sur-Cère became more frequent, Fred moved the entire family permanently higher up the mountains, to the small village of Narnhac.

Until my arrival, the family had no idea what I'd been up to during my time in the army. In my uniform, with the decorations pinned to it, they could tell I hadn't told them the whole truth.

"But I thought you were a nurse and a social worker!" my mother cried, wringing her hands together at the thought of what I'd been doing.

"I was, for three weeks," I said, smiling, "and then I became a spy."

"Well, I'm very glad I didn't know that," she sighed, flopping into a chair. "I'd have been even more worried about you than I already was!"

My father admired me in my uniform, listened to my stories and smiled privately to himself. I don't think I'd ever seen him more proud.

I was equally surprised by what my family had been up to. Fred and Arnold were both back in the army, having seen action right up until the armistice—Fred in officers' school in Auriac as part of the First French Army, and Arnold in the Second Armored Division of General Leclerc. Rosette had somehow prevented the torching of their mountain village and the execution of all its occupants with an impassioned plea to a Wehrmacht officer in charge of a raiding party. Until the Liberation of Paris, Cecile had risked death every day just to make enough money for us all to survive. Hélène had continued to smuggle arms for the Resistance and print anti-German propaganda. Rosy, too, had been busy, acting as a runner for the Maquis and risking her life many times.

But all we could talk about was Stéphanie, especially after I'd told them all that I'd seen and heard. My mother went to pieces.

My father had his own theory. "Perhaps she's in a camp somewhere and has lost her memory and doesn't know who she is?" he suggested hopefully. "We need to find her soon, so she can come home and remember her life before."

"She might be a prisoner of the Russians," Rosy said, fueling his hopes. "If she were, it would explain why there's been no word of her until now."

"She's never coming home," my mother wept, as I patted her hand. "I knew that from the moment she disappeared out of the door in Poitiers with Hipp." The rest of us sat in silent contemplation of that fateful day.

"I have something for you," I told them finally, reaching into my pocket. I handed them Stéphanie's last letter, the one Dedé had given me in Paris what seemed like a lifetime ago. I had kept it ever since. My mother couldn't read it. I'm not sure she ever did. But my father read it quietly to himself, tears rolling down his cheeks.

Sometime later Fred got a chance to read it. Opening his wallet, afterward, he folded it carefully and placed it inside. "This letter will remain in my wallet, next to my heart, until the day I die," he announced, wild-eyed. And it did.

The news, when it eventually filtered through, was almost impossible to believe. In total, more than thirty members of my immediate family had been lost to the Holocaust—Uncle Leon, other uncles, aunts, cousins, nephews, and nieces, along with Rosette's father, Kalman, Rabbi Bloch, his wife and little girl Myriam, as well as Pavel and his Polish parents. Pavel was sent to Auschwitz less than three months after we were forced to leave him behind that night in Poitiers. If only we'd defied the rabbi and taken him anyway, at least one of those poor children would have been saved.

Leon, who'd saved his brother Max, only to be arrested himself, had survived in Auschwitz almost to the end of the war. He'd been seen in the camp during the very last days. But when the Allies neared, he was among those unfortunates the guards made march toward Germany in the snow and the cold. Anyone who fell or helped another or who couldn't make it was shot. Uncle Leon never survived that bleak January march.

I'd been nineteen and full of ideology when war broke out. With all this news to take in, I had a much more realistic view of the world. Despite Fred's eternal optimism, I felt instinctively that our beautiful sister had not survived, as the rest of us had been fortunate enough to. My mother was the only other one who feared the worst. She'd been somehow diminished from the day of Stéphanie's arrest. All the vitality had gone from her, never to return.

Undaunted, Fred and Arnold undertook exhaustive research in their quest for our lost sister. They sent hundreds of letters, Fred dictating and Arnold typing, and asked anyone they thought might be able to help—the Red Cross, the Russians, and any survivors of Auschwitz they could find. But meticulous as my two brothers were, the survivors seemed reticent and the German records at the camp only included lists of those who had been tattooed with numbers, not those who arrived and were killed. It was years before we discovered the truth.

Stéphanie left her camp at Pithiviers, southwest of Paris, in convoy number 35, as ordered by the Anti-Jewish Service of the Gestapo in Berlin, along with over a thousand other French Jews. She was one of eighty thousand Jews deported from France to Auschwitz in a little over two years. With characteristic thoroughness, the Germans had painstakingly listed the names, dates of birth, and birthplaces of all those in the convoy. My sister's details were on the list, the only record we have of her entire incarceration.

The convoy carried 532 men, 462 women, and 163 children under the age of eighteen. Some of the children were little more than babes in arms. Many belonged to whole families, deported together. The convoy arrived in Auschwitz on September 23, 1942, three days after it had set off. Some 150 men were immediately selected for labor camps elsewhere, and sixty-five were chosen for labor in Auschwitz and tattooed with a special number. The same went for 144 of the women. The rest were immediately gassed—just a handful of the two million people whose lives were extinguished at Auschwitz.

Of those who survived, many were treated with the utmost cruelty. Pregnant women were beaten and kicked to death, newborn babies slaughtered, young women bled dry by an army in desperate need of transfusions for its wounded soldiers at the front. By the end of the war, only twenty-three of that original convoy of 1,157 men, women, and children were still alive. In total, only 2,500 of the Jews deported from France during the war survived.

I have read a great deal about Auschwitz since then. For many years I simply couldn't bear to. The first time I saw a newsreel about the liberation of the camps, I had to run from the cinema and throw up. Now, I know what life was like in the barracks, within the electric fence, under the watchtowers; of the thin soup and maggot-ridden bread, and the twice-daily roll calls under the constant heavy pall of crematoria smoke. In an attempt to destroy the evidence of mass destruction at the end of the war, Himmler ordered that millions of corpses be dug up, burned, and their ashes scattered far and wide, so maybe Stéphanie's remains aren't even there anymore. We shall never know, and so far I have not felt emotionally strong enough to visit the place where she undoubtedly met her death.

We do know of several people from Metz who survived Auschwitz, but not one of them was ever able to tell us exactly what happened to our beloved Stéphanie. Few of them could even talk about their experiences there and didn't want to say. When pressed, one—a cousin of Rosette—told us only: "She's dead. That's all you need to know." We can only imagine the worst.

With no body to bury and no funeral to grieve at, my family and I were robbed of an important ritual. It was hard not to agonize over how Stéphanie met her death or what her final few months and then days must have been like. But we decided to believe that she died on the day she was deported to Auschwitz. It was Yom Kippur, the Day of Atonement, and—with her broken ankle—we like to think that she was carried unwittingly to the gas chambers and killed right away.

"We shall always mark Yom Kippur as the anniversary of her death," my mother announced, and so each one of us lights a votive candle every year on that date, recites Kaddish and Yizkor, and thinks of the sister we lost.

Years later, when both my parents were dead and buried in the

Metz graveyard, we had their tombstone inscribed with the words: IN MEMORY OF STÉPHANIE, BORN 10 JULY 1921, INTERNED 17 JUNE TO 19 SEPTEMBER 1942, DEPORTED 20 SEPTEMBER 1942. Nearby was a memorial to the 1,500 people from Metz who died in Auschwitz. Underneath the memorial stone lies a handful of earth scooped up from that of the notorious Polish concentration camp.

It was small consolation when I learned that the Frenchmen of the SAP in Poitiers—who'd arrested, interrogated, and tortured Jacques and his fellow Resistance members in 1942—were brought to justice and condemned to death for their crimes. So many were being executed. The killings were not yet over.

Now that the war was over and we were occupying Germany, Captain Zimmerman—like so many others—only seemed interested in what he could make of it for himself.

"I'm hosting a dinner party tonight," he told us the first Saturday after I'd returned to the villa in Konstanz. "You're all ordered to be there. Among the guests will be three Germans I've invited. You must be civil to them."

I was so angry I could have hit him. It was then absolutely forbidden to socialize with Germans, and he was not only breaking military rules, he was asking all of us to be complicit in the violation of orders. I wasn't ready to have dinner with any Germans. My pain over Stéphanie and Jacques was still far too raw.

"It goes against all my convictions, sir," I told him. "I don't believe I could sit at the same table as a German."

"Be there or else," he said through tight lips.

I retired to my room to consider my position. Zimmerman was making it untenable, but I knew I couldn't, in all conscience, eat a meal with a German. Picking up the telephone, I dialed Colonel Bouvet's number and told him what had happened.

"Stay where you are," he said. "I'll send Ya-Ya to get you."

The thin Moroccan arrived an hour later, and I slipped out of the villa and into his car. He took me straight to the colonel. "You're staying here for the night," Bouvet told me. "I won't have Zimmerman treat you like that." I did as I was told, thus avoiding the uncomfortable dinner party the rest of my colleagues had been forced to attend. When I returned the next day, Zimmerman was on the warpath.

"Where were you last night?" he asked, the veins in his neck pulsing.

"Colonel Bouvet summoned me to dinner and to stay," I said, smiling. "I had no choice but to obey a superior officer."

"Go to your room at once! You're under house arrest," Zimmerman said, his lips white. "In fact, as of this moment, you're fired! I'm sending you back to France."

His words shattered me. He'd sacked me as if I was nothing, had done nothing. He made me feel less than a servant. Running to my room, I dialed the colonel's number, and within a short time Ya-Ya was on the doorstep.

The colonel was even angrier than I was. Sending me on to the villa of the major in charge of several antennas, including ours, he told me, "I've called him and told him you're coming. You're to tell him everything that happened between you and Zimmerman. Do you hear me? Everything!"

The commandant was equally upset. Zimmerman was a personal friend of his, and yet he knew he'd have no choice but to act. "This time he's gone too far," he admitted sadly. Looking at my file, he seemed impressed.

"You were offered a great deal of money for your war work," he reminded me, "and you turned it down. I've never heard of such a thing. Why on earth did you refuse it?"

"Because I didn't want to be paid for doing my duty, sir," I said, sitting across from him. "I'm not a mercenary. It didn't feel right."

The commandant immediately assigned me and most of Zimmerman's staff to another intelligence unit based in Lindau. In front of me, he dialed Zimmerman's number and told him I was in his office and had reported him for inviting Germans to dinner, against regulations. He summoned him the following morning. The punishment was harsh. Zimmerman was due to be promoted to head of intelligence for a large German city, but instead he was sent to a small village in the mountains. His staff was cut to a single man, Lieutenant Verin.

Lindau in Bavaria was on the north shore of Lake Konstanz, close to the Austrian border. Our headquarters was in a magnificent villa that had once been the home of Martin Bormann, Hitler's personal secretary and one of his closest advisers. Our antenna was under the command of Captain Millot, who'd followed de Gaulle to England. We became very good friends. Assigned by him to the French government of Lindau, my job was to recruit local people for intelligence work and continue with economic renaissance. Every country was jockeying for position and chattels, from land to Germany's finest brains.

My new colonel, Bavois, was a very nice man, who accepted me immediately. I was introduced as Marthe Lenôtre and he never knew my real name. As part of the military delegation, my official position was being in charge of all the passes for those who wanted to travel between Bavaria and the rest of Germany. I was given a huge office, a severe-looking German secretary, and a telephone directly connected to my antenna. No Germans could travel anywhere in the region, or have friends or family visit them, without my authorization. It was left to me how I managed it, but I knew exactly what to do. I'd learned from the Germans in Poitiers. I organized it in just the same way, with fingerprints and photographs and an identity card. More than fifty thousand people had to register, just as the Germans had made us.

My unofficial job was to recruit Germans willing to give us information on the other sectors in exchange for travel passes. Everyone was vying with everyone else for information between the English, French, Americans, and Russians. It was a hotbed of spies. One day the French military police arrived at my office to arrest my secretary. It seemed she was spying for the Americans, although she must have had thin pickings from me. I'd never liked or trusted her, and was always very careful not to show her anything important or to let her overhear conversations.

Everyone who wanted a travel permit had come to see me personally, and I watched the way they spoke to me and how they looked. I remembered all that I'd learned interrogating prisoners of war, working on hunches and gut feelings. Women's intuition, maybe. If I felt a German could be a candidate for us, I would ask him or her to come back the next day at a certain hour. At the designated time, one of our officers would arrive and wait. I'd usher the candidate into the officer's room and leave them to negotiate. Most of them accepted. We never knew if they were working as double agents but it was a risk we had to take.

Colonel Bavois told me to requisition some lodgings for myself and gave me a list. I found a beautiful villa on a little hill overlooking the lake, west of Lindau, owned by a wealthy businessman and his wife. They were in their fifties, with no children, and were initially indignant at my arrival.

"I shall take the ground floor and you can live on the first floor," I told them. "We can share the kitchen, if you behave."

The husband tried to protest but I cut him short. "Do you know what happened in France?" I said. "Do you know how many homes and businesses were seized by your countrymen? If you refuse to cooperate, I have the authority to seize this property and take it from you anyway."

His wife calmed him down and immediately agreed to my terms. I had a large dining room and a beautiful living room and an office with a large desk. I did a great deal of work at home. I had a maid to clean and cook and I hosted many dinner parties for my friends in that beautiful house. Colonel Bouvet was a regular caller. He'd given me the pin of the African Commandos and made me an honorary member. He made me feel like an adopted daughter. My work kept me extremely busy, and I had little time to feel lonely, though I often missed my family.

Most nights, I joined Captain Millot, his wife, and the other officers of our antenna for dinner. We also socialized with the Americans, English, and Russians at the Officers' Club in Lindau. I never had a shortage of dance partners, but I always suspected it was more because they wanted to find out who I was and what I was up to rather than because they were attracted to me. There hadn't been anyone in my life since Jacques, and I'd been true to my vow. I'd met several officers I found attractive and who seemed to like me, but I never wanted to have a relationship with them; it wouldn't have felt right.

In time my relationship with the owners of the villa mellowed. Once they realized I wasn't a hell-raiser, and I'd come to understand their position a little better, we became civil to each other. There were plenty of horror stories from their friends whose homes had been wrecked by their occupants. I was no vandal and I treated them and their home with respect. That first Christmas they put a little Christmas tree in my apartment—not realizing I was Jewish—and left me all kinds of cookies and goodies to eat. In turn, I told the maid to leave all the party food leftovers for them in the kitchen. I had far greater access to luxury foods than they. There were times when I wanted to explain, to tell them what had happened to my family, but I never did. At times it was difficult to resent individuals who'd never personally done anything against me or my family. I didn't want to be friends, but I didn't want them to hate me, either. I was torn.

When the wife was taken ill and had to have a hysterectomy, I went to visit her in the hospital with some fruit. She was amazed to see me. "*Danke schön, fräulein,*" she said weakly from her bed.

I'm going to have to leave this country soon, I thought as I left. I felt I was in danger of forgetting what the Germans had done to us.

One day I received a message from Fred. He'd had a letter from Eddie Seinfeld, an old friend of his, an American of Czech descent whose two sisters were in a displaced persons camp in Germany, somewhere in the English sector. "I'll sponsor them," Eddie's letter said. "If you or your sister could somehow get to see them and give them my endorsement, they'll finally be freed." The two women had been captured by the Germans and forced into labor camps. When the Allies liberated them, they found themselves homeless, a long way from home, and without any knowledge of how the rest of their family had fared.

Before I took Eddie's letter to the English intelligence HQ in a villa not far from mine, I'd been told by Captain Millot to use the opportunity to spy on the English while I was there and find out as much as I could.

"Maybe you could even try to steal some documents from a desk?" he said hopefully. I doubted it very much.

Arriving at the English HQ, I was shown into a huge room with big windows that had a view of the lake and told to wait. I was left for over half an hour. The room was completely overlooked by rooms on the second floor, and I was sure I was being watched the entire time. I stood by the window near the desk and tried to read what was on it but couldn't, for fear of being caught.

Finally, someone came in and took my letter. I may not have been able to glean any information for my antenna, but because of my visit, the Seinfeld sisters were freed to go to America and start a new life.

My job became ever more demanding, not least because of a change of command. My new boss was Lieutenant Colonel Goiset, who treated me badly from the start. Although I was only a sergeant, I'd always been given the privilege, as chief of a department, of eating in the officers' mess. Goiset resented my presence in the mess and spent every meal trying to demean me. It drove him crazy that I wouldn't rise to it. One day he bragged that the daughter of a general he admired had been in a tank during a skirmish.

Without looking up from my meal, I said quietly, "I have, too. I was once in an armored vehicle behind a tank that was blown up by a German panzer tank, killing all the occupants."

Goiset was furious. Since my intelligence identity was a secret, he didn't know who I was, but he had his suspicions. He used to carry out spot checks on the way I ran my office and would write me reports telling me to do all the things I was already doing, so they would look like they'd been his idea all along. He hated the fact that I had so much power, and even more, that he had so little over me.

One day Captain Millot contacted me and asked me to accompany two French officers on a secret mission into the American sector. As a rule, we didn't normally go into other sectors, and the request was unusual. A car came to collect me, and all three of us were in uniform. The men I was with were extremely cautious.

"The Americans mustn't find out what we're doing or why," I was told several times. "This is top secret."

The two addresses we'd been given were in a city not far from Frankfurt, along the Rhine. They were the homes of two of Germany's finest atomic and nuclear scientists, who'd been working on the V-1 and V-2 bombs for Hitler. With me acting as interpreter, the two French officers made lucrative offers to the scientists to work for the French government. The scientists were both family men, and they admitted the Americans, English, and Russians had already approached them.

Each one told me that they'd much prefer to live in France, that it would be closer to home, nearer to their friends and families, and that they felt a far greater affinity with the French.

The negotiations were extremely delicate and took three days. We lived in a nearby hotel but ate our meals with their families. It would have been too risky to dine out and be seen with them. Once the deal had been struck and the two men agreed to be moved to the French sector, they contacted their friends and former colleagues on our behalf and several of Germany's top-ranking scientists were successfully poached from under the Americans' noses. Within weeks they and their families had all been smuggled out.

Goiset was in no better mood when I returned. A man who wanted a travel permit for himself and his family had offered me a bribe of a wristwatch, and I'd ordered his immediate arrest. Bribes were commonplace, but I was dead set against the practice. At the request of Colonel Goiset, Major Renard interrogated me about the bribe. Renard had been a military judge in the First World War and condemned to death many who had revolted against the war of the trenches. He even received a medal for it, although he'd never seen any active service himself, which made me dislike him even more. How could someone who'd never fought know what it was like for those young men in the trenches? My own experiences had taught me not to judge other people for what they do or don't do. Only they know the reason in their hearts. I could so easily have been accused of cowardice when I was too frightened to lift myself out of that field the day I crossed into Germany. I only did it in the end because the fear of being called a coward was worse than the fear of dying.

After two hours of having a lamp shone in my face and Renard barking questions at me as a stenographer took down my every word, he received a call from Lieutenant Tallichet, whom I'd already alerted, and I was immediately released. It was November 1945.

Goiset continued to do everything he could to get rid of me. A month later he issued a written order sending me back to my unit, and triumphantly—in my presence, over lunch—he announced my imminent departure. Captain Millot's complaint to Army HQ resulted in the quick rescinding of my reassignment. To my great enjoyment, Goiset announced the next day at lunchtime: "Fortunately, we'll be able to keep Mademoiselle Lenôtre in our midst, after all." Repressing laughter, I thanked him.

Until he became my boss, I'd liked my work. It was very exciting and I enjoyed my life in the army. I knew civilian life would be boring by comparison. Having lived through so much excitement, it would be difficult to return to a normal life.

Not that there weren't other job offers on the table. Colonel Bouvet had already offered me a full-time job with him. Intelligence work was fast becoming pivotal in postwar Europe, and my role there would undoubtedly have been challenging. "Come and work with me, Chichinette," he pleaded. "I promise you'll never regret it." But against my better judgment, I told him no.

Frustrated that his plan had been thwarted, Goiset began to make my daily life a misery. Feeling I'd been sufficiently vindicated by his second public announcement, I decided it was time to go. My decision to leave Germany was also based on my fear that I was getting too much of a swollen head. Power is a strange commodity, and I wasn't sure I handled it terribly well. I was growing accustomed to people doing my bidding and being in awe of me. Remembering my roots and what my family meant to me, I felt it was becoming unhealthy to remain in the intelligence environment. I wanted to go back to real life and real people.

In January 14, 1946, I finally applied to leave. My life as the unlikeliest of spies was over.

New Horizons

Jacques had never been far from my mind, and now that the war was over I thought of him more than ever. We'd had so many plans, he and I. Once peace came, we were to travel the world and work in medicine, alleviating instead of inflicting pain and suffering.

"We'll go to Indochina together one day and save lives, side by side," he'd told me. The memory of his enthusiasm for the Far East filled me with a sudden urge to fulfill his dream and keep the promise we'd made to each other before his death.

In December 1945, I volunteered for the Corps Expeditionaire d'Extreme Orient, without telling my mother. Jacques's father, Georges Delaunay, wrote me a glowing reference, confirming that I'd never collaborated with the enemy or with the government of Vichy during the war.

"On the contrary," he wrote, "she has proven in all circumstances to be the best spirit of the Resistance."

I waited until I'd been accepted before I broke the news to my family. Maman was horrified and scolded me as she'd never done before. "You're only just out of the frying pan and now you've leaped straight into the fire!" she cried. "First you become a spy in Germany, and now you're taking off to a war zone on the other side of the world. What's wrong with you, Marthe?"

I did all I could to placate her, but she couldn't be appeased. Papa said little, and Fred, Arnold, Cecile, Hélène, and Rosy all wished me the best of luck.

Indochina was one of the last frontiers of the war. Although Japan was on the brink of surrendering, many soldiers laid down their weapons only when French troops landed in Saigon. Others continued fighting, and the French troops there were under constant attack. Doctors and nurses were badly needed. I was assigned to a troop ship, one of the first postwar convoys with the French Expeditionary Corps, leaving Marseille in February 1946.

In preparation, I was sent to a military camp just outside the port town and vaccinated against just about every tropical disease. Most of the women in the convoy had never been in the army before and—apart from me—there was only one other nurse, a woman named Yvette, who'd served in Europe with another commando unit and had been decorated. As a registered nurse, I was equivalent to a lieutenant. Finally, I'd been restored to my legitimate rank.

On February 6, 180 women and four thousand men boarded the ship, a huge military transport vessel. The twenty or so registered nurses were given a dorm in a first-class cabin, in which the air-conditioning didn't work. The rest of the women were ambulance drivers, nurse's aides, clerks, or technicians. It was extremely dangerous, since we carried all sorts of men on board—Foreign Legion, infantry, cavalry, Arabs, blacks, and whites—and among them were some very unsavory types. Stopping at Tamatave in Madagascar, we collected even more troops.

The women who were not officers were down in the hold, which was an open area. The first night there were several attempted rapes.

Women awoke to find men lying on top of them. The Foreign Legion immediately assigned guards to protect them.

My preoccupation, however, was with the constant motion of the ship—I was so seasick, I thought I would die. I rarely went inside after the first day. I stayed on deck the whole time with several other officers. I only went to my cabin to shower or change. I even slept on the deck, on a wooden steamer chair known as a *transatlantique.* Every day I tried to go to the dining room to eat, but each time I had to run out. I lived on sipped water and fruit.

The journey was to last thirty-six days, and took us along the eastern coast of Corsica, between Sicily and Calabria, and into the Suez Canal. When we went through the canal, a large group of us requested permission to disembark to visit the pyramids, but the Egyptian government refused. The heavily armed Egyptian soldiers who remained on board while we sailed through the canal were extremely hostile.

We were allowed off at the French colony of Djibouti, but it was stark and as ugly as sin. Across the Red Sea, Aden looked so romantic, with all its neatly positioned white buildings on a hill overlooking the water, but we had to be content with just seeing it from afar. We carried along the East African coast to Madagascar, watching people and camels among the sand dunes from the ship, and then on to Singapore and Indochina.

There was no work to do on the ship, so we behaved like tourists. I couldn't have worked anyway because I was so sick. When we crossed the equator, there was a huge fuss and the entire ship's company took part in the famous "Crossing the Line" ceremony. There was a big swimming pool in a sort of tank, and one man dressed as Neptune, carrying a trident, with his entourage, who all jumped in. Many others followed, and those who were reluctant were forcibly thrown in. Someone grabbed me and tried to throw me in, too, but I kicked and struggled and fought fiercely until my assailant gave up. Watching the behavior of some of the girls on board, I had no intention of emulating them. I'd joined the army for many reasons, but my expectations didn't include a promiscuous lifestyle.

Singapore loomed into view with all its lights twinkling. It was late evening and I was on deck, watching as we sailed past. The peace was shattered by an announcement on the loudspeaker. "Men overboard!" the voice boomed, and the searchlights were turned on. Five men, Germans from a French Foreign Legion regiment, were seen in the sea, swimming to Singapore to seek political asylum. They all made it and landed in Singapore, only to be arrested and returned to their regiment later. As deserters of the legion, they were handed over to their own men as punishment. They were treated very harshly for deserting and bringing dishonor to the regiment. Most did not survive. The officers looked the other way. It was the way of the legion.

As we neared Indochina we hit terrible typhoons and my seasickness was worse than ever. I seriously thought I would die. I was terrified of drowning, and the ship was pitching way up and then way down and I couldn't have been sicker. I tied myself to the lounger as the waves crashed on the deck in huge bursts. It was horrifying. I was washed-out and wretched with fear and sickness.

We arrived in Indochina to discover that while it had been liberated from Japanese occupation and the enemies taken prisoner, there were still a great many elements that refused to accept defeat. The woman in charge of us, Captain Torres, was the wife of Henri Torres, the famous French Jewish lawyer who'd defended the Jewish watchmaker Schwartzbad in the murder trial that had inspired me as a youth. She was an admirable woman who'd organized the Corps of French women ambulance drivers in the United States and served with General Leclerc's Second Armored Division. She came onboard to greet us and went out of her way to shake hands with Yvette and me.

"Welcome to Indochina," she said, smiling warmly. "We have a great deal of work to do."

We were quartered in a dormitory in Saigon until we were assigned to our various positions. It was dreadfully hot and muggy. Saigon was a modern city, very crowded and lively. It was great fun to be carried around the city in rickshaws. Like tourists, we visited the various neighborhoods, particularly Cholon, the Chinese town. At the center of Saigon there were beautiful hotels, excellent restaurants, and elegant shops where made-to-order clothes were completed in twenty-four hours. We admired the very slim, young South Annamese women elegantly dressed in slacks topped with long, slit tunics. Watching these women, I wondered how our men could resist the exotic temptresses.

I was sent with four other nurses to a military hospital in Phnom Penh, Cambodia. Our chief was Colonel Coleno, a surgeon who'd been garrisoned in Cambodia for more than a decade. Along with his wife and children, he'd been a prisoner of the Japanese during the war. Perhaps because of his experiences, Coleno was not a pleasant man to work for and we had several run-ins.

Half of the military hospital was for French soldiers and the other for Cambodians. I looked after the forty or so Cambodian soldiers who were ill or wounded, with a Cambodian male nurse as my assistant. In another building were the wards for native civilians, directed by a Cambodian medical director. There was a strange setup in the hospital. The Cambodian soldiers' families stayed with them the whole time, sleeping on the wide veranda outside and cooking meals for them at their bedsides.

One morning I arrived for work to find a sergeant, being treated for syphilis, lying in his bed with the eight-year-old daughter of another soldier, who'd sold her to him for a few francs. Appalled, I started screaming my head off.

"How horrible!" I shouted, and pulled her from his bed, making a huge fuss. The sergeant complained to Coleno about my intervention and I was duly summoned to his office.

"You're a visitor to this country," he reminded me sharply, "and the people here have customs very different from ours. You have no right to apply your morality to them. If you cannot accept their ways then you should go home."

"But, sir," I countered, "the little girl, she's just eight years old. That man will give her syphilis!"

He shook his head and reprimanded me for challenging his order. "Do as I say or you'll be on the next ship home," he yelled before dismissing me.

Though still appalled, I realized I'd just have to put up with it. The colonel had the power to send me home, which was the last thing I wanted. Ignoring the smirks on the faces of the Cambodian patients all around me, I set to work with new vigor.

A short time after arriving in Phnom Penh, I volunteered, along with Ghislaine, a nurse's aide, to accompany a doctor, Captain Fairmount, to a jungle area on the border of Cambodia and South Annam in the Plaine des Joncs. We traveled in an ambulance as part of a huge military convoy. It was an incredible journey, not least because once we crossed into South Annam, the road we took was literally built ahead of us. The Annamese worked like ants in their coolie hats and black pajamas, building the road so we could pass with our trucks. There were thousands of them. We advanced as they completed each new section.

It was my first contact with the local people, and I was utterly amazed. Every time they saw us they'd bow and put their hands together. I couldn't stand it. I just wasn't used to it and I didn't want it, but there was nothing I could do. Ghislaine and I—wearing our mandatory colonial hats—bowed back each time, our hands clasped together in front of our chests. The captain, who'd lived there for years, laughed heartily when he saw us.

We came across a little village where most of the people had recently died of smallpox, and we vaccinated everyone—several thousand people, the soldiers, the road builders, and us. I'd never been bowed to so much in my life.

On the third morning, I was asked to participate in a reconnaissance mission along the river, with about twenty-five soldiers. We headed south across the muddy brown waters edged by the jungle. It was nice to be out on the water and to feel the breeze in my hair.

But my pleasure was short-lived when a bullet whizzed past my ear, and another struck our boat just to the right of me. Japanese snipers. A rain of bullets fell on us; there had to be at least five or six gunmen hiding in the trees. Hitting the deck, I tried to make myself as small as possible, as the bullets hit the boat and the soldiers fired back. My mind flashed back to the armored personnel carrier and the exploding tank. I wondered how safe our fuel tank was under fire. One man was hit in the arm and fell against me, his blood staining my white uniform. Closing my eyes and screwing up my face, I prayed to God not to let me die in that filthy leech-infested river. I was terribly afraid. Fortunately, the boat driver managed to steer us out of range and into the reed beds where we could assess the damage and tend to the wounded. Nobody died.

Returning to the ambulance in which we all slept, I was glad to get back to work, vaccinating people. It was a far safer option, even if it was terribly primitive. Ghislaine and I were surrounded by men at all times, and the only way for us to wash or go to the toilet was to wade in the river, which was filthy and full of leeches. I'd come out covered in them and have to burn them off with a naked flame. Needless to say, I soon developed terrible abscesses and skin problems—all over my head, on my eyes, my legs, my breasts, even under my fingernails. They were horrible and made me very sick.

When I returned to Phnom Penh, Colonel Coleno told me I needed antibiotics but said he wouldn't prescribe them.

"I'm afraid I can't," he told me. "You'd need to stay in bed and take intramuscular injections of antibiotics every three hours, and I can't possibly spare you." So I kept working.

I shared a beautiful villa with four other nurses. Each of us had our own room. We had a "boy" and his wife to cook and clean for us, and a modern bathroom with a shower. But I was often lonely. The climate was extremely trying, and it would have been so much better to share the hardships with someone. I thought of Jacques all the time and wished he could have been with me. There were times when I became very angry with him because he hadn't taken my advice in Paris to escape.

"You must go south, Jacques," I'd told him. "Make your way to Spain. I'll meet you there. Fred will arrange everything."

I couldn't help thinking that if he'd only done what I suggested instead of returning to Poitiers, he'd be with me now.

Coleno continued to be difficult in every way. When an Annamese boy of sixteen came into the hospital with a fractured pelvis, having fallen out of a coconut tree, the colonel, who had very little knowledge of new techniques, ordered that he should be moved every day from his bed to the operating theater to have his dressings changed. The poor kid would scream in pain and couldn't heal because we kept moving him all the time. I knew it was wrong but I was utterly powerless.

One morning, right in front of me, Puthyrak Praing, a Cambodian nursing student who was working with me, deliberately flipped the stretcher the young Annamese was on, sending him crashing to the floor. The boy almost passed out with the pain. I was so horrified at what Puthyrak had done that I slapped him hard across the face.

"Don't you ever do that again!" I shouted. "Now help me get this patient back on the stretcher."

Puthyrak reported me to Dr. Sompear Hong Sat, the Cambodian medical director, who in turn told Coleno. I was duly summoned by Dr. Sompear to be given a dressing down. "You had no right to slap your student, and you are lucky you weren't jailed for common assault," he told me.

"I know it was wrong, sir," I said, "but I couldn't help it. It was atrocious behavior on his part, to do that to someone in so much pain. Nurses are meant to improve a patient's health, not worsen it."

The chief smiled unexpectedly. "You're right, of course," he said, "but try not to lose your temper again or I will have you arrested."

"Thank you, sir," I replied. Pausing, I added, "Could I possibly ask you a favor?"

"Ask," he said.

"Don't fire Puthyrak," I said.

He looked perplexed. "Why on earth not?"

"Because that's exactly what he wants. He wants to leave nursing school, but if he goes voluntarily he'll have to pay back his tuition fees. If he's fired, he won't."

The chief smiled broadly. "You don't give up, do you?" he said.

"Never."

After nine months in Phnom Penh, I was transferred to Tourane (later called Da Nang), a port in Central Annam, where Ho Chi Minh had started a war against the French. Ho Chi Minh had been to Paris to sign an agreement with the French government stipulating no further troop movements, but Admiral Thierry d'Argenlieu, the chief of the Expeditionary Corps, had other ideas and sent troops to Tourane anyway. All hell broke loose, and they desperately needed French nurses to tend to the subsequent wounded. In January 1947, I was flown there and assigned to the military hospital to be part of a team under Captain Ricard, an experienced and competent surgeon who'd worked with the U.S. Army medics in North Africa. We were taking over from a team that had been there since the fighting began in late December.

As head nurse, I was assigned to the operating theater. We slept an average of two hours a night and ate one meal a day. Drinks were brought to the door, and we'd lower our masks and use straws to keep ourselves from dehydrating. There was a constant stream of patients injured in the fierce fighting. We lived in a villa across the street from the hospital but were rarely there. The hospital was in a huge park with enormous trees. When we were needed, the staff would go to the veranda of the hospital with a loud hailer and shout, "Come immediately." After nightfall, snipers hiding behind trees in the hospital grounds became an occupational hazard, making it very dangerous to cross to the hospital. With no one to accompany us, we'd always run like hell.

In addition to being the circulating nurse in the operating theater, preparing the instruments, supplies, and equipment for Captain Ricard, I was also in charge of triage, and had to decide who needed the most urgent attention. Since a great number of the injured soldiers were soaking wet from fighting in rice fields, our first priority was to carefully remove their clothing so as not to compound their injuries. I'd insert an intravenous drip, cover the shivering soldiers in blankets, and administer drugs for shock or pain if needed. In a tropical climate, even minor injuries develop into serious infections, requiring rapid intervention. There were soldiers of many nationalities and races—legionnaires, French, blacks, Arabs, and Annamese from various tribes. The work was constant. As soon as we finished with one group, more ambulances would arrive with fresh casualties. Sometimes we cried with exhaustion and frustration, and didn't even notice we were crying. The captain was devoted to saving lives, and motivated by him, we carried on. He was a great humanitarian.

"I need you to prepare all the equipment and supplies we'd require for a small medicosurgical unit consisting of six medical staff and six corpsmen," Captain Ricard told me one day, halfway through an operation to amputate a young man's leg. "We're likely to be moved north in the next few weeks."

While we awaited the move, most of my spare time was used to assemble the essential items. I had to fight the captain in charge of procurement for every instrument, pharmaceutical, and piece of equipment on my list.

"You're breaking my heart, Marthe," he'd tell me with a pained expression, each time I asked for something else. I wasn't surprised when I heard the rumor that he was selling supplies and equipment on the black market, to the Viet Minh.

After three relentless months, our team was sent north to Quan-Tri, scene of some of the worst fighting. Madame Philippe, the nurse who administered anesthesia, refused to make the transfer to the DMZ, or Demilitarized Zone, because of the danger, and Captain Ricard told me simply that I'd have to take over her duties.

"Here, read this," he said, passing me a small book on anesthesia. "Concentrate on the sections dealing with intravenous Pentothal and the administration of ether with the masque d'Ombredane. You'll be fine."

We traveled from Da Nang, over a mountain, through the Col des Nuages, and down again. Quan-Tri was a small town thirty-five miles north of Hue. It was of great strategic importance being on Route 1, the main artery extending from Saigon to Hanoi. A river flowing perpendicular to Route 1 bordered Quan-Tri on its northern edge. To travel north on Route 1, the river had to be crossed by sampans belonging to Annamese who lived in a boat village there. Bridges were far away from the town. Once we arrived, we set up a makeshift hospital in a former school, cleaning it up and whitewashing the walls. Among the meager equipment I'd pulled together, we had one oxygen tank reserved for pulmonary injuries. A generator supplied electricity, and blood, if needed, was flown to us from Hue in a little Piper Club plane. The only blood then considered safe for our troops was the O-plus type, which fortunately caused no allergic reaction in any of our patients. Our generator was used exclusively for the operating room, but there was not enough power for refrigerators. Later, the Foreign Legion came and installed a more efficient one.

The first few nights, the two other nurses and I slept on the top floor of the hospital. When heavy rain fell on the first night, we were flooded because the roof was badly damaged. The legion repaired it for us the next morning. We set up a tent on the back lawn for

Annamese civilians injured in ambushes and for wounded Viet Minh prisoners. A second tent, set up farther away, was the morgue.

After a few days the three of us were rehoused in a villa across from the hospital. The legion helped once more by installing an enclosed shower in the back garden for us to wash in. We took turns to be on night duty. Every three hours the nurse on call would cross a large lawn and the wide Route 1, lined with huge trees, to get to the hospital. It was very frightening. One night I was crossing the road when I sensed someone close by. Raising my hurricane lamp, I saw a man barefoot and in the trademark black pajamas of the Viet Minh standing a few feet from me, frozen to the spot.

"Halte, qui vive!" I shouted, and for several seconds we stood blinking at each other. I was unarmed and—to him—represented the enemy. Suddenly, he took off, disappearing into the trees. I rushed to the hospital as fast as I could. Later that night an Arab guard accompanied me back to my villa.

The next day, when I reported the incident to the lieutenant in charge of security, he told me I was very lucky. "If you hadn't seen him, he would probably have come up behind you and slit your throat," he said.

Whenever there was a lull, I'd travel south in a military convoy to the beautiful city of Hue, on the banks of the River of Perfume and site of the old Emperor's palace grounds, to supervise the transfer of our wounded and make space for the next batch of casualties. Deadly ambushes on Route 1 were frequent but I soon gained a reputation for being lucky, as the convoys I traveled on were never attacked.

"Let me know when you're next going, mademoiselle," friendly soldiers would say. "We want to go with you."

On one of my trips home from Hue, I joined the only convoy available. After many unexplained delays, we left in the afternoon, and by dusk we were still far from our destination. As no convoy was allowed to travel after dark, we stopped at a French Foreign Legion post at the top of a hill surrounded by deep jungle. I knew most of the men there; they'd either been our patients or had visited their friends in our small hospital. The post was under the command of Adjutant Chief Dalbret, who welcomed us. Dinner that night was served under the stars, and a choir of men sang beautiful Slavic songs. I thoroughly enjoyed the music and the excellent meal. Just as a song ended, terrific gunfire broke the stillness. The noise level was unbearable. All the men around me sat staring at me instead of running to their respective posts, hoping to see me panic and hide under the table. But I just sat there very quietly, smiling, having realized it was a fake attack to test me. I passed the test.

But the trips weren't always so cozy. One day, traveling north of Quan-Tri and toward Dong Ha in a military convoy, we paused at a remote French post deep in the jungle. As we arrived, we found the camp in a state of great agitation. The Viet Minh had caught two men the previous day, hideously tortured them, and left them dead on the outskirts of the post. The outraged French soldiers had caught a young Annamese, convinced he was one of the killers. When I arrived, thick ropes tied him to a tree. He could barely stand straight, he'd been so badly beaten.

My stomach churning, I asked who he was and what he'd done.

"He killed two of our men," came the resounding reply.

"How do you know?" I asked. "What proof do you have?"

My questions were met with howls of disapproval and unpleasant comments about my gullibility. On hearing a woman's voice, the prisoner raised his bloodied head and locked his eyes onto mine. Without uttering a sound, his eyes pleaded for mercy. I could hardly bear to return his gaze.

"If this man isn't given any water soon, he'll die," I said, addressing the friends I knew or the men I'd personally treated in Quan-Tri.

"He'll die anyway," came the reply. "Water will only prolong his agony."

The prisoner kept his eyes locked onto mine, and I fought the temptation to run to the tree and cut the ropes that tied him. "Please," I said, my voice breaking, "please let me administer to him."

The situation was hopeless, and both the prisoner and I knew it. But something made him keep staring at me, and urged me to keep pleading for him.

"Okay," the NCO in charge finally said. "Give him some water. But that's all."

Taking a container full of water, I walked over to where the prisoner half stood, slumped against the tree. Holding the container in my trembling hands, I tilted back his head and allowed him to drink from it as the angry soldiers stood all around, still baying for his blood.

Beaten to within an inch of his life, facing imminent execution, the young man, who must have been the same age as Jacques, looked up at me with such gratitude at this tiny gesture of kindness that I almost broke down in front of him. His lips parched, he swallowed a great deal of water, afraid to stop, knowing that when he did, my intervention would have to end. Finally, spluttering as his stomach filled, he turned his head away and allowed me to wipe his lips. Nodding his thanks, he gave me one last look before hanging his head again to await his fate. It was all I could do to stand and walk away.

In Indochina, I often found myself grieving for the people I'd lost and thinking back to my childhood with Stéphanie and my brothers and sisters in Metz. Steph had so wanted to be a doctor, saving lives. In a different world she might well have come out to Indochina with Dedé, accompanying Jacques and me. Now Dedé had married someone else and had children, and Steph was all but forgotten by him. I still constantly thought about what had happened to her. The climate and the distance from family and friends didn't help.

Although I made many good friends, especially in the legion, had a busy social life and went out a lot, I still felt very much alone. Among my male friends, Lieutenant Jacques Durieux, a colonial coffee rancher from the Ivory Coast whom I'd met in Phnom Penh, was charming and had even talked of our getting married one day, until I told him I was Jewish. He never talked of it again. Though I liked him, he was not someone with whom I wanted to share my life.

We were just three Frenchwomen among thousands of soldiers in the region of Quan-Tri. It was most unusual not to receive a marriage proposal several times a week. Sometimes the proposals came daily, mostly from the wounded and sick who fell in love with us. I strongly believed that marriage built on such premises could not withstand the return to a normal civilian life. I turned down my two most serious suitors, and they each married someone else. I was still determined to remain unmarried, my love for Jacques still alive.

One of my acquaintances, Captain Lenay, had fought in North

Africa and Europe. Unfortunately, he had a drinking problem. He lived with an Annamese woman in a villa two doors down from ours, and when he was drunk, which was most nights, he'd beat her and throw her out of the house. We'd hear him shouting and her screaming. Like so many other men in Indochina, the captain told me his life story, how his wife, who was also in the army, had abandoned him and their young son Serge, leaving the boy in a school in England.

A captain in Hue who'd been a school friend of Lenay's told me later: "He's great guy when he's not drinking. It's just that his life fell apart when his wife left him. He was terribly in love with her, you know."

Captain Lenay went to England to get his son, and took him to his mother's home in Brittany, but she was old and sick with diabetes and couldn't cope with a child, so he decided to bring the boy to Indochina to live with him. He even bought him a pet honey bear, Miel, the most adorable animal I'd ever met, and with whom I sometimes played. Sadly, the bear later died of an infection, despite my best efforts and those of Captain Ricard who treated him in the hospital.

Serge was seven years old when he arrived. He was happy to be with his father, whom he clearly adored. Not long afterward, however, his father was brought into the hospital, extremely ill. He had typhus.

"Please look after Serge for me," he pleaded from his sickbed. "My Annamese woman's gone. There's no one at home to care for him. You're the only one to whom I can entrust my child." I promised I would.

That night, I bundled Serge up and took him into our villa, giving him a bed in my room. He was very well-behaved and my housemates adored him as much as I did. All my friends from the legion came around to play with him, and he joined in with our dinner parties and social events. But his father became more and more sick, and since we were not equipped to deal with contagious diseases, he was transferred by ambulance to Hue.

"If anything happens to me," he told me in a rasping whisper as he left the hospital, "I want you to care for my little boy." A week later he was dead.

I was shocked and upset by his death. I braced myself for the unpleasant task ahead. It wasn't going to be easy, telling Serge that he was virtually an orphan. Sitting him on my lap, I held him close and told him the sad news.

"Your father's dead, Serge," I said, blinking back the tears. "He was very sick and the doctors couldn't save him. They tried very hard but he died. I'm so sorry."

"What's going to happen to me now?" the boy asked, dry-eyed. "Who's going to look after me?"

I saw his big blue eyes fill with tears, and I stroked his head and held him to me. "I will, Serge," I said, kissing the top of his head. "I promise. I'll never abandon you."

Serge lived with me for almost a year, sleeping in my room. While I was at work, he was looked after in the day by my Annamese "boy"—the Catholic father of several children, whom I'd nursed back to health after the Viet Minh had savagely attacked him and his family with machetes. When Serge complained that the "boy" had touched him inappropriately, I went to see Lieutenant Martin, in charge of the Foreign Legion.

"I need your help," I told him. "I can no longer trust my boy to baby-sit. Would it be possible for me to leave Serge at the legion post each morning instead?"

Lieutenant Martin flashed me the broadest grin. "It would be our very great pleasure," he cried. "Many of the legionnaires already know and love your little boy."

From then on Serge accompanied me everywhere, even on military convoys sent by the legion to collect us for dinner at their jungle post. He was much loved. The legionnaires became his daily baby-sitters, playing games with him, cooking him his meals, and making him toy trucks and guns. I'd drop him off before work and pick him up when my shift ended. We had such fun with the legion, who always treated us with utmost generosity and the greatest respect.

After several months Lieutenant Colonel Berthon, director of the Health Services in Central Annam, worried about Serge's security in the embattled DMZ. He relocated me to Dalat. We stopped first in Tourane to board a military transport ship for the trip to Saigon. Serge and I, accompanied by a host of friends, took a motorboat to reach the ship anchored in the bay. Once on board, after our luggage had been carried to our cabin, the ship's captain summoned me to the bridge.

"I'm afraid you are free to travel with us to Saigon," he told me, "but not your little boy. We have no insurance coverage for a civilian."

There was nothing I could say to dissuade him, even when I explained the boy's circumstances, so we left the ship and returned to shore. I spent an anxious day wondering how Serge and I would ever get to Dalat. Later that day an aircraft carrier anchored in the bay, and that evening a large group of naval officers came on shore. As was customary, Serge and I were invited to join a local party, this time to celebrate my aborted departure. A captain, the second in command on the carrier, was among the guests. When he heard about our predicament, he told me, "Be ready tomorrow morning to come on board with Serge. I'll see what I can do."

The next morning the sea was so rough that the motor launch couldn't get close enough to the enormous aircraft carrier *Dixmude* to even moor against the hull. The captain ordered it as close as possible to a small platform leading to the rope steps up the sheer face of the hull, and then he jumped. The swell was so pronounced that he failed in his attempt and fell into the water to the cries of, *"Un homme à la mer!"*

Serge and I watched in fear as the captain disappeared under the waves. The seasoned sailors around us worried that he'd be pulled under the hull and drowned. After what seemed an eternity, however, he reappeared triumphantly holding his hat and was safely pulled into the launch.

A huge sailor was dispatched to the platform at the foot of the hull and stood there, feet well apart, ready for anything. The launch kept turning to approach the carrier as close as possible. When the distance seemed right, I was unceremoniously lifted by sailors and thrown bodily toward the platform. I remembered flying through the air and wondering if I would make it. I was caught like a feather by the giant, who put me down gently and ordered me to run up the rope steps as fast as I could. Taking a few tentative steps, I looked back to see Serge flying into the arms of our savior. Reassured, I ran to the top of the steps to be greeted by the admiral.

"Mademoiselle, welcome aboard," he said, shaking my hand.

Just as I was about to thank him, I was overcome by seasickness. Immediately, I was taken to a cabin and put to bed by a naval corpsman who took care of me as well as a mother would have. While I slept, crew members apparently lined up on deck to peer in at my open window to see the first woman ever on board.

Serge had the time of his life. He was the first child to travel on the aircraft carrier. I barely saw him during our six-day trip. He visited every nook and cranny and befriended just about every sailor on board. After a rough day and night, I was finally able to get up from my sickbed and begin to enjoy my sailing adventure. We were the guests of either the admiral or the captain at every meal. Our good life finally ended upon arriving in Saigon, and we were both very sorry to leave.

Once in Dalat, Serge and I quickly made new friends and joined in with the busy social life. There were some familiar faces from my time in Tourane and Quan-Tri, and everyone welcomed us warmly. Sometimes we'd go to Saigon for a few days to catch up with old friends there. I'd usually stay at the headquarters of the AFAT, the command post of all female army personnel in Indochina, where I was the guest of Commandant Suzanne Tillier, a pilot who had joined the Commandos d'Afrique in Tunisia as a first lieutenant in 1942. Tillier was a tall, slim woman, a natural leader. She'd been extremely active as an ambulance and jeep driver during the commando battles in Tunisia, Italy, France, and Germany. More recently she'd been promoted to chief of AFAT in Indochina, replacing Captain Torres, who'd returned to France.

Whenever I stayed with her, we'd end the evening in an opium den. Opium smoking was legal in Indochina, and many social evenings were concluded with a visit to a den by our entire group of friends. I enjoyed visiting the dens, with their quiet ambience, dim lights, attentive attendants, and hushed conversations, although I always refused the small clay pipes. Even without smoking, my brain capacity always felt intensely enhanced, probably due to secondary smoke.

Then one day, toward the end of my stay, I decided to try a pipe, knowing it was probably one of the few places I'd be able to do it legally. I thought I'd be foolish not to add this unique experience to all those I'd already lived through. Taking the pipe, I inhaled deeply and allowed the smoke to fill my lungs. But I was not a natural. Instead of relaxing with my friends, I spent the entire night in the bathroom vomiting. I will never be a candidate for addiction to narcotics.

Also in Saigon, I met up with Petit, now a colonel, who was still working in intelligence. He and his wife invited me to their house for dinner, during which he and I regaled her with the story of how he gave me a bicycle in Germany and then upgraded me to a BMW. Over coffee, he took me to one side.

"I'd like you to come back and work for me, Marthe," he said. "We have some very interesting projects, infiltrating the Chinese business community. It's economic reconnaissance mostly, but as a woman you'd be perfectly placed to go out with these businessmen and find out what they're up to. More specifically, whether they finance the Viet-Minh."

I shook my head. "No, thank you, Colonel," I told him. "My days as a spy are over. I'm a nurse now. It's what I do best."

Back in Dalat, a group of us were walking back to the hospital after breakfast in a *salon de thé* one Sunday morning when shots rang out and bullets whizzed around our feet. Turning, we saw two Annamese security men running and shooting. Their prey was a young boy, no more than twenty, who ran off the road, down a bank, and toward a lake.

"Stop him!" the Annamese shouted. "He's Viet Minh." Lieutenant Damien, one of the young French officers with us, ducked down the bank, gained on the young man, caught him, and handed him over to the authorities. I felt sick. It reminded me of the worst days of the war, when the Jews were the hunted.

"How could you do such a thing?" I asked Damien as I watched the terrified prisoner being led away. "He was no more than a kid."

The officer was stunned. "Marthe!" he said. "He was the enemy. Those are the people who are killing our countrymen every day. I should be congratulated, not chastised."

Keeping my silence, I was haunted by that young man's face for months afterward. During the German occupation, I was the hunted. That day, I wasn't proud to be on the other side of the fence.

Serge attended a French school in Dalat and had a broad education. His father had been Catholic, and every Sunday I sent him to church for mass.

"Why don't you come, Marthe?" he asked one day.

"I'm not religious," I replied. I didn't tell him I was Jewish.

He was such an affectionate, cute little boy, very bright, and obedient. He believed in me completely. We were still invited everywhere together.

Sometimes he talked of his mother, Janine, and remembered her abandoning him in England. Other times we'd talk fondly of his father, whom he'd loved very much. He called me by my first name, but I know he considered me his mother. And I considered him my son.

"I want to adopt Serge Lenay," I had told Lieutenant Colonel Berthon in Hue. "It's what his father wanted. He asked me to take care of him from his sickbed."

"All right," he replied. "I'll get you the necessary paperwork."

The adoption procedure was set in motion, and I filled in all the endless forms. I had references from everyone, from the legion to my nursing staff, saying I would make a good mother and look after the boy as if he were my own. No word had been heard from Serge's grandmother in France for almost a year. When informed of her son's death, she'd never responded, and had not inquired after her grandson's welfare since. We didn't even know if she was still alive.

Unexpectedly, I received a call from a social worker in Saigon. "I'm afraid I have some bad news," she told me on the crackly telephone line. "Serge's grandmother has sent us an inquiry about her grandson, requesting his return."

Jumping up in indignation, I cried, "But she can't! She's had no contact with him for almost a year and not much before that. Anyway, she's too ill. Her son said she was incompetent to raise a small child!"

The social worker did her best to calm me down, telling me that she'd speak to the grandmother on my behalf. But something inside me cracked. I knew I had nothing in writing from Captain Lenay, and that if it was what the old woman wanted, I'd have no choice but to give him up. By law, Serge belonged to his blood relatives, even if they were incapable or incompetent to look after him. It was more than I could bear.

After that, everything happened quickly. "She insists that she wants to raise him," the social worker told me on the telephone. "She says she can manage, and she has every right. I'm afraid you have no further right of appeal."

The social worker flew especially from Saigon to Dalat to collect Serge because she was afraid I'd fight it. I told the child everything, right from the start. He understood what was going on but didn't want to leave, any more than I wanted to give him up.

"But why can't I stay here with you, and with all our friends?" he asked, his bottom lip trembling. "I like it here."

"Because your grandmother wants you with her," I explained. "She loved your father very much, and now she wants his son with her. It's only natural."

The social worker stayed for two or three days to give Serge and me time to adjust. She even went out for dinner with us at night. I felt as if my every move was being watched. Then, on a dreadful day, he and I went with her to the small airport in Dalat, which was no more than a field.

"Good-bye, Serge," I said, holding him to me, forcing myself not to cry. I'd packed his suitcase and added some mementos of our time together.

"Good-bye," he said, his face pale with sadness.

The social worker took his hand and walked him away from me, toward the plane that would take him from me forever, and I clenched my fists and tried to contain myself until the plane took off.

Serge turned and looked back. Slipping his hand from the social worker's, he tore away from her and came running back to me, then clung to me desperately.

"Marthe, Marthe, don't let them take me!" he pleaded. "I love you."

To my great shame, I completely lost control, and we clung to each other, crying pathetically. The social worker had to literally pry us apart. By the time the plane took off, with them on board, I was overcome with grief.

The next four months, I struggled with my feelings of loss. It was as if all my losses were rolled into one. I'd lost my son. Denying myself the love of a man, I'd invested all the love I had to give in that little boy. I prayed that if I was patient, his grandmother would realize she couldn't raise a child, and accept me as his surrogate mother. Part of me knew, however, that—like Stéphanie and Jacques—I'd already lost him.

My friends from the Foreign Legion did their best to console me, inviting me to spend some time at their post in the beautiful coastal port of Nha Trang. On a security visit to a village nearby, I accompanied Lieutenant Gilbert to see what measures the locals had taken to prevent Viet Minh incursions on their soil. I wandered into the village unwittingly, only to cause an uproar. Its people had never seen a blonde before and were fascinated. Within minutes I was overwhelmed by people reaching out to touch my hair. The children, especially, almost smothered me, since I was not much taller than they. Women were screaming and laughing and pointing at me as if I was some kind of freak.

"Don't be frightened," the lieutenant told me. "They don't mean any harm."

And so I stood there allowing them to touch and stroke my hair, giggling all the while.

Having spent some time with the legion to pull myself together, I caught a train from Nha Trang to Saigon, in preparation for my departure to Europe, at the end of my tour of duty. It was November 1948, and the train crossed the difficult territory of South Annam. For security reasons, the train was divided into three sections, each with its own engine. The first was a long flatbed trailer on which stood or sat about thirty Annamese civilians paid by the French to look out for any sabotaged tracks. The second section held scores of heavily armed legionnaires, on the lookout for Viet Minh forces. The third section was the shortest and contained the passengers, all of us officers on a well-deserved furlough.

After several uneventful hours our carriage shuddered to a halt and everyone started shouting all at once. The officers left the train, yelling orders to the legionnaires, who were firing machine guns mounted on the roof of our section, uninterruptedly sweeping the thick jungle on both sides of the tracks. I jumped down from the train.

"The first two sections of the train have been sabotaged," one of the officers told me. "They've fallen into a deep ravine beneath the bridge. There are snipers everywhere, picking people off. Get back on the train."

"I'm a nurse," I told him. "I can help."

Ignoring his orders, I took half a dozen corpsmen to the ravine and organized the rescue of the Annamese civilians and our own men. The flatbed had fallen into the ravine and was upside down at the bottom. The second car, with the legionnaires in it, was still attached but hanging vertically down the gorge on the very edge of the ravine. My car sat on the track behind it. People had been thrown off against the rocks and many were badly hurt. Scrambling down the sides, clinging to the undergrowth, I assessed the most seriously injured and instructed the corpsmen what to do. A nearby Foreign Legion post was alerted and they brought additional supplies and equipment. Using makeshift stretchers made from branches, we brought the most seriously hurt to the top of the ravine and continued first aid.

"Over here, mademoiselle!" someone yelled from the edge of the ravine. "This woman's having a baby!"

Leaving a young man with badly crushed legs in the care of his fellow soldiers, I rushed to the ravine and found a heavily pregnant Annamese woman in the final stages of labor. I could barely imagine why she'd undertaken such a journey so late in her term. Holding her down, telling her to breathe, I told her: "Don't push! Do you understand?" She looked up at me, with beautiful almond-shaped eyes, and nodded.

Helicopters had been summoned for those needing hospitalization, and they flew in low over the jungle, bringing medical supplies and extra help. I organized the evacuation as best I could, returning time and again to the pregnant woman, until she was driven to a small Annamese hospital in the next village, where she gave birth to a healthy but tiny baby girl.

It took several hours to evacuate everybody and deal with the wounded. By the time they'd all been carried away, I was completely exhausted. Leaning against my railroad car, drinking water from my canteen and talking to a Lieutenant Janvier, the Annamese train conductor approached me.

"May I have your name and address?" he asked.

"Why?" I said, wiping the sweat from my eyes with the back of my hand.

"I want to report you," he said.

"What have I done wrong?" I asked, looking up.

"On the contrary, mademoiselle," he replied with a smile that revealed a row of teeth reddened by betel. "I want to commend you to the authorities."

As I tried to explain that I had only done what was expected of any nurse, one of the officers standing farther along the tracks gave him my name. His report resulted in an official commendation in my military records. "In defiance of the danger of an attack of the Viet Minh," it said, "Mademoiselle Hoffnung refused to stay put in the carriage and instead led the military rescue effort."

That, and the birth of the innocent baby in the midst of such a hellish situation, somehow seemed a fitting end to my time in that beautiful yet troubled country. France beckoned me home.

Full Circle

My return to France in December 1948 was not quite as I had dreamed it. After sailing home with a group of friends from the Foreign Legion and bidding them a sad adieu in a café on the Canebière in Marseille, I took the crowded night train to Paris. Having been surrounded night and day by colleagues, patients, friends, or by Serge, it felt strange to be traveling on my own, facing an unknown future.

Arriving shortly after dawn at the gray-stone Gare de Lyon, I stood shivering in my light cotton uniform designed for the tropics, which offered me little protection from the penetrating Parisian winter drizzle.

Wearily, I made my way to Cecile's latest apartment, on Avenue des Ternes, only to discover that she was in Poitiers, ill with the flu. Her landlady had no idea when she would return. So much for the grand reunion. Fumbling in my address book with fingers numb from the cold, I called Hélène, now a philosophy graduate student at the Sorbonne, who promised to meet me at a café on the Boulevard Saint Michel. She arrived in the late afternoon on the back of a scooter driven by her new husband, Jean-Claude, a petroleum chemist. The newlyweds had been married while I was in Indochina.

It was a meeting full of emotion for me. I had so many questions to ask, so many answers to give. Talking about what had happened with Serge brought all my grief to the surface. Hélène was wonderful. She looked radiant. Being in love obviously suited her. After the eventfulness of the war, and her dangerous undercover work for the Resistance while still an undergraduate student, it was good to see her relaxed and happy again. This was the first time since January 1946 that I'd seen any member of my family face-to-face, and it was delightful to meet Jean-Claude at last. I'd heard so much about him in her letters. It seemed fitting that Hélène had married a heroic young man who had fought in the Resistance. In April 1946, Jean-Claude had been awarded the Medaille de la Résistance avec Rosette by General de Gaulle for his activities against the occupying forces in France. He immediately felt like another brother, and I had no doubt that he and my sister were perfectly matched, just as Fred and Rosette had always been. I'd been so sorry to miss their wedding day.

Hearing that I was back in Paris, Cecile returned soon afterward. As with Hélène, there was a lot of laughter and many tears. I told her of my time in Indochina, of my sadness over Serge, and of the many strange and wonderful experiences I'd had.

"What news of Jacques Lefevre?" I asked, eager to see her boyfriend once more. During the war, he'd done so much and risked his own life to save ours. The war brought them together, but when it ended, Cecile explained, its aftereffects had separated them.

"We're still friends, but nothing more," she told me. "But I know he'd love to see you." With Cecile's blessing, Jacques and I remained friends for many years, and I don't think he ever really stopped loving her.

Cecile introduced me to her new boyfriend, Luigi Visoni, a Swiss musician who'd graduated from the Conservatoire de Paris as a violinist and pianist. We became immediate friends, too. Though an only child, Luigi showed a great understanding of the close ties that bonded Cecile and me.

Fred, I learned, had left the army and was back in Poitiers running the recently reopened Elby. Arnold had been helping him operate from makeshift quarters under very harsh conditions until he was able to get our old store back. It took a protracted three-year legal battle, but Fred finally managed to get it returned from a furrier who—despite new despoliation laws in France affecting the return of plundered goods—had refused to give it up. Now Fred wanted nothing more than for all of us to return to Poitiers and help run the family business. "It'll be marvelous," he wrote to me, "the four eldest Hoffnungs all together again, like the old days." Arnold had returned to Poitiers from Berlin, where he served with General Leclerc's Second Armored Division; Cecile had agreed to go back; and in an exchange of letters between France and Indochina, Fred had persuaded me to come, too.

Cecile left Paris for Poitiers almost immediately, leaving me behind to wait for some winter clothes to be made. Clothing was not yet available off the rack, even in the fashion capital of the world, and had to be made to order. Alone in Cecile's apartment, preparing myself for a return to a town and a job I had neither the enthusiasm nor the acumen for, I was overwhelmed by the realization that my military life was at an end and that I'd have to adjust to a more mundane civilian existence. I was sorely tempted to reenlist, and the idea of that kept my spirits up, but I knew that before I made any final decisions, I'd have to see my parents, the rest of my siblings, and Serge. Any decision I made would also have to take into account the commitment I'd already made to Fred.

With great trepidation, I took the train to Metz, where my parents and grandmother now lived. It was the first time I had been back there since we'd left, nearly ten years earlier, in 1939. Arriving at the central station, it felt so strange to be in the town that held so many happy childhood memories for me, but it also represented a phase of my life that was well and truly over.

My parents had found much the same difficulty trying to reclaim our old apartment as Fred had with our store in Poitiers. Under the new despoliation laws, they won their court case, but were still unsuccessful in reclaiming it. I was appalled to find them living in my grandmother's small apartment—stripped of everything, including my grandfather's library—while a deputy from the prefecture squatted in theirs. It was early 1949, four years after the end of the war, and yet they were still virtually homeless.

Furious, I went with my mother to see the lawyer who'd represented them at their trial and asked for his advice.

"I can do nothing if the man living there refuses to leave," he told me. "He holds a privileged position at the prefecture, which protects him."

"But what are we expected to do?" I asked.

"Why not go in uniform to the prefecture and complain?" he suggested wryly.

I made an appointment with the first deputy, the man immediately under the prefet, the highest-ranking civil servant representing the state in that department of France. I wore my uniform and all my decorations.

"I am deeply disturbed, monsieur," I told him within seconds of arriving in his office. "Having fought with the First French Army, I've just returned from Indochina to discover that there is nowhere for me to stay. My family's apartment is being squatted in illegally. May I remind you that we are in France, not Germany? The man who is squatting has no right to it. My parents won their case in court over a year ago, but the squatter openly claims he will never surrender the apartment to Jews."

The deputy was clearly taken aback. My language was polite but strong. I didn't mince my words.

"This squatter is not only arrogant, he is anti-Semitic," I went on. "I thought we fought the Germans to eradicate all that?"

He nodded his complete agreement. "Indeed," he said gravely, reaching for a pen and paper. "Now tell me what is the name of this squatter, mademoiselle. I shall look into it immediately."

I gave the deputy his name and registered his flicker of recognition. "Yes, monsieur," I told him, my eyes steely. "He is someone who works for you, in this very office."

I watched the color rise to his cheeks.

Less than a week later my parents' apartment was returned to them. The deputy arranged the eviction of the squatter personally.

My father was overwhelmed. I don't think he ever respected me as much as he did that day. I helped them move their few belongings back into the apartment by hand. We loaded them onto a cart and I began to push it along the street.

"No, no, no," my father cried when he saw what I was doing, and tried to move me out of the way. "You shouldn't be doing that. You're an officer!"

"What kind of nonsense is that?" I told him, setting off with the cart. "I'm just your daughter Marthe, that's all."

From the moment of my arrival, I'd noticed a sharp decline in the health of my eighty-seven-year-old grandmother since I'd last seen her. She'd suffered from heart palpitations for years but now complained of severe pains in her left leg, which was caused by occlusion of an artery. Uncle Max, once again practicing as a doctor in Paris, came to Metz to examine her and agreed with her doctor that she needed to have her leg amputated. As my grandmother was too weak to undergo general anesthesia, with the approval of the surgeon I packed her leg in blocks of ice for three days preceding the surgery, a procedure recommended by my uncle. Max and I were with my grandmother in the operating room, and I stayed with Grosmutter night and day until she was able to go home, where she had round-the-clock nursing care until her death several months later. At last she was reunited with her beloved Grospapa.

It was time for me to leave for Poitiers. I had little choice. Soon after arriving in Metz my mother had cajoled me into leaving the army for good and never returning to Indochina.

"Please, Marthe," she'd pleaded, tears in her eyes. "I'm begging you. Promise me you'll do as I ask. This family has been through too much already for me to continue living on the edge over you. Go to Poitiers, work with Fred, Cecile, and Arnold. Stay out of danger. Promise me you will."

Unable to resist her emotional pleading, I gave her my word, thus dashing my secret hopes of reenlisting. With no other options open to me, I resolved to honor my earlier commitment to Fred.

On the train back to Paris, I had plenty of time to reflect on my past and future. I was twenty-eight years old and still grieving for those I'd lost. Coping with my grief had been somehow easier while living and working abroad. The thought of returning to Poitiers, a place full of bittersweet memories, made me tense and apprehensive. Plunging myself into a business career was also a frightening prospect. I felt unsettled and unsure. And there was still the question of Serge.

Since he'd left on that plane from Dalat, I'd written to him and his grandmother at least once a week. I'd received only a very few brief letters in return, all written by his grandmother, and on which Serge had only scribbled his name. The letter announcing my return to France and asking if I could visit them in Nantes had not been answered at all. Regardless, I kept writing every week. "Please, Madame," I wrote. "If not for my sake, then for Serge's. Let me come and see him. I was the one person who comforted him when your son died." I longed to see the little boy who'd been my child for almost a year. Worrying about his physical and mental welfare, I spent much of my time wondering how I could obtain his grandmother's permission to raise him. I was painfully aware that I had no legal rights whatsoever.

Cecile returned to Paris on a business trip for Elby, so we had a last few nights together in the city I loved. We spent most evenings together attending plays or ballets, or eating with Hélène and Jean-Claude. At dinner in their apartment one night I was introduced to my new brother-in-law's cousin, who had emigrated to the new state of Israel, where he held an important position in the government. Jean-Claude had told him all about me.

"Why don't you come and work for us?" he asked me two days before I was due to return to Poitiers. "I have contacts with an organization helping Sephardic Jews from Morocco and Tunisia emigrate to Israel. Their Muslim governments treat them as enemies of the state since the birth of the state of Israel but forbid them to leave. We're trying to find ways of getting them out illegally," he added, his eyes bright.

"With your army background in intelligence and nursing," Jean-Claude added, "you'd be excellent for the job, Marthe."

Torn between my promise to Fred and a job that sounded both

exciting and stimulating, I didn't know what to do. "Is there any way I could do it for just three months?" I asked, reasoning that Fred wouldn't mind waiting a little longer for my poor skills as a bookkeeper.

"No, I'm afraid not," the cousin replied, disappointment etched across his face. "This is a permanent appointment only."

Swallowing hard, I shook my head sadly. "Then I'm afraid you'll have to find someone else," I told him. "I've already made another commitment."

When I finally arrived in Poitiers three days later, Fred was over the moon at having realized his dream to run the store as a family concern. I was pleased to see him so happy and resolved to make the best of the situation. As long as I can remember, I'd enjoyed a particularly close relationship with Fred. He was an intellectual, but also a man of action, a loving husband, father, son, and brother. I was proud of and greatly admired him. Though I found little reward in my work at Elby, I loved and felt stimulated by the long discussions Fred and I held on a variety of subjects. Having been prominent in the Resistance during the war, he was already establishing himself as a leader of the Jewish community of the department of the Vienne, which he served as its official representative. He established an excellent relationship with other faiths, and with the Catholic bishop, the Protestant pastor, and the Muslim imam, he organized an annual meeting to discuss understanding and tolerance. Several years later he founded the first synagogue in Poitiers since the Middle Ages. It was a privilege just to know him, let alone be his sister.

I began by living with Cecile alone, and then—after her marriage to Luigi—with them both. We found a pleasant apartment in the center of town, on the rue de l'Ancienne Comédie. Living with Cecile and Luigi was great fun. After long days in the store, Luigi treated us to private violin or piano concerts. We often had dinner with Arnold, and with Fred and Rosette and their children, Maurice and Michele, the latest addition to their family. We also had frequent dinner engagements with Jacques's parents, the Delaunays, who'd become close friends of my family.

"We may have lost our children, but we have gained so many

more," Monsieur Delaunay would say proudly at the end of another lively meal. "Thank you for allowing us to share your lives."

Having read an announcement in the local newspaper of a meeting of the Association Rhin et Danube, I met the veterans of General de Lattre de Tassigny's First Army. As the only woman veteran in Poitiers, I was asked to be their social assistant. Thus began a demanding extracurricular activity that entailed fund-raising, organizing an annual ball, and visiting sick veterans or those in prison. That job kept me on my toes, and helped acclimate me to my life as a civilian.

In December 1949, I was invited to spend Christmas and New Year's with the Foreign Legion at Sidi-bel-Abbès, in Algeria. I journeyed by train through Spain, visiting Barcelona, Madrid, and Córdoba on my way to the Gibraltar Strait, before landing in Tangier. By plane, I reached Casablanca, where the next day I boarded a train to Sidi-bel-Abbès. The glorious ten-day sojourn with my friends and former patients included invitations by groups of enlisted men, noncommissioned officers, and officers who vied with each other to entertain me at dinners, concerts, and dances, or with whom I just shared memories of our lives in Indochina. I thought the visit ended too quickly. On my return to Poitiers, I visited Seville and Grenada. It was my last official contact with the legion, for whom I will always have a soft spot in my heart.

I worked hard in my new job but never felt enthusiastic about it. Fred could see that I was unhappy and missed nursing, and he encouraged me to set up a home care nursing service, traveling to patients' homes on my motorbike at lunchtimes, evenings, and weekends, sometimes staying overnight with critically ill patients. Luigi had even less interest in the dry goods business than I did, and after a year he left for Geneva, where he'd been offered a position as violinist with the Orchestre de la Suisse Romande, directed by the world-renowned conductor, Ernest Ansermet. Cecile remained in Poitiers for a year, she and Luigi taking turns visiting each other, before she finally left to set up a home with him in Geneva.

With Cecile gone, I was alone in the apartment we'd shared, overwhelmed by the solitude of my life. Living in Poitiers didn't help; it was still so full of memories of Jacques for me. When I walked along the Clain or went swimming, when we hiked as a family in the hills or had picnics in the forests, his image always seemed to be there. I'd changed enormously as a person, and yet it seemed that the people I'd known as a teenager hadn't.

One day I met an old friend of Jacques's in the street and was very pleased to see him. "Why don't you come for dinner tomorrow night and then we can catch up on old times?" I asked, smiling broadly. For years I had been living in a man's world, and I didn't think twice about the invitation.

The poor man nearly screamed and ran away. He was in his late twenties but he said he'd have to ask his mother. He didn't understand my intentions, and I think I frightened him off. I never saw him again.

In an attempt to add some excitement to my life, I took up flying. My lifetime ambition to fly a plane, like my childhood heroes Maurice Bellonte and Dieudonné Costes, had never left me.

"One day, Maman," I'd told my mother the night after the pilots had come to Metz on their 1930 victory tour, "I'm going to learn how to fly a plane."

The Piper Cubs we flew were open to the elements, and the wind and the cold were incredible. My fellow pilots often took pictures of me in all my gear because I was covered from head to toe in warm clothes, just like Ya-Ya's "mummy." And when I got into the cockpit, I had to have two rows of cushions beneath, behind, and beside me, just to prop me up. But I did it. Unfortunately, the cost of flying lessons, compounded by mandatory lessons in glider piloting, was so high that I was barely able to afford a new pair of stockings. Sick at heart, I had to give up the sport that I loved before fully qualifying for my license.

My heartache and disappointment over Serge never abated. I was still writing regularly and had sent him several presents, but heard nothing in return. Then, out of the blue, I received a letter from his grandmother inviting me to visit. Taking a train the next day, I found him living in terrible conditions with the senile and cantankerous old woman and Serge's stepgrandfather, her husband. With some difficulty, I finally pieced together the situation.

For several years Serge's grandmother had been living in a house that her son had requisitioned on his return to France, while serving with the Second Armored Division of General Leclerc. Suffering from uncontrolled diabetes and senility, she'd ignored several summonses to return the home to the rightful owner. Her second husband, a nice old man, was completely overwhelmed by events and by his wife. Several days before my arrival they were evicted from their home, and had been taken in temporarily by a neighbor. In addition, a con man had taken what little money she had, so I went with her to see him and forced him to give it back.

Instead of thanking me, she accused me of undermining her. "Why did you take Serge away from me?" she asked, scowling. "Why did you keep him so long? You were in love with my son, weren't you?"

I thought, My God, if only you knew how he lived!

"No, I was never in love with your son," I told her firmly, "but I do love Serge. Please let him come and live with me. I promise he'll be wonderfully well cared for."

"Did you ever see my son's body?" the old woman asked then, her expression half mad.

"No," I told her. "By the time I arrived in Hue with Serge for his funeral, he was already in his coffin."

Her face lit up. "Perhaps he's not dead!" she cried. "Perhaps he's still alive!"

Alarmed, I told her that her son was most certainly dead. "He had a severe case of typhus," I said. "I personally tended to him when he was desperately ill. His doctor in Hue told Serge and me that your son died."

She took Serge by the hand. "If your father is dead," she told him, "there's only one thing we can do—throw ourselves under a streetcar."

Serge tried to pull away, crying and screaming, "No, Grandmama! No! I don't want to die!" Running to me, unhappy and frightened, he begged me to take him with me. I tried everything I could to persuade her. I promised her unlimited access to her grandson. But it was useless. Trying desperately to at least provide a permanent home for Serge, I ran from one government office to the next, but no apartment was available. In the autumn of 1949, rebuilding had not yet started in earnest and housing in France was extremely scarce.

The neighbor agreed to let them stay until something came up, and I took them to dinner in a restaurant, desperately thinking of things I could do to help. Serge remained silent and subdued the whole evening. The old man slurped his soup and never said a word. As the meal ended, the old woman became increasingly hostile, accusing me of trying to steal her grandson.

"I don't want to steal him from you," I cried, my hands clammy, "I just want to give him a better life than this."

Her eyes cold, she insisted that I leave. "I forbid you from ever visiting Serge again!" she said, her heavily lined face triumphant.

Utterly defeated, I paid the bill, left the restaurant with one last kiss for the top of Serge's bowed head, and caught the late train out.

As soon as I was able to take time off from my two jobs, I journeyed to Paris and sought an appointment with the father of a friend of mine in the Foreign Legion. The son had been a former patient from my days in Quan-Tri and was very fond of Serge. His father was a general who served as an aide-de-camp to then President de la République Vincent Auriol. Upon arriving at the Palais de l'Elysée, I was immediately ushered into his office. Through his son's letters, he knew that I had been his anesthetist and that I'd been authorized by the army to be Serge's substitute mother.

"Please help me, General," I begged. "I have to find a suitable place to live for a family in desperate need of your assistance."

The general listened to my story and promised to try to find a solution to Serge's grandmother's housing predicament. He launched an inquiry into the matter, but the old woman's suspicious nature brought all his efforts to naught. The general later wrote and told me that without her cooperation, there was nothing more he could do.

In 1958, long after I had left France for the United States, Rosette wrote and told me that Serge had written to her and Fred in Poitiers and asked me to get back in touch with him. "He wants to see you again, Marthe," she wrote. "He's asked for our help."

But I couldn't do it. It would have been too heartbreaking to lose him again; I couldn't bear to reopen such painful wounds. He never left my thoughts. I was racked with guilt that I couldn't face getting in touch with him.

Fortunately, living in Poitiers allowed me to see my young nephew Maurice, my niece Michele, and—after his birth in 1951—baby Daniel. Most of my free time was spent taking care of them, to the delight of Rosette, who badly needed a break. On weekends I'd take the two eldest to the local airport, where they watched me fly planes and gliders. I was a member of all the outings and holiday celebrations at their home, developing strong, loving bonds with them that remain to this day. My constant contact with them helped me survive despite my deep sorrow over Serge.

In December 1952, Cecile and Luigi invited me to visit them. Eagerly, I traveled to Geneva, and was dazzled by their tastefully appointed home stuffed full of antiques they'd bought in Paris. To supplement his income as a violinist, Luigi also taught piano, and he bought, refurbished, and sold them. Cecile helped him run the business. When I arrived, it soon became apparent that Luigi had a master plan.

"Come and live with us here, Marthe," he suggested, his dark eyes bright. "I've even found you a job. As you already have two years' nursing training, one year in the Red Cross Nursing School Bon Secours will qualify you for the Swiss certification as a nurse and allow you to freely work in Switzerland. Bon Secours trains its nursing students in the Cantonal Hospital, a well-respected university institution. And since you already have several years of experience in the field, you'll be paid a normal salary throughout your training. You'd be much happier working as a nurse again. You could live here with us, and my lovely Cecile would be less lonely on the long evenings I'm out working with the orchestra."

As usual, Luigi had thoroughly investigated the situation and had all the answers. He knew I wouldn't be able to resist. Returning to Poitiers, I braced myself to tell Fred.

"Go," he said, patting my arm with a smile. "Your heart's never been in this business. Go and start a new life, Marthe, with my blessings."

So in June 1953, Geneva became my new home and I enrolled in the nursing school exactly as Luigi had planned it. Shortly after starting my training, I also approached the World Health Organization to inquire about any future jobs. Two nurses—one British, one American—conducted the interview. With my military experience, I was offered a position opening nursing schools for the training of natives in the former French colonies of Africa.

"But first you must learn English," they told me. "We recommend that you go to England and work in a hospital for at least a year. Then you should enroll in a school in Paris to qualify as a nursing school headmistress."

Spurred into action by what seemed an incredible opportunity, I applied to a university hospital in London and to the school in Paris. Both answered favorably. The Paris school even offered me a grant generous enough to cover all my expenses. My path seemed set.

My professional experiences in Geneva had already taught me what discrimination foreign workers can encounter, even in countries sharing the same language. Determined to minimize the language barrier when I arrived in England, I decided that I had to learn English immediately. Geneva was an international city, home of the Red Cross and a great many U.S. and English delegations. There had to be someone who would teach me.

I placed an advertisement on the notice board at the university, and soon afterward began lessons with Henri Fournel, an impecunious medical student who was in dire need of the extra cash. To begin with, the lessons were at Cecile and Luigi's home on rue Louis Favre, but after a while I started going to his rented room on my motorbike to save him the expense of the journey. It was there, in December 1953, that I met his roommate, Major Lloyd Cohn, an American medical student. I was thirty-three years old.

My first impression was far from favorable. Major had a very dark complexion and a mass of curly dark hair. He loved the French; he'd had a French girlfriend, but she wanted him to marry her and he couldn't afford to, so they split up. He was still grieving for her when I met him. His initial behavior toward me was most irritating. He came across like a Don Juan and riled me from the outset. He tried to impress me, and the more he tried, the more I disliked him. When he left, I asked Henri, "Where on earth did you find such a terrible roommate?"

Henri was shocked. "No way," he said. "Major's a wonderful guy." He then proceeded to tell me what Major had done for him. They'd met as students in Paris after the war, and Henri helped Major with his French. Thankful for his help, Major took Henri with him to Switzerland, where he supported both of them on his GI Bill and a supplement provided by his brother Melvin, a professor in Immunology at the Pasteur Institute, and Melvin's wife Ruby, a graduate student at the Sorbonne. Though Major's income was sufficient for him alone, paying Henri's tuition and all their other expenses reduced them to spartan living conditions.

After a few more encounters I began to see Major in a different light. Slowly, I got to know him and to agree with Henri that he was a very different person than the one I'd initially disliked. The two of them often invited me to share their lunch, but all they could afford to eat was bread, cream cheese, and sardines. There was one tea bag, and the tablecloth was a newspaper. As the guest, I always had first dunk of the tea bag.

I told Cecile and Luigi how they lived; they were horrified and invited Henri and Major to dinner. That first time they came, Cecile cooked spaghetti with tomato sauce and meatballs. They couldn't take their eyes off it—they just stared at the first hot meal they'd seen in ages. When Cecile began to serve them, they couldn't stop eating. Cecile invited them regularly after that.

On New Year's Eve we went to a dinner dance in a hall where Luigi was playing with a small band. With Major and me dancing cheek-to-cheek, it was obvious to Cecile and Luigi that he was growing increasingly fond of me and I of him. During the evening several revelers lifted me onto a table and cried, "*Vive la mariée!*" Long live the bride. Was it an omen? I wondered. Walking home in the early hours of the morning, Major kissed me for the first time on the Mont Blanc Bridge. It was freezing, but I didn't care. I felt truly happy for the first time in years.

I graduated in 1954, and my fellow students threw a farewell party for me. I was touched by their good wishes. Everything seemed to be moving so fast. London, Paris, and then Africa beckoned, and I refused to think about how heartbroken I'd be at leaving Major. He wasn't due to graduate until 1956, and then he was all set to return to America to be a doctor. Stopping by his place after my farewell party, we sat and drank tea and talked for a while about nothing in particular.

"Well," I said, getting up to leave, my face long, "I'd better go home and pack, I suppose."

Major jumped to his feet. "What would happen if I asked you not to go to England?" he asked in his slow, laconic drawl.

"Are you joking?" I said, my eyes wide. "It's all arranged!"

"I've never been more serious in my life," he replied, staring into my eyes. "Marthe, will you stay?"

Without any hesitation, and to my own great surprise, I heard myself say, "Yes, Major." Looking up into his dark brown eyes, I beamed him a smile. "The answer is yes."

Hesitantly, Major added, "I can't say exactly when we'll marry, but we will as soon as I cease to depend financially on Mel and Ruby."

Luigi was furious with me for giving up my career without even a firm commitment from Major. He thought I'd been terribly foolish. "You're not even officially engaged!" he cried, pacing the floor of their home. "Is he really planning to marry you, and if so, when?"

"Who cares?" I replied, grinning at him and Cecile. "I'm happy, Luigi. That's all that matters, isn't it? I've been unhappy for too long. Whatever happiness I can get out of life, I'm going to grab."

Cecile burst into tears and pulled me into her arms.

My preparations to leave Europe for America took me to Poitiers and to Metz to say my farewells. Cecile and Luigi were now joined by Rosy in Geneva, who'd taken over Major's soon-to-be empty apartment, and the three of them gave me an emotional sendoff. In Metz, my parents wished me well and my mother clung to me, her tears soaking my shoulder. In Poitiers, Arnold, Fred, Rosette, and their children were equally emotional, as was Madame Delaunay, now a widow after her husband had succumbed to the aftereffects of his incarceration in Buchenwald. Fighting her grief, Madame Delaunay reiterated that in his last letter Jacques had expressed the wish that I marry someday.

"Very few women would have waited so long, Marthe," she told me, her bottom lip trembling at the thought of losing me to another country. "Jacques would be so proud of you."

I left her house feeling weighed down with guilt.

In June 1956, I sailed to the United States with Major on the *Ile de France*. We were married in a civil ceremony on January 30, 1958, in St. Louis, Missouri. The half-hour ceremony was held at the Justice of the Peace's office. It took place on my lunch hour during a split shift. I was a student in the School of Anesthesia of Barnes Hospital, Washington University, earning fifty dollars a month. Major was a resident in Internal Medicine in the same institution, on the same stipend. Once married, we'd get a hundred-dollar allowance for housing. Melvin and Ruby were our only witnesses. My simple gold wedding ring cost $4.50.

Ten days later, in his parents' home in Brooklyn, New York, we had an official ceremony presided over by a rabbi. Maman traveled all the way from Metz for the service and watched tearfully as we took our vows and Major stepped on the glass under the *chuppah*. I don't think she ever thought she'd witness that day.

My heart was full of mixed emotions. I missed my brothers and sisters keenly. I would have loved Fred and Rosette and their three children, as well as Cecile and Luigi, Arnold, Hélène, Jean-Claude, and Rosy, to be at the ceremony, but financial and family constraints prevented it. My father was in failing health and unable to leave France. To have my mother there, though, was the greatest blessing.

"Congratulations, Marthe," she said, kissing me warmly on both cheeks. "I'm so glad that you've finally found happiness."

Two years later, on December 12, 1960, after two miscarriages and a long and difficult pregnancy, I finally went into the early stages of labor. Major and I were traveling around Europe, en route to France—hoping that being born in France would enable our child to claim dual citizenship—and were in Agrinion, a Greek town in a mountainous region northeast of Athens, when my water broke. The baby was six weeks' premature. Taking me to a private clinic where no one seemed to speak French or English, Major paced the corridor outside the maternity ward, like any anxious father.

The labor was surprisingly easy, although I'd already been warned that it could be very dangerous. "Don't let her get pregnant again," the doctors had told Major in America. "It might kill her next time."

But I was determined: I wanted a child more than anything. I felt strongly that my greatest achievement would be to give life to a new human being. It would be the best legacy I could think of for Stéphanie and Jacques and all those members of my family whose lives were so cruelly cut short. To have survived the war as a Jew was good enough; but I felt that to continue the family line, for the sake of Grospapa and my parents, was the most important aspect of my survival.

"Don't push!" the midwife told me. She was the only person in that hospital who spoke limited French. My mind flashed back to the pregnant Annamese woman, in labor on the edge of a ravine.

I remembered Hélène and Rosy as tiny babies, like little dolls. I'd watched over them with Cecile. My father had wept each time another one arrived.

With one final, supreme effort my firstborn child burst into the world, a world largely at peace, where war on such a grand scale was a distant memory. I heard a baby's cry, and the next thing I knew, this tiny creature was laid in my arms as I wept tears of joy.

"It's a boy," the midwife told me, standing at the bedside. She summoned Major in from outside.

"Oh, Major," I sobbed. "We have a son . . . Stephan Jacques."

Major nodded and smiled.

"Welcome, Stephan Jacques," he said, reaching forward and kissing his forehead. "Welcome to the world."

Epilogue

In 1998, when I was seventy-eight years old and in France visiting my family, I decided to approach the authorities for copies of my military records. I wanted to regain my French citizenship in tandem with my American status, which I could now do under new laws.

I think the French Army was surprised that I was still alive, but it gave me what I needed. For years my brother Fred had insisted that I apply for the Medaille Militaire, and so—at his insistence—I delicately raised the question in the Bureau of the Military Archives in Pau, in the Pyrenees. I was given the relevant application forms, and several weeks after submitting them, received an acknowledgment and advice to reapply should I not hear anything by July 1, 1999.

The date passed and I completely forgot about it. I knew that whatever happened, I wouldn't reapply. Then, in December 1999, unexpectedly, the French Minister of Defense notified me that I'd been awarded the medal for my services during the war. Even though I'd applied for it, I was still absolutely staggered.

The simple ceremony took place on Bastille Day, July 14, 2000, in a suite of the Sofitel Hotel in Beverly Hills, not far from where I now live. The Medaille Militaire, created in 1852 by Napoleon III and once awarded to Winston Churchill, was presented to me by Monsieur Yves Yelda, the French Consul to Los Angeles, for my "exceptional courage" while on "special missions" in the Black Forest in April 1945. According to the citation, my small part in the war "facilitated in large measure the success of the last operations of the French Army."

My husband Major, my sons Stephan and Remi, Stephan's wife Barbara and little daughter Anna, along with some close friends, stood watching as the gold medal was pinned to the lapel of my royal-blue suit, which I had made specially for the occasion. Despite my best efforts, tears of pride rolled down my cheeks.

I considered then and believe still that I accepted that medal for Jacques and for every single member of my family, alive and dead, who were all as brave as, if not braver than, me—Stéphanie, Uncle Leon, my parents, brothers, and sisters, and all those who deserved the medal much more than me. I'd never previously told my children what I'd done during the war. Even Major knew only the scantest details. I always felt that people would think they were tall tales. Until that day, many of my neighbors and close friends had no idea what I had done in the French Army during the war.

And what of my family and friends? How did they all fare? What else did life throw at them after such experiences? Deemed a near miracle by Major and me, our second son Remi Benjamin was born on April 25, 1964. My father died a year later, my mother in 1983, after three trips to America to see me married and to help with each of my babies.

Fred died in June 2001, after a long illness. His son Maurice killed himself three weeks later. Of Fred's other children, Michele works for the Direction Financière de la Société de Construction Aéro-Europeénne in Paris and Daniel is a doctor in Poitiers. The youngest, Serge, works in Poitiers for the local newspaper.

Cecile and Luigi never had children. Luigi died in 1998, and

Cecile still lives in Geneva, although in poor health. Arnold never married, and he worked with Fred all his life. He lives in Poitiers. Rosy, too, remained single, and worked as an executive secretary in Geneva. In February 2002, she died after a long and valiant battle with cancer.

Hélène became a professor of philosophy in Paris. She and her husband, Jean-Claude, live in Paris. After her experiences of the war, Hélène said she had no right to bring children into this world. They both love children and are devoted to their nieces and nephews.

Uncle Max, whose health worsened after his incarceration, died in the early 1970s. His wife Fannie died some years later. Their daughter Ruth lives with her son in Jerusalem and runs the French library there. Uncle Benoit, his wife Fannie, and their son survived the war, but Benoit died later of cancer. His wife and son did not survive him very long.

Jacquie, who took on the Hebrew name Gavan, is a father of three and grandfather of two and works as an electrical engineer in Israel. His brother Josie was killed in the Sinai war of 1967 at the age of thirty-one. Mindele, their sister, lives in Toronto and is married with two sons. Their parents died in Israel several years ago.

Madame Delaunay died in 1988. She and my family remained in close contact until the end. I still have a pair of white leather shoes she gave Stephan when he was a few months old.

My friend Sophie Weyne lived, like Cecile, in Paris as a non-Jew and escaped arrest. After the war she married Henri Nichols. They live in New York and have one son, Claude. Odile de Morin married Maurice de la Servé and they had children. She died some years ago. Annette Boutin became a social worker and remained in Poitiers. I have also remained in touch with Janine Rieckert, whose brother Eloi was shot alongside Jacques. She married and had four children and lives in La Rochelle.

Dedé, Stéphanie's fiancé, married in 1945 but later divorced. He died quite young. Rosette's mother, Madame Korn, survived the war in a hospice in Poitiers but was dead within ten years. When the Germans came to arrest her for being Jewish, the doctor in charge, Dr. le Blé resisted and they went away without her. Her husband Kalman, Rosette's father, was arrested soon after we escaped and deported to Auschwitz, never to return.

I lost contact with Serge Lenay and never had the courage to try again, until recently. After rekindling my memories of him by writing this book, I realized that time had soothed my pain, and I wanted him to know how much our precious year together meant to me, and to tell him how very sorry I was. My cowriter discovered him listed in the phone book in a suburb of Paris and gave me the number. On impulse, I picked up the phone. Serge is now in his sixties, happily married with four fine children, two girls and two boys, and a teacher by trade. He had never forgotten me, either. Major and I have already visited him and his family and, now that we have been so happily reunited, we shall never lose contact again. I have found my lost "son."

Now in my eighty-second year, somewhat arthritic and infuriatingly deaf, I can look back on my life, and that of my entire family, and hold my head high in pride. We were more fortunate than most—we largely lived up to our name of Hoffnung Gutglück, Hope and Good Luck. Despite all that we went through, the years of daily terrors, none of us ever really lost hope.

War taught me many things, among them that, like anyone, I could be a coward one minute and brave the next, depending entirely on circumstance. They say that war brings out the best and the worst in people, and I certainly saw both sides. When I think of the dozens of people who risked their lives for us, it almost helps compensate for all the sad and bitter memories of those who were so cruel. War also made me accept the inevitable and savor the important gains, like my two wonderful sons and the granddaughter I might so easily have never lived to see.

Through the memories of those we've lost and our shared sense of unity and pride in what we've gained, I've somehow managed to keep hope alive, against what often seemed impossible odds.

Bibliography

Augustin, Jean-Marie. *Les Grandes Affaires Criminelles de Poitiers.* Mougon: Geste Editions, 1995.

Baillie, Kate, and Tim Salmon. *The Rough Guide to France.* New York: Rough Guides, 1997.

Bauer, Lt. Colonel E. *The History of World War Two.* Surry Hills, Australia: Galley Press, 1984.

Beevor, Anthony, and Artemis Cooper. *Paris After the Liberation 1944–1949.* New York: Penguin, 1995.

Berenbaum, Michael. *Witness to the Holocaust.* New York: HarperCollins, 1997.

Bouvet, General George-Regis. *Ouvriers de la Premiere Heure.* Paris: Berger Levrault, 1954.

Collins, Larry, and Dominique Lapierre. *Is Paris Burning?* Victoria, British Columbia: Castle Books, 2000. Reprinted; first printed by Simon and Schuster, 1965.

Foot, M. R. D. *Resistance, European Resistance to Nazism, 1940–1945.* London: Eyre Methuen, 1976.

Garçon, Maurice. *Les Cinq Etudiants de Poitiers, dans Procès Sombres.* Paris: Artheme Fayard, 1950.

Gilbert, Martin. *Never Again: A History of the Holocaust.* New York: Universe, 2000.

De Gmeline, Patrick. *Commandos d'Afrique, de l'Île d'Elbe au Danube.* Paris: Presse de la Cité, 1980.

Gutman, Israel. *Encyclopedia of the Holocaust,* volume 3. New York: Macmillan, 1995.

Klarsfeld, Serge. *Le Mémorial de la Déportation des Juifs de France.* Paris: Beate et Serge Klarsfeld, 1978 (they are the editors and publishers).

De Lattre de Tassigny, General J. *Histoire de la Premiére Armée Française, Rhin et Danube.* Paris: Librairie Plon, 1949.

Levy, Paul. *Elie Bloch Être Juif sous l'Occupation.* Mougon: Geste Editions/Histoire, 1999.

Mercer, Derrik (ed.). *Chronicle of the Twentieth Century.* London: Longman Chronicle, 1988.

McLachlan, Gordon. *The Rough Guide to Germany.* New York: Rough Guides, 1998.

Parrish, Thomas (ed.). *Encyclopedia of World War Two.* London: Secker & Warburg, 1978.

About the Authors

Marthe Cohn, at the age of eighty, was awarded France's highest military honors. It was the first time her children and grandchildren had even heard of her exploits. She lives in Palo Verdes, California.

Wendy Holden, the coauthor, has written numerous books and spent eighteen years as a celebrated journalist. She lives in England.